THE
MAN
IN
THE
MIDDLE

978-1-4336-7288-0

Published by B&H Publishing Group
Nashville, Tennessee

Dewey Decimal Classification: 261.7
Subject Heading: BUSH, GEORGE W. \
PRESIDENTS—UNITED STATES \
CHRISTIANITY AND POLITICS

Published in association with the literary agency
of Wolgemuth & Associates, Inc.

Unless otherwise noted, Scripture quotations are from
the Holy Bible, New International Version, copyright
© 1973, 1978, 1986 by International Bible Society.

At time of printing, all Web sites were checked for accuracy.

1 2 3 4 5 6 7 8 • 16 15 14 13 12 11

THE
MAN
An Inside Account
of Faith and Politics
in the George W. Bush Era
IN
THE
MIDDLE

TIMOTHY S. GOEGLEIN

PUBLISHING GROUP
Nashville, Tennessee

This book is dedicated to the six loves of my life:

My wife, Jenny; our sons Tim and Paul; my parents,
Stanley and Shirley Goeglein; and my mother-in-law Beverly Carson.
Theirs has been a sacrificial love, none more than Jenny, my soul mate.
They have taught me that the best life is the one enveloped
in unconditional love, given and received.

Soli Deo Gloria!

Contents

Far better it is to dare mighty things, to win great triumphs, even though checkered by failure, than to take rank with those poor spirits who neither enjoy much nor suffer much, because they live in the gray twilight that knows neither victory nor defeat.
—THEODORE ROOSEVELT[1]

For you, LORD, have delivered me from death, my eyes from tears, my feet from stumbling, that I may walk before the LORD in the land of the living. . . . What shall I return to the LORD for all his goodness to me?
—PSALM 116:8–9, 12 (NIV)

Orthodoxy is my doxy—heterodoxy is another man's doxy.
—BISHOP WILLIMAN WARBURTON[2]

Foreword

At any given time, a handful of people—several hundred out of more than 311 million Americans today—are called by a president to serve on his White House staff. For seven eventful years Timothy Stanley Goeglein was one of those select few working at 1600 Pennsylvania Avenue. This book is his story of his time on the White House staff in years of controversy, conflict, and war.

This volume is an inside look at the policy battles and presidency of George W. Bush, told by a man who served as the White House liaison to the conservative community.

I know Tim Goeglein well. I recruited him for his post and worked with him closely during my nearly seven years at the White House. We became close colleagues and friends. I relied on the advice, insights, and advocacy of Tim and his colleague in the Office of Public Liaison, Matt Smith, who led the Bush Administration's outreach to our fellow conservatives. And so, up the chain of command, did the President of the United States.

Tim's book is pugnacious, often dealing revisionist blows to mistaken conventional wisdom about President Bush, his decisions, methods, strengths, and intentions. Tim patiently marshals facts and evidence to set the record straight in a powerful defense of the Bush era.

This volume also gives the reader a view of what life inside the White House gates is really like. People who labor in the White House often find it hard to explain to friends or family what the pace and burdens are of working for a president. Tim's glimpses inside the real West Wing are revealing.

You are there as Tim helps prepare for the National Cathedral prayer service days after 9-11, as the Senate takes up the president's nominees for the Supreme Court, as a president attends the funeral of Pope John Paul II, and as a conservative administration takes on the tough challenges facing the country.

This is also a personal book offering Tim's views on issues and events. No two people (especially two conservatives) always think alike. Nor do people present at a moment see it through the same frame. So it is interesting now to hear—unvarnished and unfiltered—my colleague's reactions to events and issues at which we were both present.

Tim also writes of the toll of service inside the pressure cooker that is the White House. He describes the pressures, stresses, and strains that cause anyone who has been honored to work there to feel a kinship with others who do, regardless of party or philosophy. You get a real sense of the costs paid by those who abandon the comfortable patterns of their career and family life to answer a president's call to service.

This volume is candid, and so it is necessarily an intimate story of error, forgiveness, and redemption—Tim's error, the forgiveness he received from his president and colleagues, and the redemption made possible by Tim's faith and character. I suspect this part of the book was difficult for Tim to put on paper, but his doing so only increases my admiration for his honesty and recognition that we are all fallen creatures, capable of mistakes, and needing the help of a greater power.

For 222 years, the American president has played a pivotal role—for good and sometimes for ill—in the life of our nation and, increasingly the globe. The post a president occupies is the most powerful in the world. The space in which he labors—the Oval Office in the West Wing of the White House—is the most important center of political power in the world.

It is a place so powerful that it overwhelms many. Vladimir Putin, for example, when visiting Washington for the first time, came into the Oval Office, took a long look around its splendor, and exclaimed, "Oh, my God!" If it can take away the breath of a former KGB agent raised in the atheistic Soviet Union, you can imagine what it can do to almost anyone.

For eight years, a good man occupied that office. George W. Bush made vital decisions on behalf of a people he loved, to protect their freedoms and way of life from enemies bent on our destruction. He had the courage to propose reforms of big institutions important to our people and our future. He stood for timeless conservative values that were engrained in his heart and soul, not drawn from a poll or focus group. And he made a difference—an enduring and big difference for the good for our country.

It was Tim Goeglein's honor to serve this man and our nation. This is the story of that service, a chronicle worth writing and one well worth reading

—Karl Rove

Prologue

A thankful heart is not only the greatest virtue,
but the parent of all other virtues.
—CICERO[1]

It takes struggles in life to make strength. It takes fight for
principles to make fortitude. It takes crisis to give courage.
And it takes singleness of purpose to reach an objective.
—MARGARET THATCHER[2]

This book is about the presidency of George W. Bush, seen from inside the White House, through my own perceptions of being there for seven years, and dating from the first day of the first Bush administration on January 21, 2001. I was one of the longest serving White House aides to the president, dating from my time on the first Bush campaign in Austin, which I joined Labor Day weekend of 2000.

I was a special assistant to the president and the deputy director of the White House Office of Public Liaison, one of the four political offices. Though mine was a long title, I had comparatively little influence. In Washington, the shorter your title, the more influence you have; the longer, less. I welcomed not being in the inner circle, as it were. By nature I am an outsider's insider or an insider's outsider. I relished my role as an insider's outsider because this is a position of utility and value for any White House; with this role comes unique responsibilities and none more so than the honest ability to reflect back into the White House what one is hearing from people of credibility, reflection, and intelligence.

I am a conservative. My chief responsibility was to be the president's point man to what is commonly called "the base"—the whole of American conservatism—evangelicals and Mass-attending Catholics, the major veterans groups, the think tanks, public policy groups, and a number of the leading and elite cultural institutions. There was a special emphasis in my work with my fellow traditional conservatives, better known as values voters, but also with the broad spectrum of the American conservative movement, with whom I am completely in sync and where I find my natural political and cultural home.

Because I served closely with Karl Rove, he gave me entree to the president and the senior staff at the White House and in the agencies. His was an act of trust in me for which my gratitude is endless. It was a remarkable seven years, a true labor of love, and as a result, I spent a lot of time with the president at fairly close range. On many occasions and in multiple settings, I observed a president whom I came to love and respect. I personally witnessed and ultimately became a beneficiary of his natural warmth, prayerfulness, and loyalty to family, friends, and staff.

I was never a confidant of the president. Excepting rare occasions, he did not seek my counsel or advice. Although I spent a lot of time in the West Wing, I was not of its subculture. My role and utility were to be the man in the middle, the reliable, loyal conduit for the president's agenda to the outside groups, but also a reliable arbiter for getting timely and key information into the White House bloodstream. It was a role tailor-made for me because of my love for people. As a Christian, I came to see it was my vocation in those years.

Conservatives have often focused like a laser beam on their various disagreements with President Bush: his unwillingness to wield the veto pen on national spending issues; his creation of No Child Left Behind; his Medicare expansion legislation; immigration reform; the initial stimulus; and the overall federal spending record of his eight years at 1600 Pennsylvania Avenue. These issues are an integral part of his record and will continue to be closely examined and debated for years to come.

Yet what I, as both an eyewitness and a full participant, have come to conclude about George W. Bush's presidency is that, on major decisions, he was not only right but also wise in his prudential judgments and in the way he led. Contrary to the beliefs of some in the media and most of the Left, and contrary to the uneasy feeling among some of my fellow conservatives, much of what President Bush stood for and advocated into policy on large matters of state during those two administrations was not only in the best interest of the country in the short term but also in the long term.

On the most lethal threat to our national security in this new century, the combination of radical jihadism and nuclear proliferation, the president confronted and then put into place a foundational road map that will likely guide the United States forward for decades to come in security, intelligence, homeland, and foreign policy. This is a huge accomplishment but little recognized.

On the most important domestic issue facing any president, the shape and scope of the Supreme Court and the attendant composition of the federal judiciary, the president made outstanding appointments that will impact millions of Americans for decades to come.

Also, he was the most pro-life, pro-family, pro-marriage, pro-religious liberty president of the contemporary era, and this achievement will grow with time. There is much more to the Bush record of achievement, which I discuss in the following pages.

Far beyond the issues, I found in George W. Bush a man of enormous integrity, quiet strength, kindness, and good humor. He embodied all that conservatives say we believe most about the connection between high character and public life. This is often overlooked in men and women we choose to lead us. My conclusion is that President Bush's legacy is not only one of wise domestic and foreign policy choices on a host of critical national and international matters facing our great country but also a form of distinguished leadership, rooted in his personal character and humanity that is a model for those who will follow him in the Oval Office. Despite the criticism and fault-finding mostly rooted in ideological differences and borne out of an over-the-top toxicity, the Bush legacy, I believe, will ripen in a positive light.

That legacy begins in his basic, personal decency. The president was gifted with an easy rapport with ordinary Americans, the ability to make difficult decisions and remain unwavering, the ability to show no rancor despite personal attacks that some days seemed unending, a friendliness and personal regard rooted in uncommon loyalty, and a singular courage that was moral before it was physical. That courage was often employed to raise the dignity of every person.

Some of my former colleagues have written critical books, for which there will always be a ready audience. Books of this sort sometimes are valuable in that they point toward identifying problems, but they rarely fill in the blanks, solving nothing. Instead, they provide titillation and entertainment but do not seem to serve any meaningful, long-term purpose. My goal is the opposite.

I am not writing a full-blown biography or history of the Bush administration, but rather my raison d'etre is to craft a personal portrait by a friend, a White House insider who was on the outer ring, and on occasion, a person who was honored to pray with the president. I will not unveil anyone's uncomfortable secrets except my own, but I am keen to lift the veil on a president who perhaps has been overprotected when it comes to the portrayal of his inner feelings or personal character. I am keen to dust off some of that opacity because I am a lover of portraits that reveal something important about its subject. I hope to paint a portrait in words of my time at the White House and in Washington. The goal is to capture a fair and balanced depiction of the president's achievements illuminated by insights, anecdotes, and small details about the forty-third man to occupy the Oval Office.

Sir Desmond MacCarthy said that a biographer is "an artist upon oath."[3] By God's grace I have been given all kinds of brushes and colors in my paint box. I hope to reflect on what was right and best about George W. Bush, many of my colleagues, and the great people I worked with outside the White House. This book has given me the occasion to think carefully about my time as part of the Bush White House and to look broadly at the ideas we promulgated as a cornerstone of American public life from 2000 to 2008. It allowed me to ask why we believed what we believed in real time, not upon reflection where hindsight is often 20/20.

While this book is partly a White House memoir, it is also partly a personal reflection on some of conservatism's important thinkers, writers, scholars, and political figures as well as partly a retrospection on the immutable first principles of conservatism as they apply to the political and cultural scene where I have spent much of my professional life. It matters greatly to me why and how these principles should help provide the way forward for America in the twenty-first century. These principles are rooted in a view that justice and order are the biblically directed chief duties of government and best exemplified in the most important virtues—prudence and courage. They are first among equals of all the cardinal virtues, and they open the door in public policy to make the sanctity of every human life, the sacredness of marriage, the sacredness of the nuclear family, and the protection of religious liberty foundational to all we believe as Americans.

It is conservatism that recognizes we cannot have a healthy, productive economy without healthy, productive families and that the unchangeable taproot of both is a religiously sanctioned morality and code of ethics. It recognizes that economic outcomes have moral implications. It is a conservatism of personal responsibility that values hard work, saving, and compassion for those who cannot help or provide for themselves. It is a conservatism that shapes, molds, and impacts the culture. This uniquely American conservatism confirms the danger of decoupling economics, ethics, and morality; they are of a piece, rooted in the Judeo-Christian worldview which is consonant with the United States Constitution, a noble and exemplary document whose influence and force of nature for good in world history is probably second only to the Holy Bible. It is also a conservatism that believes our rights come directly from God, not from government or other men. The state is not our master but rather our servant; we give the state its power, not vice versa. It is a conservatism that recognizes family, not government, as the center of our lives.

Ronald Reagan said: "The family is the basic unit of our society, the heart of our free democracy. It provides love, acceptance, guidance, support, and instruction to the individual. Community values and goals that give America strength also take root in the home. In times of change and challenge, families keep safe our cultural heritage and reinforce our spiritual foundation. As the mainstay of our national life, family life must be preserved."[4]

This book has prompted my own thinking about America's future—about whether our exemplary country can survive without faith as our primary foundation, about the correlation between faith in God and faith in ourselves, about the legitimate role of faith in the public square, about the impact of secular extremism on Western civilization's greatest gifts to America such as religious liberty and genuine tolerance, about the relative passivity of Christianity and Judaism and the relative vigor of Islam, about the political correctness that continues to fog our heritage and best traditions, about whether those of us who firmly believe in the Judeo-Christian tradition are willing to exchange our dominant role in America's cultural formulations for becoming a merely influential minority.

The second president of the United States, John Adams, wrote: "Statesmen may plan and speculate for Liberty, but it is Religion and Morality alone, which can establish the Principles upon which Freedom can securely stand."[5] I have been the personal beneficiary of Adams's view.

The tone of my book is powered by a deeply felt sense of gratitude to God, friends, colleagues, and great mentors who have enriched my life beyond measure. Yet mostly my gratitude and thanksgiving well up for my wife and parents—the ordinary, extraordinary people who have loved me and been at my side at every important juncture of my life. The root of my happiness as a boy was the happy and faithful marriage of my mom and dad. They taught me, by their indomitable spirit of faith, that the ultimate value in life cannot be measured materially in money or things, but by whom and with whom you can enjoy the things God gave you. My mother once told me to always strive to find the childlike wonder in every day, in the words of Lewis Carroll, the "child of the pure, unclouded brow, and dreaming eyes of wonder."[6] My parents gave me a protective, loving, faith-filled carapace that shielded me from many of the slings and arrows of life and endowed me with an unsurpassed love of God and country. They taught me by their example that my chief end was to do my duty with excellence and joie de vivre, and they instilled in me appreciation and cheerfulness that make life worth living.

Churchill wrote, "Writing a book is an adventure. To begin with, it is a toy and an amusement; then it becomes a mistress, and then it becomes a master, and then a tyrant. The last phase is that just as you are about to be reconciled to your servitude, you kill the monster, and fling him out to the public."[7] I am uncertain about the monster part, but I know this book, and any book, calls for a singular sacrifice from one's family, and mine has shown the patience of Job and the love of Christ. I also owe a singular debt of thanks to Kathy Wills Wright, whose idea this book was and whose encouragement was unwavering, and to seven great friends, Hannah LaJoy, Jonathan Aitken, Donna Rice, Ryan Cole, Joshua Shepherd, Paul Batura, and Tom Minnery whose intelligent reading and encouragement were invaluable. Also, my excellent editor Gary Terashita made this a stronger and better book. Kim Stanford of B&H is a gifted editor, and her tireless, selfless work brought this book across the finish line. My gratitude is deep.

I owe special gratitude to Jim Daly, president of Focus on the Family; Alan Sears, president of The Alliance Defense Fund; Ed Feulner, president of The Heritage Foundation; Frank Cannon, president of The American Principles Project; and Colin Hanna, president of Let Freedom Ring for personal kindnesses and support too numerous to mention.

Finally, a note of thanks to my colleagues at Focus on the Family. Every man should be so blessed to have coworkers who are so uniformly excellent, and powered by their love of God.

The late Irving Kristol said conservatism at its best "is hopeful, not lugubrious; forward-looking, not nostalgic; and its general tone is cheerful, not grim or dyspeptic."[8] I believe he was right. Conservatism is not a passing ideology or a political program. Rather, conservatism is a way of life, powered by grace and enjoyment. Conservatism, at its highest, is comprised of an ethical stance, a sense of the salvific and a sacramental vision of life. Therein lies its vitality and its future.

Bloomington, Indiana
24 June 2011

Chapter 1

Forgotten Is Forgiven

When pride comes, then comes disgrace,
but with humility comes wisdom.
—PROVERBS 11:2 (NIV)

Humility is the mother of giants. One sees great things from
the valley; only small things from the peak.
—G. K. CHESTERTON, THE FATHER BROWN STORIES[1]

The worst day of my life began as one of the most luminous. The contrast between the glory of that morning and the horror of that evening bordered on the surreal.

During my seven and a half years at the White House, working as a special assistant to President George W. Bush as the deputy director of the office of public liaison and as one of Karl Rove's aides, I was rarely at my desk later than 6:30 in the morning. I loved getting to work early, going through my e-mails, reading through the morning papers, preparing for what almost always turned into a crushingly busy day. The pace was usually in overdrive, and I was raised to be of service, to be energetic and cheerful in my vocation. I loved my job. The sense of playing a small part at the large center of our nation's public life was a gift from God. My White House colleagues felt the same way, and one of the little known things about the Bush White House is how much the staff liked and respected one another and how close we were. This rarely happens in any White House team. I am sure there were exceptions, but by and large we loved our work, we loved working with one another on behalf of a president in whom we believed.

After I got through what one of my interns once called "the White House morning chores," I walked through Lafayette Park, across the street from the White House, to the Hay-Adams Hotel for breakfast with a longtime friend. The park is quiet and beautiful most mornings, ringed by large trees and redbrick sidewalks, with the famous statue of Andrew Jackson on horseback in the middle.

My friend and I had not seen each other in a long time. His young family and ours were neighbors for many years on the same quiet circle in Northern Virginia, so our meeting was a mini-reunion. Our hour together went by all too rapidly. As we departed the hotel, he remarked to me what a beautiful morning it was, one of the best of the year. We shook hands and promised to meet again soon. On my way back to the White House, I remember saying a small prayer, thanking God for great friends like Dennis. My wife and I both believed these White House years were good years for our family, despite the busyness of it all.

I was on my way to a meeting in the Eisenhower Building, where my office was located, next to the White House. I stopped into my office to quickly check my e-mails and to get a file folder. When I popped open my e-mail, I saw a note from a reporter I knew during my decade on Capitol Hill, working for U.S. Senator Dan Coats of Indiana as his press secretary and communications director.

I opened the e-mail, read it once, felt the blood drain from my head, got down on my knees next to my desk, and was overcome with a fear and trepidation as never before. My only prayer, which I repeated again and again, was "God help me. God help me." I knew instantly this would be the most impossible day of my life, and my heart was pounding as if to burst from my chest. I sat back down and responded to the reporter's e-mail. She told me she learned I plagiarized part of a recent column I wrote in my local hometown newspaper, *The News-Sentinel*. Was it true, she wanted to know? It was indeed true, and I told her so instantly by return e-mail. When I sent that e-mail reply, acknowledging what I had done, in all my guilt and shame, I knew events of that day would move rapidly toward my resignation from the White House and service to a president I loved and respected.

Every one of the principles I held and espoused, every one of the values I was raised by—truth in all things, character above intellect, unquestioned integrity before God and man alike—every mentor who ever invested part of his or her life in me, I had violated and violated completely. My hypocrisy was now transparent, and I was guilty as charged. What a prideful fool I was, and it was all my fault without excuse or exception. Mine would be a public failure in the front ranks. Whatever punishment was to follow that day and in the weeks to come, I deserved completely.

The avalanche of media coverage began almost immediately. One of George W. Bush's aides was caught in a plagiarism scandal. My colleagues were incredulous and disbelieving: What were the details? What was the context? Surely it could not be true? I had become close friends with many of my colleagues in various offices at the White House; and as they learned of the story, their e-mails and calls of disbelief began pouring in. Surely, most said, this was a mistake or an oversight or due to busyness or sloppiness. Surely, they said, in all their friendship and love, I could not have "meant" to plagiarize.

But I did it knowingly and repeatedly, as stories in the days to follow would show. There were no extenuating circumstances or justifications for what I did. It was not a mistake or an oversight. It was not due to sloppiness. I was deceptive, and it was all rooted in vanity and pride.

The more my colleagues' regard and friendship came to me, the more painful it became because of the violation it represented. I utterly violated their trust in me. I personally put a premium on collegiality and worked to foster that kind of civility and diplomacy of which I was now unmasked as a violator. I earned their trust and built wonderful friendships and relationships only to let them down completely. I not only violated their trust and friendship, but I also violated the trust and friendship of the man to whom I owed so much, the president himself.

Mine was a high-profile role, relational in tone and quality. As people around the country with whom I worked learned of my story, they began to call and e-mail in response to the major cable and radio networks who were broadcasting my story of plagiarism. Even as I write these words, the horror of that morning and the events of that day come back to haunt me with the pain and awfulness I inflicted on others but most especially the three people I love most in the world, my wife and sons. I embarrassed them all deeply in a betrayal rooted in self-centeredness and ambition, both of which were venal.

I resigned that afternoon, writing a personal letter of apology to the president. I departed the White House that Friday shattered and fearful, exiting the White House gates as I had done a thousands times before and vowing to myself that, even as I returned to work to foster a smooth transition for my successor, I would never again darken the doorstep of the West Wing. I had always held up as nearly sacred ground that part of the White House because of the thousands of decisions—many of them life-and-death decisions of war and peace—that are made there, which so deeply impact the direction of our country.

Upon my arrival home that afternoon, I gathered my family into our living room and, in no uncertain terms and placing no varnish on my rottenness, explained to my wife and sons what I had done. The look on their faces crushed me, so completely had I betrayed their love and trust in me. When I asked for their forgiveness, they gave it to me willingly but in a state of disbelief. The evening remains a blur, and when I finally went up to bed, I shut my door, turned off the lights, and literally collapsed on the floor, like a house of cards, a completely broken man, wailing in pain.

All my professional goals, all my dreams, all I spoke about and encouraged and advocated in the lives of my own sons and in nearly twenty years of working with outstanding interns and other young people in Washington, all that undergirded my worldview as a Christian had gone up in flames, roaring and snapping like so much kindling. My life caved in, and it was all of my own doing. With it I wounded the people I loved most in the world, and that seemed to me unforgivable. The anguish I felt that night—mental, physical, and spiritual anguish of the deepest sort— is the realest thing I have ever encountered or imagined. As a Christian, I was gripping the cross of Christ and holding on for life. I genuinely hated myself with a loathing that bordered on the diabolical.

My personal collapse evoked Dante's powerful stanza on humiliation, repentance, and contrition, and it stung deeply:

> What better can we do than prostrate fall
> Before him reverent; and there confess
> Humbly our faults, and pardon beg; with tears
> Wat'ring the ground, and with our sighs the air
> Frequenting, sent from hears contrite, in sign
> Of sorrow unfeign'd, and humiliation meek?[2]

A sleepless night of tossing and turning ensued, further blighted when I heard the morning newspapers snap down on the stoop outside and below the bedroom window. I knew my awful story would be there for all our friends and neighbors and parishioners and community to read. The shame would deepen, and it did, like the incessant drip of a broken faucet. All those yet to see the story of my fall and scandal would read about it that

Saturday morning, and another day of shame would commence, which I deserved but my wife and kids did not. We could not bring ourselves to leave the house that day.

In Washington, when high-order transgression takes place in the political classes, it is *de rigueur* to cut off the offender. To excise the cancer. To rid him or her from the system and move forward toward the inexorable goals of politics and policy. When a staffer embarrasses the representative, or the senator, or the president, a divorce must take place leading to *persona non grata* status for the victimizer.

I knew I was finished. I believed my friendships would end; my phone would go silent; the e-mails would cease; the head-of-steam mantra of nearly eight years at the White House would dissipate—poof!—overnight, resulting in my own personal denouement, fall, disgrace, and destruction. *The nadir had seemingly arrived,* I thought, *and this chapter in the book of my life would be slammed shut for good.*

Only that is not what happened.

In all my pride and arrogance, grace broke through and prevailed. At the very moment I was crushed under the weight of my own sin and wrongdoing, God's mercy materialized as if in a dream. What followed was a miracle in my life and the life of my family. The combination of grace and mercy we were about to experience shattered those Washington myths about which I had been warned. This period of twinned grace and mercy commenced on the Saturday morning after the worst day and night of my life, and it would prevail, opening up new chapters I did not deserve.

People were not enabling or making excuses for me; they knew the enmity I deserved. But they believed in second chances and forgiveness, and I learned people want you to get back up and start again. They won't abide excuses or cheap explanations, and I had none to offer. But they deserved to see and hear my contrition in words and actions.

At almost exactly 10:00 a.m., our phone rang. It was my mother and father, my best friends in the world after my wife. They said they were calling to tell me they loved me. I broke down, and then apologized for disappointing, hurting, and embarrassing them. But they told me again, they loved me and forgave me. They wanted me to know they would be with Jenny and me and the boys through all the days ahead.

About fifteen minutes later I received another call, this one from a well-known, well-loved Washingtonian. I will never forget his words: "Tim, I can only imagine how tough this morning is for you. I just want you to know two things: Our friendship remains and I want to help you and your family. Call me when you feel you can." I thanked him but again found it tough to speak in response to his generosity of spirit.

A neighbor knocked on our door, saying she "heard some news" and just wanted to know how we were and if there was anything she might do. A church friend phoned from Florida, where she was vacationing, and asked how she might pray for me and my family. The outpouring of love came in spite of my own infamy and wretchedness. On this, the day after my crushing failure, the phones did not go silent; the e-mail flow from those who were concerned about me and my family did not cease; friends did not rush for the tall grass but rather offered to help us; colleagues did not abandon us but offered their prayers; neighbors did not shun or spurn us; our church family reached out and embraced us. My pastor, Chris Esget, asked me to come spend time with him, which I did, and his friendship and counsel were boundless.

My time with him, of confession and absolution, was solemn; and I came to see the revelation of my sin actually started a process of restoration and liberation. Also, I came to see I could not experience joy without first mourning my sin. In fact, I entered a period of grieving over what I had done and saw that its weight was devastating. That grieving brought me closer to God because the enormity of my sin—against God, my family, my friends, my colleagues, my editors, the people who read my columns—was immense. I brought pain and sorrow to those whose love is my privilege. I fell short of what God wanted for my life. I knew that in my repentance I was honor bound to know the gravity of my sin and it was ugly.

Regret, remorse, contrition, and confession, however, were not enough. I had to experience sorrow for my transgressions because I offended both God and man. My brokenheartedness over what I had done brought me comfort; it was, for me, the pathway to God's fathomless forgiveness and love. The writer Henry Blackaby wrote that God's "infinite grace is sufficient for the most terrible sin."[3] I lived the reality of that insight.

All day Saturday after my resignation and at church the following day—walking in those doors was one of the most difficult things I have ever done—I found unbounded and unmerited love. It would be replicated in the days and weeks ahead. The narrative was the same: solid friendship and support where and as needed. We were overwhelmed and humbled.

Monday dawned; I never wanted so much for a single day *not* to arrive. I headed for the White House to begin packing and preparing for a flawless transition for the person who would take my place. When I walked into my office that Monday, I wept bitterly; the memories of the people and the dynamism of what occurred there were overwhelming. My colleagues in the Office of Public Liaison had become a second family. Their generosity of spirit during those tough days touched the depth of my soul.

Shortly after I arrived, I received a call from one of the best men I have ever known in Washington, Josh Bolten, the president's chief of staff. We met on the first Bush campaign in Austin, where he oversaw the policy shop. We held a high regard for each other dating from that time. Would I please come over and chat with him in his West Wing office, he asked? "Josh," I told him, "I appreciate this call more than you know, but I vowed to myself never to enter the West Wing again, so badly have I screwed up." No, he said, it was important for me to come over and talk with him.

I walked into his beautiful corner office, the sun streaming in the nearly floor-to-ceiling windows overlooking Executive Drive and the Eisenhower Building, his Harley Davidson memorabilia here and there. He hugged me and shook my hand as I entered, and before I could say anything, he asked, "How are Jenny and the boys doing? How are you? I forgive you, Tim."

"But Josh," I told him, "I have embarrassed the president, and you, and all my colleagues, and I have violated"—he stopped me. It was over, he said, and it was a new day. A fresh start. He asked me to sit down on the couch next to the fireplace over which hung my favorite portrait of Lincoln in the White House. We chatted about the momentous events of the last eight years and about the work we collaborated on most recently, the confirmation of President Bush's third attorney general, Mike Mukasey. Josh's kindness moved me to tears. I pledged to him a smooth transition as I exited the White House, which he appreciated, and as I departed he said, "Oh, and the boss wants to see you this week," meaning the president.

I knew instantly what that meant: a much-deserved woodshed moment. I imagined the president, Josh, and perhaps my immediate boss Barry Jackson, Karl Rove's successor, would formally level the boom. I knew it would be as unpleasant and awkward as possible, and I knew I deserved it.

Only that scenario never materialized.

When I arrived later that week to see the president in the Oval Office, I expected to be greeted in the anteroom by Josh, or Barry, or one of the deputy chiefs of staff. But only the president's executive assistant was there. Then I heard the president's voice: "Timmy, is that you? Please come in." Now my mind began to race. This meeting would only be the president and me, which would make it all the more awkward and unpleasant. I assumed he would read me the proverbial "riot act." I would offer a heartfelt apology, and we would say our farewells and be done with it.

Only that is not what happened.

What followed was the greatest professional moment of my life, far greater than being offered the job at the White House by Karl Rove; far greater than even the highest high points of my time there, among them both presidential inaugurals and the initial swearing-in in the East Room when we were a new staff in 2001.

I walked in; closed the door (my heart was pounding), turned to the president, and said, "Mr. President, I owe you a . . ."

"Tim," he said, "I want you to know I forgive you."

"But Mr. President, I owe you . . ."

"Tim," he said, "I have known mercy and grace in my own life, and I am offering it to you now. You are forgiven," he said again.

"But Mr. President, you should have taken me by the lapels and tossed me into Pennsylvania Avenue. I embarrassed you and the team; I am so sorry."

"Tim, you are forgiven," he said again, "and mercy is real. Now we can talk about this, or we can spend some time together talking about the last seven years."

I was stunned. The leader of the free world, on whose administration I brought shame, not only told me he forgave me multiple times but proceeded to ask me to sit down and have a conversation. I walked over to one of the two couches, and he said, "No, sit here," pointing to the chair of honor in front of the fireplace in the Oval Office. That is the place where the vice president, or head of state, or distinguished guest sits during presidential visits or meetings, not the place where former aides who have resigned in a scandal sit. This was mercy personified in a way difficult even to describe.

We spent about fifteen or twenty minutes together, reliving many remarkable moments from the previous two administrations. This time together sealed our friendship as brothers in Christ, and I asked if I might say a short prayer for him, the First Lady, and the Bush family. We prayed together.

Before I departed, I glanced around that majestic office for what I thought was one last time: the matching blue- and gold-striped chairs in front of the fireplace where we just sat; the luminous rug the First Lady designed with the presidential seal near the president's desk; the gold curtains framing the three floor-to-ceiling windows with flags unfurled nearby; the two beautiful paintings on either side of those windows, one of them "A Charge to Keep" by artist W. H. D. Koerner whose title was taken from the president's favorite hymn; the large Palladian door topped by the famous white shell leading to the Rose Garden; the Remington statue of the horseman on the table below the painting of the Texas fields alive with bluebells; the fresh flowers on the coffee table in front of the matching couches; the two great portraits dominating the room of Washington, looking upward to the left in confidence about the future of America, and of Lincoln; the elegant, graceful grandfather clock to the left of the president's chair; and at both the Churchill and Eisenhower busts, the former next to the fireplace and the latter to the left of the president's desk. To me this was sacred ground, and I felt overwhelmed.

We embraced. I told him I loved him and the First Lady, that it had been the professional honor of a lifetime to serve him and the country, and that I would never forget all he had done for me and my family. I told him he and his family would remain in my daily prayers without fail. Even as I was saying this, the refrain of Jesus' words, "Take heart, son; your sins are forgiven" (Matt. 9:2 NIV) kept going through my mind. I was in a state of semi-disbelief over what just transpired.

As I headed to the door, I was certain I would never see him again. It was a bittersweet exit. I choked up and knew this was the ending of something significant in my life.

Only, it was not the end. It was the end of the beginning.

"Tim," he said, "I would like you to bring Jenny and your two sons here to the Oval Office so I can tell them what a great husband and father you are."

"Pardon me, sir?" I was stunned by this added note of unfettered grace. He wanted to affirm me in front of my wife and sons. And I heard from his scheduler two days later for an appointment to come back to the Oval Office.

The forgiveness he modeled to me that day was rooted in the forgiveness in his own life, dating from 1986, when he decided to give up drinking for good, forever swearing off alcohol, and recommitting to faith in "the Almighty," as he called God most frequently.

When we arrived as a family to see the president the following week, both of our boys were in their blue blazers, rep ties, and khaki pants. We waited in the Roosevelt Room, the president's conference room across the hall from the Oval Office. Jenny and I told the boys that when the door to the Oval opened, they were to look the president in the eyes, firmly shake his hand, and thank him for seeing us. On cue the young aide arrived and escorted us across the hall—both Josh and Barry joined us this time with the president. When the door opened, the president looked at my boys and said, "I'll bet before you came in, your parents told you to look me in the eyes, shake my hand, and tell me how nice it is to be here today, right?" There was spontaneous laughter, and a wonderful family time with the president ensued. He gave each boy presidential gifts; photos were snapped; hugs all around and handshakes; we departed in a daze of gratitude.

We thought a giant chapter in our lives had ended and looked around one more time at the White House and its remarkable grandeur and history. All the people who meant so much to us on a day-by-day basis in the Bush administration, we thought, would become part of our memory.

Only that is not what happened.

We were not forgotten; we were not shunned; we were not cut off; our friendships continued; our sense of belonging continued in a healthy way outside of work relationships; we witnessed faith in action repeatedly on the part of former colleagues, none more so than from my professional family in the Office of Public Liaison at the White House. All three of the former directors—Lezlee Westine, Rhonda Keenum, and Julie Cram—reached out to our family and showed us pure love and friendship. As a family we were invited to Andrews Air Force Base for the president's final departure from office in January 2009, and the emotional bonding that took place there sealed our friendships for a lifetime. It was all undeserved; the peace and reconciliation that flowed from the president's heart pervaded my former colleagues' hearts too.

I knew I had one more difficult apology to make. I did not want to make this apology by e-mail or phone or fax or letter; I wanted to make it in person, man to man. I knew I would be in Fort Wayne later in the year and made an appointment to meet the executive editor of *The News-Sentinel*, Kerry Hubartt. I betrayed him and the editorial page editors of his newspaper who were valued friends through the years, none more so than Leo Morris, the page's editor, and Kevin Leininger, a columnist and a former editor on the opinion page. I made a plan to meet Kerry for coffee, and what ensued was yet another remarkable session of grace. I offered my categorical and unconditional apology for what I had done, and I told him I took full responsibility. I asked for his forgiveness, which he offered unconditionally.

Small demarcations of God's grace continued to unfold in the months after I left the White House, none more important to me than when a man I knew professionally, a fellow Christian, reached out to me and invited me to join him "and three other friends" for coffee "just to talk about how you are doing." That circle of four men turned out to be the most important time of healing and confession of my life; we met every other week for a year. They counseled me, prayed with me, allowed me to open myself up in a way that made me vulnerable; but it was the greatest form of ministry and healing I have ever experienced. Though they all lived in Washington at that time, one by one, with a single exception, they moved to other parts of the country; but I remain in regular touch with them; and the bonds of our friendship are immutable.

What I have found is a joyful peace having passed through that furnace of public disgrace, where I discovered the most holy grace possible. It is as if God worked through me for years and then in one horrid moment allowed me to be stripped of worldly masks, reformed, and moved to an image closer to His. A friend of mine wrote to me: "You were formed in the fire just as surely as metal is cased in a foundry." Every Christian experiences rebirth, and the process of grace must be attendant. My sin was real, and only through apology, atonement, and learning from it could I find a way forward.

Another friend wrote to me: "God doesn't give us our due penalty for our sins but rather takes them on Himself and instead gives us beauty for ashes." That moved me to tears. I know from my own experience that if a rebel returns to Him with a penitent heart, giving up the claims of self-ownership, He redeems everything. I have shared with anyone who will listen that conceit and arrogance are inimical to the life of a Christian, that humility of spirit is liberating and leads to the heart of God.

I worked for President Bush from the first campaign in 2000 until my resignation in early 2008. The grace he showed me upon that exit was a reflection of his faith in Jesus Christ. It was also a deep reflection of who the man really is. His grace set me out on a journey of recovery, where I found healing and peace as a result. His grace was an extension of a casual, warm, earthy, companionable, and self-effacing man who always understood that power is ephemeral, the source of his genuine humility.

Chapter 2

Home Free

All the good things which are connected with manners and civilization have . . . depended upon . . . the spirit of the gentleman, and the spirit of religion.
—EDMUND BURKE[1]

In 1979 I was sitting at the dining room table of my parents home on Autumn View Drive in Fort Wayne, Indiana, giving serious thought to the pending presidential election between President Jimmy Carter and then Governor Ronald Reagan. I was sixteen years old then, having virtually no political views but having a legal pad in front me, working out the outline for a speech and debate team presentation I was preparing. I could not have articulated it at the time, but my parents' growing concerns about the fate of the country—economically, socially, and in foreign policy—impacted me strongly and would eventually help set the direction and course of my life, moving me from an upbringing where political issues were discussed occasionally to a lifetime where those issues have formed the collective centerpiece of my personal and professional life.

Born in January 1964, I was raised in a mostly apolitical home as a young boy, even as my parents were becoming steadily more politically interested and aware by my teenage years. My father, entrepreneurial and independent by nature, was a painting contractor, who founded his own business in the 1960s, building it into a reputable concern through hard work and sheer grit. To the degree he thought about current affairs in Washington, it was through the prism of how politics affected the bottom line of our family business. There were four kids in my family—I am the third—and my father prized his role as breadwinner. The country was in a terrible recession by the late 1970s, getting worse by the day; and he became more attenuated to how economic decisions in Washington were impacting our family business in Indiana. Layoffs became a necessity for him, and it pained him to tell yet another loyal employee with kids that work was scarce. With four children and a mortgage of his own, my dad was increasingly, deeply concerned.

My mother, a housewife with a decidedly intellectual bent—neither she nor my father had a college degree—was equally concerned about the direction of the country but was especially worried about the fallout from the sexual revolution. She started taking courses at the regional campus of Indiana University in our city, and she found herself at odds with a few professors who espoused a worldview out of step with the one she grew up with in the 1940s and '50s as the daughter of Macedonian parents—my maternal grandfather was an immigrant from Macedonia, coming through Ellis Island in 1916—and a wide and close ethnic circle that always placed family at the center. This was our social circle growing up. So the economic recession that concerned my dad and the cultural recession that concerned my mom made a huge impression on me just at the time in my young life when I was really beginning to think about politics and culture.

I remember my mom returning home one day from campus incredulous: One of her professors spent part of the class "redefining" the family, conveying to her students that the concept of the traditional nuclear family—father, mother, sister, brother, grandparents, aunts, uncles, cousins—was outdated, a source of repression for women, and an institution that had to be broken apart and put back together again. My mom said many of the younger students absorbed the professor's comments like sponges, but my mother spoke out civilly and unapologetically in defense of the traditional family—having grown up in one and started one herself—but was casually dismissed by the professor.

My parents were both cradle Lutherans, my mother from the more conservative Missouri Synod and my father from the more moderate Lutheran Church in America. The LCA congregation I was raised in was comprised of lots of families with young kids. One of our pastors, in the 1970s, began to post on the church bulletin boards social and opinion pieces from various publications concerning foreign policy and security matters in South and Central America. These position papers had one thing in common: They always seemed to cast America as the oppressor.

These statements provoked divisiveness in an otherwise small but unified church.

As this continued, my parents came to feel more and more alienated, isolated from a worldview that was decidedly less than orthodox. They made what proved to be one of the most difficult but necessary decisions of their married life: They decided to depart from the mainline church that was the religious cradle of our family's life and move to the Missouri Synod, where my mother was baptized and confirmed as a young girl. My parents did not know they were part of a national trend away from religious heterodoxy in America. The mainline had begun its historic decline.

This tumult of economic distress in the country; the social climate that seemed to champion a worldview at odds with ours, spawned in part by a cultural revolution; and the increasing churchly politicization of issues normally outside the bounds of the local parish, all began to congeal into an issues framework that impacted my family most directly and began to shape and impact my own mind and heart. I began to think seriously about all these issues and sought a reliable intellectual guide that comported with my parents' values, which were now my values and which could help explain the time in which we were living.

Ours was always a home with two daily newspapers, the weekly magazines *Time* and *Life*, and a plethora of books. Reading was a principle stressed from a young age.

By happenstance, as these ideas and debates were swirling in my mind as a teenager, I was in a bookstore with my dad, Riegel's Pipe and Tobacco Shop in downtown Fort Wayne. In those days Riegel's had one of the best collections of maps, newspapers, magazines, and journals from around the country and the world. My father, a pipe smoker, sometimes went there to purchase tobacco, and while he was at the counter making his selection and purchase, I happened upon a magazine with a huge presidential seal on its cover reflecting my ongoing debate of Carter versus Reagan and featuring a cover story on the presidential campaign in which I was taking an increasing interest.

The magazine was *National Review*, founded in 1955 (the year my parents graduated from high school) by William F. Buckley Jr. I had never heard of *National Review* or Buckley, much less the American conservative movement. My father purchased the magazine for me, slipped it into the same bag as his tobacco, and when we got home, gave it to me and asked me to let him know what I learned from it. I read the entire edition straight through. That cover story confirmed why Ronald Reagan deserved to be the next president of the United States. What appealed to me about the magazine is that it used rapier humor to make serious points; it had book and art reviews aimed at the general, intelligent reader; and it conveyed an overall sense that America was an exceptional country, which I believed but which had never been put to me in quite that manner.

But the most important thing *National Review* did for me was to introduce a whole new world of ideas, books, letters, authors, history, music, and culture that comported with the worldview I saw as worthy of defense, even in my world of local parish and community. This conservatism was long before Rush Limbaugh and Sean Hannity, long before the advent of conservative talk radio and cable TV. It was having its impact just as important think tanks and cultural institutions were coming together, and it was influencing a rising generation of young Americans like me. This post-Goldwater, pre-Reagan conservatism was giving voice to a broadly, widely, and deeply felt concern about the direction and standing of the United States of America. It was comprised, in Tom Wolfe's immortal words, of people "who for one reason or another had not gone along with the official gag for the last quarter century. I think that's about what it amounts to."[2]

I came to see that the toxicity of Vietnam, Watergate, and the Carter malaise played significantly into this brew. For those of us who were born in the early 1960s but who grew up in the '70s and '80s, the idea-matrix formed in American conservatism with Buckley, Reagan, *National Review*, and a host of other worthies issued a kind of silent call to come join a movement centered in what are known as the "first principle": A love for serious faith rooted in the Judeo-Christian tradition; the promulgation of the traditional family and its rich benefits as the foundation of American strength and confidence; skepticism of big government, high tax rates, and draconian regulations; and a love for ordered liberty underscored by the United States Constitution and its attendant federalism that put a premium on a true balance of power between Washington and the states.

The Reaganite conservatives of my generation saw the United States as having that same "rendezvous with destiny" FDR championed: with Lincoln, we viewed our country as "the last best hope of earth"; with Kennedy, we wanted to ask what we could do for our country; and especially with Reagan, echoing the pilgrim fathers, we believed America was and is "a shining city upon a hill." We were not nationalists; we were patriots, loving our country with good cause and gratitude that Providence allowed us to be born and raised in America. Reagan's victory over Carter was my first entree into the political scene, and that historic 1980 election seemed a confirmation of the things I was coming to believe in so deeply.

So as the first Reagan administration commenced, I began following the national debate much more closely. *National Review* and another publication, *Human Events*, opened up a big world of ideas to me. I began systematically and voraciously to read all the major conservative writers and thinkers, among them Whittaker Chambers's *Witness* and *Cold Friday*; Richard Weaver's *Ideas Have Consequences*; Alexander Sohlzhenitsyn's *The Gulag Archipeligo*; Milton Friedman's *Free to Choose*; F. A. Hayck's *Road to Serfdom*; William F. Buckley Jr.'s *God and Man at Yale* and *Up from Liberalism*; and Russell Kirk's *The Conservative Mind, Eliot and His Age, Edmund Burke: A Genius Revisited*, and *The Roots of American Order*.

In many ways, with the exception of Kirk and Buckley, the Anglo-American conservatives had the biggest impact on me. Johnson, Coleridge, Burke, Newman, Chesterton, Lewis, Waugh, and T. S. Eliot became my philosophical, political, and literary heroes; and the collective sense from this concentrated world of ideas propelled a desire in me to live a life marrying ideas and action. This was consonant with the men of the American founding who influenced me most: Washington, Adams, Madison, Jay, Marshall, and Benjamin Rush. Also, I saw in Prime Minister Margaret Thatcher not only a great woman but also a leader who successfully combined the best conservative ideas into a life of political action, and she became another hero, with Reagan.

In a twist of fate, I came to know Buckley and Kirk as personal friends, but above all I came to see that their ideas and the conservative movement they created after World War II most impacted my intellectual life. Without the infrastructure of the modern conservative movement (born in disgust with the New Deal and the Great Society and the attendant, massive concentration and redistribution of power in Washington), the political and cultural era that formed the foundation of my life would never have occurred.

Yet I knew even as a young conservative that, as precious to me as these ideas and principles were, my life would not be dedicated to pure policy or academia. I loved and needed interaction with people too much. The writer Joseph Sobran once said he desired "a literary, contemplative conservatism to the activist sort that was preoccupied with immediate political issues."[3] A part of me had a foot in that camp, and yet my inclination sought ballast between ideas and action. I wanted to be in the arena. In part, this came from my great admiration for Buckley, Reagan, and Thatcher. They were able to synthesize important and often complex ideas without compromising their substance and never forgetting the importance of humor, which was a central principle in my own home growing up. As a young child, I was a severe stutterer and only because of the incredible patience of my family was I able to put that era of deep frustration behind me. In all my various speech frustrations, I remember being liberated by laughter and good humor.

My earliest memories are centered on a love of people: learning their lives, their stories; trading ideas about art, music, history, sports, culture, the things of life. I believe conservatism is not a political program, a cultural program, or any program at all. It is a concentrated way of life built on hard work, family, friendship, faith, and community. Chesterton said he believed in the "democracy of the dead,"[4] that he put great stock in his ancestors and those who came before him. Chesterton was probably antimodern in some ways, which I am not, but philosophically we were of the same breed. My own worldview was taking shape.

Critically during these years I also read the United States Constitution, the Declaration of Independence, the Bill of Rights, the Federalist Papers, the Anti-Federalist Papers, Tocqueville's *Democracy in America*, Treveylan's *History of England*, and a host of other foundational documents and classic books. These works instilled in me a rich sense of Anglo-American history, which has only deepened across the years.

I was particularly influenced by Tocqueville's dual observation about America in the 1830s, that the Puritans successfully manifested both the "spirit of liberty" and the "spirit of religion,"[5] and that these together created a strong and lasting representative government supported by a concrete moral foundation. He said the American Constitution was a document of both political and moral prudence, a truly noble achievement. In this way liberty and genuine religious belief went together. He wrote: "Despotism may govern without faith, but liberty cannot. . . . How is it possible that society should escape destruction if the moral tie is not strengthened in proportion as the political tie is relaxed." This was perhaps his most important observation, that freedom and faith are inextricably linked in America. "Liberty regards religion as its companion in all its battles and its triumphs, as the cradle of its infancy and the divine source of its claims. It considers religion as the safeguard of morality, and morality as the best security of law and surest pledge of the duration of freedom." He believed religion in America was "the first of political institutions."[6]

As a young man, I was most attracted to journalism as a profession. It seemed to afford a catbird seat on the major issues of our time but also would allow me ample interaction with people from every walk of life. I was deeply influenced as a kid by the work of Ernie Pyle, a fellow Hoosier, and perhaps the greatest American wartime journalist of all time, born in little Dana, Indiana. His generalist grasp of the central issues of his lifetime—the implications of war, sacrifice, an emerging American century—combined with a rich, commanding prose style appealed to me.

Inspired by Pyle, I proposed in 1976 that the local CBS affiliate in my hometown allow me and a group of friends to write and produce a weekly TV show called *News for Little People* to air on the Saturday evening newscast, which we did for a year. That was followed by a radio show *Kids Views on the News*, which was produced by these same friends on a local radio station in 1977. That was followed by *Kids' Almanac*, another television show, which aired daily on our local independent TV station just after reruns of *Superman* and before *Leave it to Beaver*. That was followed by *Mikeside*, a radio program I produced and hosted for twelve years on one of the largest stations in the Midwest, the 50,000-watt WOWO, which combined all my loves of writing, producing, and interviewing. So while my cultural and vocational bent toward conservatism and first principles was growing and deepening, my professional bent tended toward the media as the expression and outlet for all I believed and loved.

I would eventually graduate in 1986 as the Richard G. Gray Scholar from the ivy-covered walls of the Ernie Pyle School of Journalism at Indiana University in Bloomington, one of the great journalism schools then and now, producing two radio shows during my college years. All the while, I kept one hand in politics; and during my junior year of college, this combination of media and conservatism combined in a way that would change the course of my life forever, although I could not have known it at the time.

A friend from my home town, Betsy Shoppe, was good friends with the founder and president of the conservative group Eagle Forum, Phyllis Schafly, who did the remarkable: led the nationwide effort, against the cultural tide of her time, to defeat the Equal Rights Amendment. One of Phyllis's key Midwest lieutenants, Betsy effectively identified and helped mentor young conservatives like me. She wrote me a letter asking if I might like to be considered for an internship in Washington, D.C. with U.S. Senator Dan Quayle who had been elected the same year as Reagan. Though I was eighteen at the time, I had only been to Washington twice, once on a family vacation in the early 1970s and a second time for an eighth-grade class trip in 1978. The idea intrigued me, so I entered the interview process on campus and was selected to spend three months working for Quayle on Capitol Hill.

Though my college years at IU were among the best of my life, for the first time that summer in Washington, I met people my age from all over the country and the world who shared a similar passion to impact the shape and course of our country and world. In those years my passion for tennis was equally high, and I came to see you could play three sets in an hour, be social, and build lasting friendships and relationships across the ideological spectrum. Many of my closest friends were liberals with whom I agreed on virtually nothing, but as steel sharpens steel, our conversations helped me sharpen my ability to debate, discuss, and disagree agreeably. I also spent that summer reading Boswell's *Life of Johnson*, the great British novels of the nineteenth century. I came to see that the interior life is as important as the exterior life and that literature and civilization go together in an important way. Mine became a literary world in significant ways that summer, and I began to read and reread a bevy of the classics—poetry, prose fiction, and drama.

I loved my Washington internship from the first day. I had a remarkable start. Sometime during the first two weeks of my time in the Quayle office, the senator himself came walking through the mail room where I was probably opening my nine-hundredth letter of the day. He asked me who I was and where I was from, and a short conversation ensued. When I referred to his maternal grandfather, the famous publisher from Indianapolis, Eugene Pulliam, and to how important the conservative *Indianapolis Star* editorial page was to so many of my classroom debates at IU, the senator asked me to continue our conversation in a hallway chat on the way to his next event of the day, a meeting of the Senate Armed Services Committee. He asked me, once there, if I would like to come into the anteroom and listen to the hearing for a little bit before going back to the mail room, which of course sounded wonderful. I had never been to a congressional committee hearing before.

I will never forget when that committee room door flung open because standing just inside the room—we nearly hit him with the large door—was Arizona Senator Barry M. Goldwater, who was defeated for the presidency in 1964 by President Lyndon Johnson and who became, for me, by osmosis through *National Review* and my conservatism, a large and central figure. But there he was, warmly greeting me in his houndstooth-check jacket, white mane of hair, and rugged face. I tried to express, in a fleeting moment, how much his patriotism and love for America meant to me over so many years. I am certain he didn't hear me because he made a quick joke and then exited the room just as we were entering. But it was a great moment for me and one that confirmed the glory in the variety and intrigue of a life in public service. That summer of 1985 was momentous in my life, and I loved working for Dan Quayle, who treated me and all his interns and staff, with kindness and good humor.

Another central event of my life—apart from Washington, politics, literature, and tennis matches with new friends—happened that summer, too. When I returned to Fort Wayne to spend two weeks at home before returning to campus, I took a Greyhound bus to Toledo to visit a friend from IU. His father was a prominent doctor there, and they invited me to spend a few days playing tennis and golf and relaxing before the new school year commenced. On the bus, sitting by myself and looking out the window, I had a moment of powerful transcendence. I had been a serious Christian my whole life; among the things I loved best about campus life, in fact, was being a deacon in my church, University Lutheran in Bloomington.

This moment seemed to echo, for me, what T. S. Eliot identified as those rare moments of life when time and the timeless seem to intersect and the divine seems to be present in a way that is almost surreal. Like C. S. Lewis, and Wordsworth before him, I was having a moment "surprised by joy—impatient as the wind."[7] I felt the presence of Christ with me, and I felt, if not compelled then surely prompted to make a silent reconfirmation and confession of faith, almost a recommittal of the vows I took as a young confirmand in the eighth grade, all those years ago. Would I really commit my life, as a young adult, to the Christian life? If so, what were its dimensions, and why should I do so? But I did, in that moment, and experienced an unsurpassed rush of peace and contentment.

Silently I said I was rededicating my life to Jesus Christ; that in all my sin and inadequacy, I believed in Him and that His resurrection was real, that He alone was the Son of God, reigning coeternal with His Father and with the Holy Ghost. Evelyn Waugh wrote that understanding the world would be "unintelligible and unendurable without God."[8] That is the thesis sentence of my life. On that bus on the way to Toledo, I was not sleeping; I was not dreaming; I did not experience a trauma. This moment for me was unadulterated joy.

When I arrived in Toledo, I remember my friend John, a fellow Christian and serious Catholic, asking me the typical question: How was the trip? The temptation was to share with him that transcendent moment, but I demurred, not for cowardice or awkwardness but because I wanted to internalize the beauty and the singleness of it all. To this day, all these years later, I am almost mesmerized by its power and simplicity.

Summer gave way to early fall. Returning to IU for my senior year and despite the great Washington experience I had, I was certain my professional choice would be working for one of the television network affiliates somewhere in the Midwest. I loved Indiana; it will always be my home; and I knew that with my family and most of my friends there, I wanted to begin my career in the Hoosier State. I began to put feelers out as the school year commenced and continued producing the weekly radio show at one of the two campus radio stations. My senior year was a particularly fruitful one academically, and as I moved toward the final spring semester, I felt certain I would depart campus, enter the first newsroom of my professional life, and begin what I prayed would be a life in electronic journalism.

But just as my friend Betsy intervened to act as a bridge to an internship with Quayle in 1985, another friend, Curt Smith, the press secretary for U.S. Representative Dan Coats, a relatively little-known conservative Republican congressman from Northeast Indiana, called me and asked if I would consider doing an internship on the other side of Capitol Hill in the summer of 1986. He reasoned that I spent one summer in the Senate; wouldn't it be great on my professional resume to have another summer on Capitol Hill, this one in the House of Representatives and working with him on press and media matters? I applied, was accepted, and headed back to the Beltway for a second summer.

When one of my mentors, a highly regarded professor of broadcast journalism at IU, Richard Yoakum, who had enjoyed a distinguished career at NBC News, learned I was heading to Washington, he offered to help me get a weekend internship at NBC News there. It worked, and in May I flew to Washington to intern in the House of Representatives for Rep. Dan Coats during the week, and for the news program *1986* with Roger Mudd and Connie Chung on the weekends. It was an amazing summer and one of the best professional experiences I ever could have had. I visited *Meet the Press* on a number of Sundays, watching from the wings as Tim Russert asked his insightful questions.

Dan Coats and Roger Mudd were gentlemen in the front ranks. They treated me with grace and multiple kindnesses, all the while showing me the best of public service and the best of American journalism.

When both internships concluded at summer's end, I returned to Indiana with no plans for a working life in Washington. I came to love Washington, though, and after those two summers the cultural and historical appeal of the city was real for me. The confluence of the national life of our country—media, politics, policy—was a luminous combination to a young man; and in those years I took every opportunity to attend regular events and lectures at The Heritage Foundation, which was rapidly becoming the nation's premiere conservative think tank, a veritable factory of ideas. I was a regular attendee at the Heritage Noontime lecture series, one of which would lead to one of the most important friendships of my life, with William F. Buckley Jr.

In the fall of 1986, after graduating from Indiana University, I went to work for the NBC affiliate in my hometown, WKJG, the second oldest TV station in Indiana. I was hired by the station's general manager, the legendary Hilliard Gates, who played himself in the movie Hoosiers. Hilliard was one of the great sports announcers of his era and became the gray eminence of Indiana sports broadcasting. For the first six months, I produced the 10:00 p.m. news and was later promoted to executive producer, responsible for both the early and late newscasts, which I loved. I was there during a transition time for local news across America, working with that last era of journalists who read serious history and literature, many of them having worked in newspapers before a life in radio or TV, like the late David Brinkley and Walter Cronkite. They were incredible mentors. Dick Florea, the news director, was one of the men in that league, becoming a lifelong friend. His commitment to unbiased journalism was his hallmark. Melissa Long, the station's anchorwoman, taught me television journalism, and we became fast and lasting friends. After a year and a half there, I was ready to move into a larger TV market. Providence intervened at just this time.

Chapter 3

From Coats to Bauer to Bush

God cannot give us a happiness and peace apart from Himself, because it is not there. There is no such thing.
—C. S. Lewis[1]

In 1988 Dan Quayle became vice president, and Dan Coats was plucked from near obscurity by Indiana governor Robert Orr and appointed the new U.S. senator from Indiana. Without peer Coats was the right man for the job because his character and integrity were unassailable. He was, and is, one of most virtuous men in American politics, loved roundly and widely by men and women on both sides of the political aisle, a Wheaton graduate and serious Christian, a family man par excellence. This Quayle-Coats series of events proved professionally irresistible to me, and I contacted Curt Smith, my friend and the press secretary for Coats, and told him how much I respected Coats and said that if there were ever any openings on the new Senate team, it was one of the few positions that would lure me to Washington.

A few months later, while I was sitting in the newsroom at WKJG, I received a call from Curt. The senator, he said, wanted to make me his first deputy press secretary, overseeing all the senator's radio and TV. This would be a pivotal position because Coats had to stand for election twice in four years instead of getting a full, six-year term like most new senators. Would I take the position, and if so, could I be in Washington to start in the next three weeks? I knew this was a remarkable offer, but I also knew it would be a large step for me, a major shift from a state I loved to the nation's capital. It also meant a shift away from extended family, to whom I was very close. This would be the hardest part about moving. I loved my family, my city, and my state. During my years with Senator Coats, there was no person who taught me more or served more as a personal and professional mentor than Curt Smith, the senator's first press secretary and a man of extraordinary gifts but whose humility became a benchmark. He hired me, and by doing so, set my life on a new professional trajectory.

We prayed as a family about this wonderful offer; we discussed the upsides and downsides; and in my mind and heart, despite the tug toward family, home, and the familiar, I knew being part of two hard-fought Senate elections would be the faith and action slot I had envisioned for myself and prayed about regularly for much of my young adulthood. Coats was a fiscal conservative; a security and foreign policy conservative; but above all, a values conservative whose original election to the House of Representatives in 1980 was a culmination, in part, of religious conservatives becoming actively engaged in the political life of our state and our nation.

Coats had built a career in the House as the primary defender of the traditional family, the sanctity of every human life, and a prime defender of marriage. His support of the Reagan defense buildup, his anticommunism, his defense of the Reagan tax cuts and pro-business policies, his original membership in the House's Conservative Opportunity Society, and his close friendship with Jack Kemp made him the ideal candidate for appointment to the Senate. He was prudent and winsome by nature, and that carried over into how he shared his faith and conducted himself. He had a knack for surrounding himself with a team of people who were both mega-talented and committed to the conservative first principles. This team of folks went on to hold important jobs in later years: Sharon Soderstrom became chief of staff for Senate Republican Leader Mitch McConnell; Ziad Ojackli became a vice president of the Ford Motor Company; Dave Hoppe became the president of Quinn-Gillespie, a major lobbying and public relations firm in Washington; Mark Souder went on to become a congressman from Indiana; Tom Keller, Vice-President of the Russ Reid Washington office; Rob Schwarzwalder, Senior Vice President of the Family Research Council; and Mike Boisvenne, who worked at a pivotal spot in the Green Zone in Iraq for several years. Mike Gerson became a columnist for *The Washington Post*.

Four years and two hard-fought but victorious Senate races later, Coats became a full-time, six-year-term U.S. senator in 1992. Shortly after the second victory I became the press secretary and later communications director. The staff was unified and close; the issue set was enormous. Coats became a leader in the Senate Armed Services Committee and in the Senate Labor and Education Committee, often going toe-to-toe with the late Senator Ted Kennedy. Coats and his tenure in the Senate proved to be one of the beacons of American conservatism in those years.

Dan Coats is one of God's great men. His civility, genuineness, kindness, and gentlemanliness are unparalleled in the Senate. When former U.S. Senator Paul Simon retired from office, he invited Senator Coats to come speak at the college in Illinois where Simon was a public policy director. Simon and Coats agreed on virtually nothing, and yet the civility and mutual respect between them was a hallmark of the way Dan Coats built relationships. On the plane to Illinois, Simon told me that, in all his years in politics, he never met a better man than Coats and that he admired Coats more than anyone he had ever met in the Republican Party in a public life spanning forty years. Similarly, Coats and Senator Joe Lieberman became fast friends when, on a foreign CODEL trip together, they noticed each other reading from the Scriptures, Lieberman from the Torah and Coats from the Bible. A short chat sprang into a conversation, which built into a long-lasting friendship of warm and mutual regard.

When I saw Lieberman many years later at a dinner honoring Bill Buckley and Jack Kemp, the senator told me, in almost the same words Simon used several years before, that there was no one in politics he admired more than Dan Coats. I learned a lot from Dan Coats—he was the ultimate mentor—but nothing more important than how to relate to people of the other party, other faiths, and other political views. He always told me that, as a Christian, he actively sought out personal relationships; and when differences arose, he chose to keep it professional, never personal. His personal integrity and good grace never faltered, even under the most stressful circumstances of two hard-fought Senate campaigns in the 1990s and another one, when he was sixty-seven years old, when he won back his old Senate seat.

One of the highlights of my years with Dan Coats was meeting Ronald Reagan. He returned to Washington after his presidency to dedicate the Ronald Reagan Center, which also serves as the Republican National Senatorial Committee building. After the dedication ceremony ended, a Secret Service agent asked three or four of us to temporarily move closer into the building to make ample room for the mass exodus for those departing the ceremony. I found myself literally jammed into a small hallway near the front door and thought I would merely walk through the new building and look for an exit out the back or on the side. But when I walked into the next room, I found myself in the middle of a VIP reception with members of the Reagan cabinet and none other than Ronald and Nancy Reagan. I turned around, and standing in front of me was the great man himself, with a ready smile and wink in his eye: "Mr. President, it is a great honor to meet you. You inspired me to enter politics."

"Well, this is just great," he said. "Thanks for all you are doing."

We shook hands; he kindly introduced me to Nancy, and I promptly departed on cloud nine. A photo was snapped of our thirty second meeting, which I treasure.

When he decided to retire in 1998, Dan Coats left the Senate with a full plate of well-deserved accolades and honors. He would later serve as President George W. Bush's first ambassador to Germany; and, as the man who took the lead in the Senate on the successful nomination and confirmation for Supreme Court Justice Samuel Alito. My decade in the Senate serving him and my fellow Hoosiers was pure joy. I came to hold Coats in the highest regard. Next to my own dad, Coats is the man I have admired and respected most in the world. I owe him so much. As it turns out, he would give me some pivotal advice upon his retirement.

I went to say my final good-bye to him in his office in the beautiful Russell Senate Office Building overlooking Constitution Avenue and the Capitol grounds. I told him I had a wonderful job offer but was uncertain about the next best thing for me and my family. His eyebrows expressed surprise: "Tim, you have worked at this end of Pennsylvania Avenue for ten years. You really ought to consider involving yourself in at least one presidential campaign," he counseled. Before that conversation I thought I might be done with politics. It had been a wonderful ride, and I told the senator I felt I worked for the best man in public life. By this time I was happily married; I had two young sons, ages two and six months old. Life was good. But Coats told me working for a presidential campaign would be the next logical step for someone who had enjoyed serving in the public arena for that long. He was right.

Two weeks after that discussion, I had a series of long and in-depth conversations with the well-known Washington consultant and journalist Jeff Bell, a man who once knocked off a sitting U.S. senator in a New Jersey Republican primary, Clifford Case, and nearly beat Bill Bradley in a hard-fought contest to become the next U.S. senator from the Garden State. Jeff was now working for Gary Bauer, the president of the Family Research Council, who was giving serious thought to running for president in the GOP primary in 1999 and 2000. Would I serve as Gary's communication director for the campaign? he asked. Would I meet with Gary the next day at his Family Research Council Office across the street from the National Portrait Gallery, near Chinatown, in downtown Washington?

I knew Gary a little. I deeply respected his principled stance on a host of issues. He was one of the smartest men in Washington. Gary was a Kentucky native, had a hard-scrabble upbringing in the town of Newport, near Cincinnati, and was the father of three children. He built the FRC into a social conservative juggernaut in Washington, and his debating and communications skills were unparalleled. He graduated from Georgetown Law School and rose to become Ronald Reagan's political director at the White House. Along the way he befriended Elliott Abrams, who would later become George W. Bush's deputy national security advisor; Bill Kristol, the editor of *The Weekly Standard*; and Dr. James Dobson, the founder of Focus on the Family, with whom Gary would write a book following his White House years.

I have never had a shorter, more productive interview in my life. Gary said he wanted to hire me; knew of my work with Coats; was prepared for a rough and tumble primary; and would fight till the last breath to articulate a conservatism that stood for low taxes, small government, a strong national defense, a strong defense of Israel, and traditional values, with a special emphasis on the pro-life cause. I was in sync with that credo, told him I was honored to be asked to serve, and for the next year I had one of the most dynamic experiences of my life. During the Bauer presidential campaign, serving as the communications director, I lived on airplanes and out of suitcases, traversed the country from Louisiana to Alaska, from Iowa to New Hampshire, from California to Kentucky, seeing the country and learning a whole new coterie and matrix of media and communications people. It was both exhausting and exhilarating.

Gary Bauer is one of the most eloquent, gifted speakers I have ever been privileged to hear. When Gary offered me the job as his communications director, he asked if I would like to join him for an event in Mississippi the following week just to get a feel for how he connected with an audience and what issues were on the minds of potential voters. We flew to Jackson for the speech—I had never heard Gary speak prior to that trip—and went to a standard political circuit dinner, the kind I attended a million times: chicken or beef, iced tea, and dessert. There were about three hundred people in a hotel ballroom. After two or three forgettable speeches by people from the local pro-life and family groups, Gary was introduced, followed by slight applause, as most of the people in the room did not know him. For the next twenty-five minutes he gave one of the most remarkable, heartfelt, passionate speeches I have ever heard. In fact, the room was dazzled. There were times when you could have heard a pin drop; other times he had people in tears; a section of the speech on World War II, Korea, and Vietnam was breathtakingly good. When he finished, there was a slight pause, and then the room came unglued with applause and a five-minute standing ovation. All Gary used for notes was a standard index card.

There were many highlights in the Bauer campaign: Gary beat Quayle in the Iowa Straw Poll, which was a significant upset and probably helped curry Quayle out of the nomination process early. Gary was routinely judged the most passionate and articulate of most of the nine presidential debates, which included Steve Forbes, John McCain (with whom Gary began a close friendship), Elizabeth Dole, Patrick Buchanan, and George W. Bush. He garnered a national reputation as a serious, smart, social conservative who had deep and informed convictions about lasting matters of national concern. One of the true highlights of the Bauer presidential bid had nothing to do with politics per se. It was the genesis of one of the most important friendships of my life. Frank Cannon was Gary's campaign manager. He was smart, tough, funny, brilliant, and indefatigable. He built an impressive campaign team from sheer moral imagination. Frank had John Wayne levels of true grit.

Gary's denouement from the presidential campaign ended after a pancake-flipping contest before the New Hampshire primary in February 1999. Gary lost his footing on the stage, fell backward off the rickety platform, managed to get up and stand with his wife Carol, recovered his legendary good humor (though he could easily have broken his arm), and was applauded for his sheer tenacity. He lost the primary in the Granite State, endorsed John McCain, took me along for a ride with McCain on the campaign bus The Straight Talk Express in South Carolina and then to a campaign stop that confirmed for me that, though my regard and respect for McCain was significant, I could not abide one of the most disappointing speeches he ever delivered.

Gary asked me to fly with him, McCain, and the McCain campaign entourage to Virginia Beach, where McCain was going to deliver a speech on traditional values. Little did Gary know, or virtually anyone know, that the speech was designed to be a fairly frontal assault on religious conservative leaders, with Pat Robertson in the bull's-eye, and in Pat's own backyard. Gary, learning of the speech's content only when we arrived in Virginia Beach, advised that the speech not be delivered in its present form without serious editing. He was overruled. McCain delivered one of the most ill-advised speeches of his career and later came to see it as the mistake it was, later apologizing to men like Jerry Falwell.

I continued to work with Gary at his political action committee, The Campaign for Working Families, as I thought and prayed seriously about returning to the private sector now that I had "the presidential thing" out of my system. It was an intriguing experience, but I was eager to reconnect with my wife and boys and get on with life after the Senate and a hard-fought presidential primary campaign. McCain eventually lost to George W. Bush, and everyone knew the Bush-Gore matchup would be a campaign for the ages.

Mine was a wonderful professional bridge from Quayle to Coats to Bauer. All were excellent men and each very different from the others. I was blessed to have worked for gifted conservatives, and their genuine faith and commitment to living the values they espoused were heartening and confirming against the sometimes cynical, skeptical narrative and tone of Washington. I believed then, and do now, that politics can be a noble and ennobling vocation. Through my work with all three, I learned that I love people, I love policy, and I love politics. My serendipitous journey from Fort Wayne to Capitol Hill, from Capitol Hill to the presidential trail, from radio and TV stations to the various offices and campaigns had been a great ride. I thought my life in the arena had now come to its natural close after the Bauer campaign. How wrong I was.

While working for Gary in his political action committee, I was in touch with one of my closest friends in those years, Mike Gerson. We were both on the original Senate staff of Dan Coats; dined together regularly; were in each other's weddings; and gloried in the births of each other's kids, the two Gerson boys and our two sons. Our families became close. Mike was working as the chief speechwriter for Governor George W. Bush in the Austin campaign, and we exchanged e-mails following Gary's campaign exit and endorsement of McCain. Mike expressed to me the possible need, in the Bush-Cheney campaign, of a conservative outreach person, someone who knew the territory but would also proactively reach out to key conservatives and people of faith on behalf of the governor. I agreed such a role was necessary, but my own personal interest, I expressed, was media driven not coalition driven; the communications side of politics was my area of expertise.

Mike and I remained in touch, and in the meantime I began a now-and-again conversation with one of Karen Hughes's deputies. Karen, who served as Governor Bush's communications director, and I got to know each other on the Republican Primary campaign trail when I was still working for Gary Bauer. We would see each other at various debates or media venues and always had plenty to chat about.

Gary decided to attend the Republican National Convention in Philadelphia and kindly asked me if I would like to join him. I had never been to a convention before; and after the year we spent on the campaign trail, I thought this would be one last way to say good-bye to lots of people I met over the course of the last year. On the night George W. Bush was to deliver his acceptance speech, a friend phoned me and told me he secured an extra ticket on the floor of the convention and would I like to be there? It took no prodding or lobbying, and the speech turned out to be one of the most underrated speeches of Bush's career. It was a rousing, creative, uplifting, inspired speech, and my only thought afterward was how disappointing it was going to be to have to follow the campaign from the sidelines in 2000.

As the crowds departed the convention hall after the speech, I got into a large elevator, and by coincidence Karen Hughes was standing right in front of me. We exchanged pleasantries, asking about each other's families; and as she departed, she said to me, "You know, we would like to get you on board." She then disappeared into the masses of conventioneers. *What did she say?* I asked myself. *Who is the "we" in that sentence—the campaign? What did she mean by "on board"—on board the campaign in Texas?* I was nearly speechless.

Later that week, and for several nights in a row, I went out for long walks around our neighborhood. I prayed a simple prayer during those outings: "Lord, I ask You please to give me direction in my life. I am asking You to open the right door for me and my family professionally and to show us where you want us to go next." Returning home about 9:30 from one of those walks, I noticed my BlackBerry light was flashing with new e-mail. I had an e-mail from that deputy of Karen's in Texas. Would I consider coming to Austin, joining the Bush-Cheney campaign as director of media coalitions, for a sum of money that meant a nearly 75 percent pay cut? Oh, and I needed to be in Texas in two weeks, with no time to spare. She needed to hear from me right away.

I believed, despite the economics of it, it was an offer I could not and should not refuse. This was an answer to my prayer, and it followed my vocation and my heart. There were only three months left in the campaign. I would be working six and a half days a week with no breaks. Jenny and I would have to rent our home rapidly, find a new place to live in Austin, and drive there within the span of ten days. With the exception of the Gersons, who moved to Austin, we knew no one and nothing about the city. We had never been to Texas.

When I married Jenny, I married up. Despite the incredible pressures this would put on our family, Jenny said yes instantly about my taking the job, despite being the mother of two young boys. Almost everyone advised us not to move to Texas as a family, saying that Jenny and the boys should remain in Washington and only I should move. But we wanted to be together, and I could not consider being separated from Jenny and the boys even for three intense months.

The next fortnight was a blur: We rented our home in Alexandria to a woman we had never met; we found, via the Internet, a tiny, two-bedroom apartment near downtown Austin, peopled mostly by day laborers; we packed and loaded our Dodge Caravan to the gills; and we set out on a driving tour that would prove the opening act in a new chapter of our lives to rival anything we ever experienced before or may ever again.

We arrived to one of the hottest summers in Austin's history. It was 100 degrees on the day we arrived, and the thermometer rarely if ever fell below 100 for the next two weeks. It was so hot Jenny could not be outside with the children during the day. In fact, the Texas heat was so intense our rearview mirror melted off the windshield. I tried to take the boys to the pool one late night when I arrived home, only to find the pool water was like a steam kettle.

I was dazzled and a little overwhelmed my first week in the Bush-Cheney campaign. The largest press staff I had ever been part of was four people. This campaign had twenty or more. I was used to receiving ten to fifteen e-mails an hour; now I was receiving that many every quarter hour. With the exception of one Sunday, I worked six and half days a week for the next three months, meeting some of the greatest people I will ever know, most of whom would go on to become my White House colleagues: John McConnell and Matthew Scully who were on the speech-writing team with Mike Gerson, Josh Bolten and John Bridgeland in the policy division, Ken Mehlman and Matt Schlapp in the politics division. I only knew Karl Rove fleetingly, but our friendship was seeded in that campaign and would bloom in the months and years ahead. The man who was my deputy in the Coats office and the Bauer office, my great friend Matt Smith, would be the last person to join the Bush-Cheney campaign in Austin, and so our professional journey together would continue.

The joy and excitement of election night would soon dawn, and it would prove to be the wildest night in contemporary American presidential politics. America would hold a presidential election. No one would win. No one would lose. And little did I know I would soon be boarding a plane in the middle of the night for Florida to be part of the most famous recount in American political history. Nor did I then realize mine was becoming a typical American story, in the narrative style of novelist Cynthia Ozick, of a young man going out into the world to find himself.

Chapter 4

Recount

We mean all sorts of things, I know, by Beauty. But the essential advantage for a poet is not to have a beautiful world with which to deal: it is to be able to see beneath both beauty and ugliness; to see the boredom, and the horror, and the glory.
—T. S. ELIOT[1]

The strangeness and otherworldliness of standing in the middle of Congress Street in Austin on election night, November 7, 2000, surrounded by hundreds of other people, for hours on end in the drizzle, waiting for an election result naming the new president-elect, with no ultimate conclusion, was the oddest evening of my life.

It was the first day of what would turn out to be one of the strangest and most discomfiting elections in American history, on par with the momentous election of 1860, which not only divided the country in half but roiled it into toxic disagreement for years to come.

The evening, however, began with a buoyancy after months on end of continuous days and nights of campaign work.

Our two sons and the Gersons' two sons were now being looked after by a babysitter at the Gersons' Austin apartment. We assumed it would be a late night and were glad all four boys would be together. I remember arriving in downtown Austin and going straight to the famous Stephen F. Austin Intercontinental Hotel for the election eve party. The room we were in had multiple TV sets, each tuned to a different channel. As one commentator would announce a statewide result, the crowd would rush, en masse, to hear what was being said. Then another announcer, on another TV set, would give another result. The crowd would rush toward that TV. This went on, like a Ping-Pong match, all evening. After a couple hours of that, we began to pour into the streets of Austin. The drizzle was becoming a heavier rain. There were multiple, bright, and loud JumboTrons placed around a large stage, flickering to and fro among the various satellite TV trucks. The buzz of excitement among the crowd was palpable.

The closeness and camaraderie of the Bush-Cheney campaign team was genuine, and we actually felt it that evening. I had been around two major Senate elections and another presidential campaign, but I have never seen such unity and goodwill among a political team as we had on that team in 2000. The campaign staff gelled and found great pleasure in one another's company. We had deep respect for one another, which would only deepen in the days and months ahead. I think, in part, this was because the roles among the most senior staff were clearly defined. That made for good working conditions. Karen Hughes, Karl Rove, Joe Allbaugh, and Don Evans—the four senior-most members of the Bush-Cheney team—all had specific duties, and their teams understood expressly their jobs.

Karen handled all communications and media relations. Karl was the chief tactician and strategist, doing special on- and off-the-record interviews with key reporters, writers, editors, and producers, along with special outreach on both the political and the policy sides. Even then Karl was the famed architect and was a model of clarity and efficiency. Joe made the trains run not only on time but cost efficiently. He loved to joke about cheap hotels and airfares. Don, the campaign's chairman, was the gray eminence par excellence, the president's best friend and confidante.

Even though I did not know him well, I was immediately drawn to Karl. I remember distinctly two meetings in his smallish, glass-enclosed office in Austin. He would hear every word by everyone in the room, absorb it all like a sponge, and have an immediate reaction that either gave a green light or a red light. There was no fuzziness or delay or muddled thinking. Karl was good at making decisions and giving clear instructions about how to proceed. I liked working this way. He was always on point, on message, and sharp and direct in calling the shots. This is how Karl worked in the White House as well, and those skills, I believe, were honed and polished in that first presidential campaign, despite the vast experience he had long before Governor Bush's run for the White House in 2000. Karl's direct, no-nonsense manner appealed to me but was always layered with roaring good humor. In those early but rare meetings of which I was part, I learned of the high-decibel laughter I came to love and expect, even when the stresses and pressures were higher than a kite.

As the election evening wore on, the uncomfortability factor seemed to rise in increments. The states were reporting in, but the results never seemed definitively to point toward victory or defeat. That was the heart of the oddness of it all. There never seemed to be that moment of clarity and closure when we had a sense the election momentum was ours or theirs. All of us were trained to believe that as the state's wins or losses rolled in, we were to be preoccupied by an electoral college count that would finally give us success or failure. There was, however, one recurring refrain that night: Keep an eye on Florida.

I received updates from fellow conservatives all day long from around the country, many from key battleground states, and so I was feeling good about how it was all coming together despite the lack of definition that evening. Conservatives worked hard for George W. Bush. We came to see him not only as a committed conservative but also as a man of faith who was comfortable in his own skin. We liked the fact his yea was yea and his nay was nay. After Bill Clinton, this was a welcomed distinction.

The comfortability factor really rose for President Bush among social conservatives dating from his answer in that December 14, 1999, Iowa Republican Primary debate when he was asked who his favorite philosopher was. Succinctly, and without pause, Bush answered "Christ, because He changed my heart." It was as if the whole dynamic of the primary began to shift among the conservative and Christian base with that single answer. Evangelicals, who had not yet decided on a candidate and who were particularly listening and watching closely for a nominee they could support and a nominee who could beat Al Gore, reacted overwhelmingly to that single phrase, and their support never wavered.

Governor Bush was not only bold in answering as he did. In that single reply he demonstrated that he did not mind being cast as an evangelical Christian. That single response opened him up to the vast reservoir of support among the "values voters," largely religious social conservatives, who were eager to learn whether the governor was not only pro-life but also would make that policy position a benchmark for his Supreme Court justices and federal judges if he got the nomination. I believe that for men and women of faith, it was the most important comment of the debates. I discuss this a little later in the book in my chapter on the values voters and our importance to the president's political success.

In addition to the strong support Governor Bush was garnering in those early primaries, he was also gaining the support of key social conservatives in a systematic but off-the-record outreach effort where I was spending lots of my time. One of the most important such meetings occurred a month after I arrived in Austin. My friend and fellow campaign aide Ted Cruz, a former Supreme Court clerk for Chief Justice William Rehnquist and later a candidate for the U.S. Senate from Texas, phoned me one day and told me Paul Weyrich, one of the leading traditional conservatives in the country, was in Austin and wanted to have breakfast to discuss Governor Bush's record and the campaign. Ted asked me to join him. Paul, who later became a close friend and ally, had a reputation for blunt talk and core, unswerving convictions, and so I knew the meeting would be foundational to our coalition efforts in the Bush campaign.

We met for a breakfast all of us thought would last an hour or so. It ended up going nearly three hours. Paul queried Ted and me on nearly every issue possible in a spirited, lively session. I came to see the repartee among the three of us was rooted in common principles and values; and by the end of the breakfast, Paul told us that, in all his years following presidential politics, he had never felt more comfortable with the core convictions of a candidate on the issues he most believed in, which were a strong national defense, the sanctity of every human life, the foundation of the traditional family, and American sovereignty. The breakfast ended in unity and common purpose. This kind of one-on-one outreach was a cornerstone of the first Bush campaign, and conservative support was one of the keys to victory.

This kind of outreach came back to me on election night in Austin as state after state began to go for Governor Bush. Confidence was building about what was happening. The hour was getting late; the loudness of the music ticked up a notch; floodlights were turned on, illuminating the beautiful Texas state capitol building. The rain continued its misty downpour. There were lots of smiles and goodwill amid the exhaustion of the Austin campaign team. Things seemed to be steadily going in the right direction now, but it was not to be.

There seemed to be no finality. A culmination moment of victory or defeat never came. Even as the music played on, it all seemed a prelude to nothing. It was the most hollow night of my life. Slowly a sense of puzzlement descended upon us (and the country) like a fog. Reports began to filter out that in fact there may have been a problem in the vote counting. Then there was speculation the problems in Florida were more serious than anyone first thought. Reports on TV began to say the vote counting in Florida might come to a halt.

The 2000 presidential election became the closest presidential campaign since 1876 and a stunning and bizarre example of modern-day political theater. It was beyond the scope of anything anyone was familiar with: No winner was emerging, and the hour was now late.

The JumboTrons were switched off. The crowd noise, so piercingly twinned with music in the background just hours before, fell to near silence. There was now a hush in the streets of normally busy Austin. Someone came onto the stage and told us the governor would not be making an appearance.

Knowing our sons were with a babysitter, we departed; and on the way to collect them, after midnight on November 8, we heard on the radio that in fact Governor Bush was the winner, which seemed amazing in light of the otherworldliness of what we experienced in downtown Austin. Vice President Gore conceded to Governor Bush, telling him, "We gave them a cliff-hanger." Governor Bush replied that Gore was a "formidable opponent and a good man." In that moment the governor became President-elect Bush. Hearing the news seemed anti-climatic.

But a strange night became stranger. By the time we packed our boys into our van, headed to our little apartment, and prepared to turn in for the night (or was it now morning?), we heard on the radio that Gore retracted his concession because of voting concerns in Florida. Gore called the president-elect again around 2:30 a.m. saying the Sunshine State was now "too close to call." Bush was necessarily incredulous. "You mean to tell me, Mr. Vice President, you're retracting your concession?" It was true, Gore replied, "You don't have to get snippy about it." Like the rest of America, we went to bed without any resolution about who would be sitting in the Oval Office in just two months.

Variously, over the next forty-eight hours, like a small army, campaign colleagues were systematically deployed to various cities in Florida, with the heaviest concentration in Tallahasee, Miami-Dade County, and Palm Beach. One by one, my colleagues seemed to disappear, each of us waiting like soldiers for our Florida assignments. A formerly buzzing campaign headquarters became like a hushed library, and on the fourth day after the election, Karen Hughes came to me, asked me to pack for four days or so, because she was sending me to Miami-Dade County to assist in the media efforts there.

She said I would be leaving that evening by private plane with ten other staff members. The plane would make three stops before mine, dropping me and three others at a private hangar in the dead of night. My specific task would be to help the media coalitions effort in Miami as the recount got underway. We arrived at two in the morning, rented a car, and began driving ourselves to a hotel in the heart of Miami. I remember having to wait endlessly, as a drawbridge went up and down in the middle of the night, in the center of the city, seemingly for no reason. For me it represented futility, disorder, and nullity.

I remember thinking: What am I doing in Miami at two in the morning after the tumultuous election we have just been through, waiting for a drawbridge in the blackness of the Florida night? What will this time in Florida actually mean? Laughter broke out spontaneously at that very moment in our car of colleagues. Everyone was thinking the same thing. The bizarre nature of the time we were living in, and being right in the center of it, bonded us. It was the single most important professional experience of our lives. We were apart from our families and friends, apart from the familiar; and we entered a period of uncertainty unparalleled in our lifetimes.

We arrived at the Miami-Dade County Courthouse the morning after our arrival. It is the ugliest building in America. Story upon story of solid concrete. The recount room looked like a casino, with four ballot counters per table, as if at a poker match. Lawyers loomed over all the tables, literally looking over the shoulders of the participants. I half expected poker chips and a dealer to materialize. It all seemed a huge mockery of our political process. On the day before the vote counting actually began, we stood on the courthouse plaza for our first scheduled news conference to set the stage for what was to transpire in the week ahead.

A grand total of one cameraman showed up, and he spent periodic moments going into the shade of a nearby tiny palm tree, sipping what looked like white wine or ginger ale. The camera whirred, unattended by a reporter or cameraman, and a congressman who was a strong supporter of Governor Bush, but not from Florida, was the man speaking into the lone camera, doing his best to provide a talking head for what was surely a gathering news storm. The cameraman then packed up his gear, and that was that.

By the next morning satellite TV trucks and crews and the typical media avalanche descended on Miami like a swarm of bees, the ground zero of the presidential election of 2000. All that week, across Florida in the disputed counties, there was growing concern about hanging chads, uncounted ballots, badly handled ballots, inspectors peering at ballots with magnifying glasses, and the seeming bread and circuses that went on and on. It all fed a growing frenzy that this was not how American democracy, much less a presidential election, was to be conducted. It is not that it was just messy or undignified. Rather it was unseemly and unworthy of our great country's reputation and honor. It was rapidly becoming toxic, partisan, and divisive. Americans were increasingly glued to their TV sets, watching the whole show unfold and unravel. Our national angst was of epic proportions.

As the counting began in Miami-Dade, protestors for both sides flooded the Miami-Dade County Courthouse plaza and the streets around it. Police cars and sirens were adding to the dramatic scene. People dressed like Santa Claus and Raggedy Andy marched with signs; horns were honked constantly at streams of protestors with signs. All the while, upstairs in the counting room, virtually anytime there was a disputed ballot, commissioners overseeing the recount seemed to rule in favor of the Gore camp. It was a partisan bloc despite the fact certain of the commissioners called themselves independent. On and on the counting went, with periodic starts and stops. Would everyone's ballot be counted? Would everyone feel secure that their vote was certain to be part of the final tally? These questions began to loom in the ether. The crescendo of animosity built day by day as the commissioners were under severe pressure to stop what clearly became an outrageous, shameful exercise.

Every time the Bush-Cheney camp protested the unfair counting procedures, the other side mocked and scorned us. The emotional toll was huge. We were called revolutionaries, and the first charges of stealing an election were now bandied about routinely. I think it was former U.S. Senator Bob Dole who chided the critics, saying of us that ours must have been a "Brooks Brothers revolution" because our levels of civility and diplomacy were high, the ultimate bourgeois protest.

I remember the particular strangeness of Thanksgiving Day 2000. Dick Cheney was sent to Florida to speak to a special holiday luncheon to which all of us in the campaign were invited. His job was to encourage us, thank us, and help boost our morale. He did a fantastic job, but the whole presentation was marred when someone had the idea of adding to the program mix the singer Wayne Newton, who said he wanted to sing us his signature song "Danke Schoen." The problem was twofold. First, with few exceptions, no one in that room was of Newton's generation. Second, and tragically, when he mounted the stage to sing, he promptly forgot the lyrics, culminating in what appeared to be a kind of *Saturday Night Live* skit. Newton's well-intentioned but strange performance added to the angst.

Afterward I went to my hotel room and phoned my wife and kids in Texas, and my parents who were spending Thanksgiving at my sister's home in Pennsylvania. I remember looking out my window at the ocean on a mercilessly hot day in South Florida and feeling utterly alone, cut off from those I loved most in life. My life seemed completely unsettled. I despaired, thinking: *Why is half my family in Pennsylvania and the other half in Texas, and I am here alone in Florida? What does it all mean?* I am an upbeat person by nature, and my morale had been high, even through the hurdles of that November. But for the first time I felt tired, sad, lonely, and helpless; and I missed my family and friends deeply. Speaking with Jenny and the boys made me even sadder because of us being apart.

My dad, my best friend, came onto the telephone line after a discussion with my mom. It was a providential moment for me. He told me, "Remember Tim, there is a purpose in all of this. We are praying for you. Don't lose your optimism. It will all work out. Be thankful to God for this. He will give you peace." I remembered Saint Augustine's charge that despair is a sin. Here I was, a thirty-six-year-old married man with two kids, needing my father's reassurance. Yet my dad, who was always there for me, even in the toughest times of life, was there again when I needed him most. It was the most heartening telephone call of my life. That conversation recalibrated my thinking: I was not a victim but the beneficiary of a momentous chapter of American political history. Win or lose, I was part of something larger and more important than myself. I came to see that there was in fact an alternative to despair, and it was a hope-filled sense that each and every day should be lived to the maximum. Carpe diem, for me, was to be Christ-centered, despite the outcome. When I put the phone down, I fell to my knees in prayer, thanking God for the trials and difficulties of the time I was going through. I also prayed for our divided country. I said to God that I was trying to find the thankfulness in all of this. I prayed that God would give me strength to trust Him in all situations and that He would give me peace and quietude in an otherwise chaotic and difficult time. He answered my prayer; and during the rest of my days in Florida, I never again experienced a moment of despair or apprehension, despite the many ups and downs. I remembered Dante's great line, "In his will, our peace,"[2] and found great solace in reading the Psalms each morning and evening.

Soon after that isolating Thanksgiving Day, the counting was stopped in Miami-Dade County, and a significant victory for the Bush-Cheney effort was declared. Over the course of my thirty-two days during the Florida recount, I would eventually spend time in nine different cities. A long night of sleep was four hours. During those thirty-two days we took only one day off. A small group of us decided to spend part of an afternoon at Epcot, at Disney World, since we were deployed to a neighboring county near Orlando. The whole day felt existential. The country was embroiled in the middle of a presidential election crisis, and for those of us in the campaign, there was no sense of normality or continuity.

Yet when we got to Epcot, we were jolted back into reality. Moms and dads, kids, and grandparents were enjoying themselves quite apart from what was happening in presidential politics. Were these Epcot families living in a bubble away from reality, or were we? The recount became so all consuming and the apartness from our families so "normal," that it took this scene of domesticity to remind all of us the depth of what was happening.

Without peer, the best five days for me during the Florida recount occurred when I was asked to work with former U.S. Senator Bob Dole in reaching out to veterans across Florida. The charge was to build momentum and support for Governor Bush and to use Senator Dole as the key spokesman. During the ten years I worked for U.S. Senator Dan Coats, I got to know Dole's staff and became friends with a number of them. But I did not know the senator, even though upon Dan Coats's retirement from the Senate, Dole and Coats would become law partners in Washington. Dole spent a lot of time in South Florida where he and his wife, Senator Elizabeth Dole, had an apartment.

Over the course of those five days, we traveled nonstop across the state, where Senator Dole spoke to veterans rallies and gatherings, appeared on a lot of TV and radio programs on behalf of the campaign, and wrote an important *New York Times* op-ed which helped make the case for Governor Bush and the necessity of having every veteran's vote counted. In working at close range with Dole, three things struck me immediately: (1) He read almost nonstop during our time together, mostly newspapers. (2) When he was not reading, he was preoccupied with the latest election news and spent a good deal of time watching the cable networks. (3) He was a gifted, incredible raconteur. I have never laughed so hard or been more intrigued by living history than during my time with Dole that week.

He was kind enough, on two occasions, to ask me to breakfast with him at a table overlooking the pool, cabanas, and sea on the ground floor of his South Florida apartment building. He regaled me with stories, one of which I have never forgotten. I asked him, "Senator Dole, during your career you have met everyone, done everything, been everywhere. Of all the men and women you have met, tell me about the most personally meaningful experience you have had." Without hesitation he told me it was his time with President Eisenhower. Dole told me that after his first election to the House, following his World War II experience, he received a call from Ike, a fellow Kansan. The president invited the young, newly elected congressman to visit him at his farm in Gettysburg where the Eisenhowers retired.

Dole told me the president proceeded to give him a personally guided, hours-long tour of the Gettysburg battlefield, complete with the president's own personal narrative about decisive turns in the famous three-day battle, the turning point of the Civil War. I asked Dole what he thought about that experience with Eisenhower. Dole paused. "What do you think I thought? I thought I had died and gone to heaven. It was Ike!" Perfect.

Everywhere we traveled, Dole received an outpouring of love and affection; his wit and winsomeness were suited for the role he was asked to play, and the attention he garnered for the Bush effort in Florida among veterans and their families was incalculable.

As the Florida political recount went on and on, seemingly without end, the legal and court battles were continuing apace, culminating in a series of Florida Supreme Court decisions that would eventually propel the whole election to the United States Supreme Court. But before that, on November 26, 2000, the Florida secretary of state certified that George W. Bush won the state. Dole pointed out that "the margin of victory that was certified [in Florida was] smaller than the electoral college itself, with its 538 electors." Still Gore would not concede.

The culmination of the whole Sunshine State effort officially came to a close on the heels of the Supreme Court's 5–4 decision on December 12, 2000. In the campaign offices there in Tallahassee, all of us gathered after the Court's decision was handed down. The clerk's office at the Supreme Court let the campaign know they had a decision, and it was faxed over. My friend Ted Cruz, a former clerk for Chief Justice William Rehnquist read the decision closely for five minutes. James Baker, who oversaw the Florida effort for President Bush, was looking over Ted's shoulder as Ted was reading. Baker then asked Ted, "What does it mean?" Ted said, "It means it's over; we won." Baker phoned Bush, and said, "Well, Mr. President, how does it feel?" The room came unglued with hugging and multiple cheers. More than a month after that rainy, indefinite, lugubrious night in Austin, the winner emerged through a blizzard of butterfly ballots, hanging chads, recounts without end, state supreme court decisions, angry protests, and a national constitutional debate. Echoes of the election of 1800 between John Adams and Thomas Jefferson always seemed close at hand.

Vice President Gore called President-elect Bush later that day to concede for good. Gore said: "Just moments ago I spoke with George W. Bush and congratulated him on becoming the forty-third president of the United States, and I promised him that I wouldn't call him back this time."

In that phone conversation Gore also echoed Senator Stephen A. Douglas's remarks to Abraham Lincoln after losing the 1860 presidential campaign: "Partisan feeling must yield to patriotism. I'm with you, Mr. President, and God bless you."[3]

After the Supreme Court decision, I returned to my hotel room and tried to put the clangorous, emotional swirl of the previous thirty-two days into some context. It was as if my psyche, and those of my colleagues, had been on a roller coaster for the previous month: This day up, this day down, this day slow and climbing, this day a rush downward. That month away from my wife and kids, all spent in various cities, was episodic, disturbing, and animated by various permutations of restlessness.

It is tempting to say there was a huge party, or celebration that flowed out of the victory. But it was not so. The atmosphere was one of a new reality dawning: A new administration had to be built from the ground up. We were way behind schedule in doing so, and many of the key people who would play a part in the new administration were strewn among Texas, Florida, and Washington, D.C. People were keen to pack their bags, reconnect with families, and begin to sort out how or if they would play a role in the new administration.

That day planes were chartered to return to Washington, and among the media and press staff, I was one of the few who was married with children. The anticipation of getting home was singular. I remember walking onto the tarmac, climbing the stairs into the plane, only to discover it was sort of like musical chairs. If there was not an empty seat, you would have to wait for the next ride home. That was me, so I sheepishly exited the plane. The next morning Ben Ginsburg, a lawyer at the Patton Boggs firm in Washington who played a foundational role in the 2000 Florida recount and I returned to Washington together on a separate charter loaded with snacks and TVs.

We landed on a brutally cold, icy, and windy day at Dulles Airport. I have never been happier to see my family than I was that day. I could not stop hugging my wife and kids, and of course the sense of joy among the four of us was huge. We had not seen one another in several weeks. The victory we did not get to enjoy in Austin was now ours as a family. My time away in Florida had been worth it, as had been the sacrifice of moving from Washington to Austin. But Jenny had borne the brunt of the pressure on our young family, and I will never be able to repay her adequately for that sacrifice. By God's grace a new chapter would soon dawn for us. Yet the reality of those thirty-two days in Florida would never escape us, so indelibly was its imprint on our personal and professional lives.

Chapter 5

I'm Calling You to Change Your Life

Far and away the best prize that life offers is the chance to work hard at work worth doing.
THEODORE ROOSEVELT[1]

Happy the man to whom never comes the thought, of what use is my work?
—T. S. ELIOT[2]

I was told many times as a boy by my maternal grandfather, "The only constant in life is change." He knew of what he spoke. He left Macedonia as a sixteen-year-old, made his way to America via Ellis Island, and lived in multiple places in a long life spanning almost the entire twentieth century. He saw gigantic, tectonic shifts in America. On a much smaller scale, but with his vision in my DNA, I lived the most changing, changeable year and a half of my adult life in 1999 and 2000.

I had left Dan Coats's employ after ten years in the U.S. Senate as a part of his senior staff; served as Gary Bauer's presidential campaign and political action committee spokesman; served in the Bush-Cheney campaign in Austin; served in the *Bush v. Gore* recount epoch in Florida as a part of the media and communications team for thirty-two days; and now returned to Washington with no job. There was a battle royale over whether to release federal funds to allow for a presidential transition office during the *Bush v. Gore* case, but Gore prevailed in that battle, and no funds were allowed for such a transition office. This meant that when the governor was finally victorious, there was no infrastructure for a formal presidential transition in place in Washington to prepare for the new administration. Instead, there was a privately funded transition office, skeletal in nature, operating in Tysons Corner, Virginia, about fifteen miles west of Washington.

It was by no means a certainty that just because I was a part of the Bush-Cheney campaign in Austin, or the recount team in Florida, I would necessarily be asked to join the formal transition team to the White House, especially in the historical and fraught atmosphere of the winter of 2000 after the Supreme Court decision. There was ample speculation that Dan Coats might be in the running for the position of secretary of defense, and I assumed I might be a part of that team to help prepare him, but that was indefinite, and so when the phone rang two days after I returned from Florida, I was pleased to accept an offer from Karen Hughes to join the media affairs transition team that would help staff the prospective cabinet members in the new administration.

Shortly thereafter I was assigned to the team that would help prepare Treasury secretary designee Paul O'Neill. All the while, there was a separate team, housed elsewhere, preparing for the inauguration. Even though I was assigned to the O'Neill team, it was uncertain whether I would go to Treasury with him if he were confirmed, to another agency, or to a place in the White House, which was always my first choice.

As temporary as this transition phase was, I was certain I did not want a policy position in the new administration or a position at Treasury. Secretary designee O'Neill and I got along well, but it was clear to me early on that for all his remarkable intelligence, we did not share the same views about economic or monetary policy. He was comfortable in the Ford legacy as a deficit hawk, felt at home in corporate America, where he was a star at Alcoa, and had much in common with his friend Alan Greenspan. I was a supply-sider in the Milton Friedman and Jack Kemp tradition, and I knew from quick research that these were not the ideas that motivated the secretary-designee.

When you are up for a cabinet slot, one of the rites of Washington, D.C. is that you take part in what is called a "murder board." Smart people sit in the same room as the nominee and fire questions at him or her to make sure the person is fully prepared in a mock congressional hearing session. O'Neill passed with flying colors. He was gifted intellectually, but his answers confirmed for me his views of economic policy were not in the conservative tradition, and even at that early stage I was a little puzzled that he was the choice. But he treated me with great respect, and I enjoyed our small span of time together.

During the O'Neill phase of the transition, I received a call from one of Karen Hughes's deputies, Tucker Eskew, who worked for Governor Carroll Campbell in South Carolina before joining the Bush-Cheney media team. Tucker became a good friend during the Bush-Cheney campaign in Austin and was helping Karen put together the White House media affairs team. This is an important division within the White House. The media affairs team divides up the United States into media regions and assigns someone to oversee and coordinate all the White House press in those regions among newspapers, magazines, TV, and radio within geographical boundaries.

Tucker asked me if I would like to be considered to be a regional media affairs director, and of course that appealed to me. My roots were in the Midwest, and because I was a press secretary and communications director for a U.S. Senator, I concluded that Karen and Tucker might be considering me for that slot. I could not have been more pleased, and because so many of the people I met in the media and communications division in the Bush campaign, and later in Florida, were going to be working in the White House media affairs division, it seemed a natural fit for me. I truly loved working with my colleagues—Jeanie Mamo, Scott Stanzel, Scott Sforza, Taylor Griffin, Ken Lisaius, Taylor Gross, Erin Healy, Andy Malcolm—and was pleased to be reunited as colleagues with some of them in the Eisenhower Building next to the White House where the media affairs team works. The media and communications team was one of the strongest, best groups of people in the whole of the Bush-Cheney campaign; and we were united, having been through the "wars" in Austin and Florida together.

Also, I knew media affairs would be working closely with the outstanding speechwriting team taking shape for President-elect Bush, the same trio who did such outstanding work in the campaign—Mike Gerson, John McConnell, and Matthew Scully—three of the best men I have met in Washington. History will show them to be among the best White House speechwriting teams ever. They were graceful and elegant in their prose; and unlike many speechwriting teams, they also had a core function in foreign and domestic policy.

But my whole professional future was turned on its proverbial head one morning when the phone rang as I was sitting at my transition office desk in the General Services Administration Building at 1800 G Street NW near the White House. We moved to the GSA complex from our temporary offices in Tysons once the election was decided. "I'm calling for Tim Goeglein," said the voice on the other end of the line. My heart began to beat rapidly. I recognized that voice immediately. It was Karl Rove.

"Tim," he said, "I'm calling you to change your life."

"Karl," I said, "You're a funny man."

I thought he was joking, only he wasn't laughing. "Tim, there is an office at the White House called Public Liaison. It is one of the offices that will be working with me at the White House. The president-elect wants to make you a special assistant and the deputy director of that office. You will be the middle man, the point man, for the conservatives and the faith-based groups. Are you interested?"

There are few moments in a person's life when his life is literally changed in an instant. This was one of those moments for me, and I recognized it instantly for what it was. I did not know what a "special assistant to the president" meant, and I had never heard of the Office of Public Liaison. But I learned rapidly it was the primary outreach office for the president at the White House, that Karl would be overseeing it, and that my role would be to help direct it in the new administration. Plus, for the first time in my professional life, my faith and my conservatism would play a central role. I was deeply honored by the offer and promised to give Karl a firm answer the following morning.

I shared the news with Jenny that afternoon; her love and support would be central, as we both knew the pending demands of a White House assignment. Our boys were young, the days at the White House were long, and this would be a family decision and commitment of genuine sacrifice. My prayer that afternoon and evening was intense. Prayers first and foremost of thanksgiving. Prayers for strength—mental, physical, and spiritual. But also prayers for a commitment to excellence of service both for the new president and for the country.

I phoned Karl the next morning, conveying how honored I was to be offered the job and that in accepting it I would strive every day to be excellent in what I did. He asked me to meet the following day with one of his chief deputies, Chris Hennig, who would debrief me on the four offices at the White House Karl would oversee as an assistant to the president and senior advisor. In the White House commissioned officers' structure of senior staff, there are three levels. The senior-most level is comprised of the assistants to the president. In the Bush White House, that was Karl Rove, Karen Hughes, Chief of Staff Andy Card, National Security

Advisor Condi Rice, Press Secretary Ari Fleischer, and others comprising a small inner circle. The second level is comprised of deputy assistants to the president, who are senior staff but work for and directly report to the principals. The third group is comprised of the special assistants, and this is the level where I would be working.

Chris debriefed me on the four offices Karl would oversee in the new administration—the Office of Public Liaison, the Office of Political Affairs, the Office of Inner-governmental Affairs, and a new in-house think tank that would help generate ideas, absorb the intellectual climate of Washington and the country, and where and when necessary impact that matrix, the Office of Strategic Initiatives. Chris introduced me to the woman who would become the first director of public liaison and my first White House boss, Lezlee Westine.

It is rare in life you befriend someone from your first meeting, but that was the case with Lezlee and me. We were two of the first people Karl hired. Our office would grow to fifteen people, though in previous administrations, Republican and Democrat alike, there were often up to forty-five people in public liaison. We would be doing a terrific amount of work for the new president with less than half the staff normally allotted to that office at the White House.

Lezlee was tailor-made for public liaison, which is the key outreach office to all the groups, coalitions, foundations, public policy organizations, niche groups, various VIPs, and associations across the country. She is first and foremost a people person, having the gift of reaching out and building relationships that could be leveraged to the benefit of the president in a unique manner. Her forte was business, with a special gift for connections with high-tech industries, and that is the wing of the Republican Party she came from. A Georgetown University-educated lawyer, her claim to fame was that she led the effort to flip Silicon Valley support from Al Gore to George W. Bush, a feat that almost everyone doubted could be done in 2000. But her creativity and brilliance met and exceeded that goal, winning that part of the business and entrepreneurial class for President Bush, which proved incredibly important for the Bush-Cheney effort in California.

My portfolio would be precisely as Karl described it to me in that original phone call, to be the president's man in the middle—the liaison to the conservative community comprised of the economic, social, and security/foreign policy wings of the movement. Happily, I was of all three wings, a conservative without prefix or suffix. I would also be the point person for the major think tanks and public policy groups and their leadership—The Heritage Foundation and Ed Feulner, the Hudson Institute and Herb London and Ken Weinstein, The American Enterprise Institute and Chris DeMuth, the Manhattan Institute and Larry Mone, the Hoover Institution and John Raisian, and the congeries of state-based think tanks organized under the umbrella of the State Policy Network headed by Tracy Sharp.

I built fast and natural alliances with the Free Congress Foundation headed by Paul Weyrich, Americans for Tax Reform headed by Grover Norquist, the Family Research Council headed by Ken Connor and later by Tony Perkins, Concerned Women for America headed by Bev LaHaye and Wendy Wright, Eagle Forum headed by Phyllis Schafly, and the National Right to Life Committee headed by David O'Steen and Darla St. Martin.

Also, I would be the point man for a host of faith-based groups and ministries: the Southern Baptist Convention, the Ethics and Religious Liberty Commission of the Southern Baptist Convention, the National Religious Broadcasters, Focus on the Family, Liberty University, the American Center for Law and Justice, the National Association of Christian Schools, the Alliance Defense Fund, the National Conference of Catholic Bishops, the National Cathedral Foundation, and a host of mainline and other evangelical groups. Though we had a person in public liaison who was the formal connection point with the American Jewish community, I also worked with key people there, namely Nathan Diament at the Union of Orthodox Jews, among others.

One of the great passions of my portfolio was the work I did with some of the major American cultural institutions, making sure they had a person in public liaison they could call on. I worked closely with the National Endowment for the Arts, the National Endowment for the Humanities, The Metropolitan Museum of Art, the National Gallery of Art, The National Archives, the Library of Congress, among others.

I worked to make purposeful relationships the centerpiece of my work as a reflection of the foundation of my life, Jesus Christ. Both Karl and Lezlee encouraged me to convey unfiltered into the White House the thoughts, views, and ideas of some of the key people affiliated with those groups. John Jay wrote: "To see things as they are, to estimate them aright, and to act accordingly, is to be wise."[3] It was my professional goal from the beginning of my service to the president to convey the opinions I heard in that transparent light.

On January 20, 2001, George W. Bush was inaugurated the forty-third president of the United States of America. It was a cold and rainy day, in the middle to high thirties. The president delivered a remarkable speech, calling upon the American people to seek "a common good," one rooted in civility and compassion. Civility was the centerpiece of his speech, which hit expressly the right note after the tumultuous Florida battle. In this much-underrated inaugural speech, the president showed why America is "a nation of character." The highlight for me was not only the speech itself, evoking the Jeffersonian image that an "an angel still rides in the whirlwind," but also the beautiful and heartfelt prayer of invocation from Franklin Graham that began the ceremony and the benediction by the Reverend Kirbyjohn Caldwell that concluded it. Those two prayers are a beatitude.

It was a glorious day altogether, made meaningful by having the president's parents there—the first father-son presidents since John and John Quincy Adams in the eighteenth century. Joining on the Capitol dais were the president's mother Barbara and the First Lady's mother Jenna (both looking on regally while covered in rain protectors); the First Lady, Laura, in a beautiful blue coat trimmed in black, and the president's dad, George H. W. Bush, standing just to the president's left behind President Clinton and Vice President Gore, who was stoic and without a top coat. Gore returned to Washington for the ceremony from a family vacation. Connecticut Senator Chris Dodd stood next to Gore in black coat and white scarf, all looking on while the Chief Justice of the United States, William Rehnquist, administered the oath of office.

Laura Bush held the family Bible as Rehnquist administered the oath to the new president, in a black robe trimmed with fancy gold stripes. The two Bush daughters, named for their grandmothers, looked on as Vice President and Mrs. Cheney stood behind them—their own daughters not far away. After the oath the new president gently and tenderly held the neck of his father with his right hand as he kissed his mother in joy. This was the most tender moment of the day.

I invited my mom and dad and my Aunt Anita (my mother's sister, who is like a second mother to me) to join Jenny, me, and the boys for the inauguration and one of the balls that night. I shared a special dance with Jenny and she was stunningly beautiful. I am certain we have never had more fun as a family than we did that day. The beauty of the music, the luminosity of those prayers, the gentle power and lucidity of the president's evocative inaugural address, the precision of the military, the ruffles and flourishes undergirding the high ceremonial nature of it all combined for a great day, a day of new beginnings.

We absorbed it all and prepared to go to the White House afterward for what we thought was an informal reception among the new staff. Once we went through White House security and made our way to the East Room, I was told I was to follow one of the White House military staff while Jenny, the boys, and my parents and aunt were to take a seat. We assumed there might be a short program of some kind. Little did we know Vice President Dick Cheney would be formally swearing in the newly commissioned officers, that he would deliver a rousing set of remarks on the purpose of public service, giving us a memorable charge and challenge for the presidency. Then, in another surprise, the Bushes themselves arrived to greet us and welcomed us to a reception on the state floor of the White House, their first public event there. As a lover of history, I walked slowly through the state rooms. I was overcome by a combination of awe, wonder and surprise—the sense that I was part of history, or something greater than myself—and it was a blessing to have my family there to enjoy it with me.

Afterward we wended our way to the Eisenhower Office Building, next door to the White House at the corner of Pennsylvania Avenue and 17th Street NW, directly across from Blair House and the Renwick Gallery of Art. This staid building, with as much history as the White House itself, is where most of the White House staff works. My new office would be located there. Our suites were on the first floor of the 17th Street side of the building. What a glorious old pile that building remains: twenty-five-foot ceilings, black-and-white tiled floors with parts of fossils in the stone work, giant mahogany doors replete with door handles left over from when the building was the Department of War in the nineteenth and early twentieth centuries, and plenty of filigree. Each door handle contained an insignia from whatever branch of the military that office represented.

I kissed and hugged my family, and before they departed, my mother offered a prayer that the work I would perform at the White House would be to God's glory. She then invoked a special blessing upon our new president and vice president and their families. More hugs. More kisses. They departed. I sat at my desk. A blank legal pad was on the desk in front of me. I was speechless. It had been a whirlwind ride to that spot, and something momentous was now getting underway. Public service was my vocation, but how to make it work and put it all together? The task seemed overwhelming. Where to begin?

Karl was right. He had indeed called to change my life.

Chapter 6

Stem Cells before the Storm

*The care of human life and happiness,
and not their destruction, is the first and only
legitimate object of good government.*
—THOMAS JEFFERSON, THIRD PRESIDENT
OF THE UNITED STATES (1809)[1]

Summertime in Washington, specifically August, is when the city seems most European. Official Washington flees the city to the Outer Banks in the Carolinas, the Maryland and Delaware and New Jersey beaches—anywhere but hot and humid Washington. The traffic seems magically to dissipate; many tourists with young kids do not come to Washington in August because it is too close to the beginning of the school year; and overall, the tempo and energy of the city regresses to the kind of sleepy southern city Washington was until the fury of World War II fundamentally changed it into a big government town.

August 9, 2001, dawned as one of the most relentlessly hot and humid days of that year in Washington. The congressional recess was underway, so Capitol Hill was desolate. The president and the senior staff departed Washington to the president's Prairie Chapel Ranch in Crawford, Texas. The Supreme Court was already on its summer hiatus. Many of my White House colleagues were taking their vacations so even the "eighteen acres," as the White House is often called by those who work there (so named because the grounds are a national park), seemed quieter than usual. Karl asked the week before whether I was planning to be in town that day, and I told him I was, even though I had no idea why he wanted to know.

A colleague in the White House domestic policy office also asked whether I would be at the White House that day, which I confirmed. When I heard the president say he came to a decision on stem cells early that week, I assumed the ninth would be the day of his announcement.

That August day deserves to be remembered as one of the most significant dates in the history of the young Bush administration. In a highly anticipated decision and in his first national speech to the country in prime time since his inauguration seven months earlier, President Bush announced he would authorize federal funding of research only on existing stem-cell lines. Having campaigned as a staunch believer in the sanctity of every human life, the president's speech was a confirmation of that commitment. Normally placid and quiet Washington erupted into partisan divisiveness immediately. The speech elicited the cheers of supporters and the jeers of the president's critics as almost no single issue had since the president came to office. I had never had a busier day in the White House. Immediately upon learning the subject of the speech, I began preparing for it by working behind the scenes to reach out and prepare our coalition allies and friends for what was to unfold that evening.

When the dust settled and the emotional tug of that announcement was better understood, the speech came to be viewed as among the most important domestic decisions of Bush's entire presidency and one that, in the long light of history, will be seen as the most important, prime-time pro-life speech ever discharged by a U.S. president.

The president said he made a decision to allow federal funds to be used for human embryonic stem-cell lines, but only on cells already taken from those embryos. He said the federal government would not support new human embryo destruction for research purposes going forward. It was a courageous decision, completely consistent with the pro-life policy he laid down in multiple venues and debates on the campaign trail.

The decision had a prudent, pragmatic element: The president made clear that research conducted in the private sector, without government funding, had already produced stem-cell lines with the ability to reproduce themselves repeatedly; and federal funding could be used on those existing stem-cell lines but not on any new human embryos. He said the life-and-death decisions had already been made on those earlier embryos. The new policy, the president said, "allows us to explore the promise and potential of stem-cell research without crossing a fundamental moral line by providing taxpayer funding that would sanction or encourage further destruction of human embryos that have at least the potential for life."[2]

It is tempting to say I had a heads-up or insider's view of what was coming down the pike in that speech because, among conservatives and people of faith, the president's pending decision was the single issue I heard more about than any other, day in and day out, for months before the policy was announced. In fact, I had no idea what the policy would be even though I was feeding significant amounts of research, information, input, and other data to my colleagues in the Domestic Policy Council from people who wanted to impact the final decision.

The American pro-life community rightly knew the decision would impact many other related policies for the rest of the administration. Although the president reinstated the Mexico City Agreement as among his first decisions as president—no taxpayer funding for overseas abortion—and spoke by phone to the massive annual pro-life march after his inauguration, a major question mark hovered over how the president would decide the new stem-cell policy. The heavy lobbying going on in those weeks leading up to the president's announcement was the most intense I had yet witnessed in the new administration.

For months before the decision was announced, scholars, public policy experts, researchers, theologians, and others came to the White House to spend significant amounts of time with colleagues of mine in the Domestic Policy Council and with the president himself. In our regular daily meeting with Karl, I would recommend thoughtful men and women who might be worth consulting on the issue of stem-cell research. Over the course of several months, I got excellent feedback from various quarters at the White House that in fact those views were being heard, as were the views of those who did not share the president's pro-life convictions. The consultation process, I came to see, had worked well, and the ability to convey views and information worked as it was intended.

Immediately upon learning of the prime-time speech, I asked Karl and a few of the senior staff what the decision would be. Although the trust factor was huge among us, there was a solemn agreement that the decision would remain closely held, for fear of leaks, because the president deserved the right to make his own announcement, a decision which I respected and thought the prudent one. When I was asked repeatedly what the decision would be by many of our outside friends and allies, or for any insight on what the decision might be, I was bold to say that although I truly did not know, I knew the president to be a man of his word, that his pro-life promises in the campaign, and in the early pro-life decisions in the administration on both policy and personnel matters, were proof-positive his stem-cell decision would be consistently pro-life. I said the president respected the bright lines between what the late Pope John Paul II called "the culture of life and the culture of death."[3]

The whole stem-cell process did something extremely important for me professionally: It helped me sort out what my role was and what it was not in the White House hierarchy, and this proved invaluable in the seven years that followed. My role at the White House was not, at any remove, one of policy making or policy formulating but instead one of information sharing and distribution. The role of being a reliable conduit was critically important to how the White House process worked. If and when I was asked my opinion during the policy formation process, I was happy to offer it. But my role was to be a reliable middleman, to absorb and feed into the White House the best of what was conveyed to me from equally reliable outside stakeholders. In other words, when the proverbial engine was firing on all cylinders in the Office of Public Liaison, the best public service I could render was to impart data points that helped the policy people inside the White House make good choices but also to make sure that, once those decisions were made, I faithfully and accurately transmitted not only how but also why those decisions were made. When this process is running smoothly, key constituencies can in turn convey to their own networks key presidential policy choices.

As the stem-cell policy unfolded, my role as a communicator came into sharper focus. My duties were to convey the policy in a clear, concise, synthesized, and consistent manner. I had to call upon all those relationships and friendships I had been building for months in order to mobilize them for action on behalf of the president's and administration's decision. All this was accompanied by building alliances that had a specific purpose: to make sure we used every available avenue—social media, e-mail, teleconferences, newsletters—to get the message out. Also I came to see that God had prepared me—as He prepares all of us through various life experiences— how to communicate effectively and efficiently a highly controversial decision with major ramifications. Years of being in forensics at Paul Harding High School, on the radio, and in debates prepared me to convey the policy in substance and tone fitting of a major presidential decision.

One of the roles I played in the stem-cell decision was to recommend or suggest the names of well-informed people who could be organized into high-level discussions with the right policy people. The goal was to explore common principles, which was important to the president and his senior team because it was key that everyone who had a stake in the outcome of the president's decision had the ability or opportunity to be heard. Karl gave me license to make recommendations of who those people might be, and that bond of trust is what made working for him such an honor. I knew that, rightly done, one of the goals would be to influence opinion shapers and formers. In order to do that, we had to tap into preexisting networks of like-minded people. This was an elemental part of my job for the president, and we worked systematically to meet that goal.

Two hours before the president's Prairie Chapel announcement, I received a call from a White House colleague who knew how important it was I convey precisely and exactly not only the president's final policy decision but also his reasoning behind it. This colleague asked if we might get dinner together, and of course I said yes. We walked to the nearby Old Ebbitt Grill on Fifteenth Street NW, near the White House, across the street from the U.S. Treasury Building. The Ebbitt is one of the great administration hangouts, regardless of which party is in power. That dinner proved to be a timely gift.

My colleague told me he wanted me to know two things ahead of the announcement. First, foundational principles came up again and again in the policy-formation sessions leading up to the president's decision. One was whether an embryo was in fact a human life. The other was more pragmatic but with an ethical gloss: If those embryos were going to be discarded under any circumstance, should they not be used to possibly discover remedies for various illnesses and diseases?

My colleague told me that, over the course of the preceding months, as the president met with various experts, these two principles came up repeatedly, and the president wanted to hear informed opinion and reasoning on both. Among the most thoughtful and learned people he met with was the University of Chicago bioethicist Leon Kass, who also did a lot of work with the major think tank the American Enterprise Institute. Leon would later become chairman of the newly created President's Council on Bioethics. My colleague told me the president was seeking clarity on both principles and thus deliberated his way through to an ethical, moral decision.

I told my colleague presidents usually used rare prime-time speeches to discuss issues of war and peace, or when a particularly difficult political issue arose, and not to deal with domestic social issues with heavy moral tones. But my colleague told me the president realized the national and international importance of stem-cell research had gained such huge momentum with its heavy matrix of moral, scientific, medical, and research ramifications. He wanted to elevate it to a singular place of importance. My colleague told me the president's announcement would confirm his pro-life stance while welcoming what science could offer to preserve life.

There were a huge number of stakeholders—a word used in Washington to denote people who have a particular interest in a given policy decision—on the stem-cell issue, so we began to work overtime to reach out and explain the policy while providing as much information as we could immediately after the speech concluded and continuing into the next morning. In fact, we worked nonstop to schedule a number of teleconferences and small-group meetings with key constituencies: think tanks, pro-life groups, members of the Catholic community, ethicists, scholars, a number of important medical researchers, and faith-based leaders, both evangelicals and Jews alike. We also made a point to reach out to some who strongly disagreed with the president.

We had an outstanding relationship with the United States Conference of Catholic Bishops, but they let us know they would strongly oppose the new policy. Their president at that time said the policy was "morally unacceptable" because the policy allowed the use of cells removed from human embryos. But most other conservative Catholics of standing supported the new policy, or at least understood the president's reasoning and respected his view.

The ministry for which I now work, Focus on the Family, a leader and reliable benchmark for American evangelicals, was pleased with President Bush's policy. Although Focus would have strongly preferred no funding whatsoever, it saw the utility and moral consistency in what President Bush decided and applauded the fact no taxpayer money would be used to destroy human embryos for research purposes. Focus's bioethics analyst Carrie Gordon Earll said, "What [the president] is talking about is using cell lines with embryos that have already been killed. We grieve the loss of those embryos, but the truth is they are gone, and we can't change that. He is not talking about destroying any more with the involvement of federal dollars."[4] She captured the policy exactly as the president intended it. I feared some among our conservative base might not make this distinction, but most did, and most came to see the president's new policy as the triumph it was for this relatively new issue area inside the pro-life movement.

Perhaps most surprisingly a number of people in the American medical and scientific communities believed the president's policy was a good one. They knew allowing for continued federal funding on existing cell lines was a prudent choice. The debate in those communities was mostly centered in whether there were an adequate number of cell lines. At the time the president limited the research to twenty-one such lines.

The criticism, however, was razor sharp, bilious, and nearly unrelenting. Most Democrats said full taxpayer funding of all embryonic stem-cell research was the only acceptable policy, skating around any ethical or moral reasoning. Both House Minority Leader Richard Gephardt (D–MO) and Senate Majority Leader Tom Daschle (D–SD) weighed in immediately but struck different notes and tones in their reaction. Daschle chose a prudent rhetoric, thanking the president for realizing the federal government could have a role in funding and research but wanting the Senate to address the policy head-on, presumably to lift the Bush restrictions in some fashion. Gephardt, on the other, chose a lower road. He said the president had "done the bare minimum in order to try and publicly posture himself with the majority of Americans," which was demonstrably false, and said full funding needed to proceed with "full force."[5]

Two of the White House pro-life highlights that flowed directly from the president's new stem-cell policy were the East Room events highlighting the so-called "snowflake children." Couples from around the country, most of them infertile, adopted frozen embryos, had them implanted in the woman's womb, and nurtured them through birth into childhood. These were among the most loving, caring, welcoming young parents I ever met. Their children flourished from the love and attention they received. We invited several of the moms, dads, babies, and young snowflake kids to come and meet the president. They shared with him their stories, with the refrain that "we were all embryos once." The president successfully put a human face on an otherwise abstract scientific argument about the ethics and consequences of destroying human embryos.

Short of a full ban on all federal funding, this was the most consistently pro-life decision the president could have made. It confirmed the growing view that President Bush was the most pro-life president in American history. That honorific would be borne out over the next eight years through two administrations in a host of policy and personnel decisions. The president said he found himself, in making the stem-cell decision, at a "difficult moral intersection," but he chose rightly, and that decision prompted his successor, President Obama, not only to overturn the Bush policy but also to use the full force of the Justice Department against a federal judge who ruled not only to uphold the Bush policy but with it Congress's intent in preventing unethical federal funding of embryonic stem-cell research. On this issue alone the pro-life/pro-choice contrast between George W. Bush and Barack Obama could not be starker, proving that elections have consequences.

The Obama administration reinterpreted existing stem-cell funding laws when the president changed the policy, concluding that research on embryonic stem cells could be separated from the deliberate killing of embryos from which cells for research are extracted and used. The

Bush-era law was specifically designed to protect embryonic humans, and Judge Royce Lamberth agreed when he temporarily blocked the Obama administration's anti-life policy.

Lamberth wrote: "Congress has mandated that the public interest is served by preventing taxpayer funding of research that entails the destruction of human embryos."[6] He was correct, and like President Bush before him, was subjected to an immediate round of meretricious character assassination. The judge's critics called him "brain dead" and "crazy" for merely restating what the clearly stated Bush policy and congressional intent had been. Despite the political wrangling and rhetoric, the Bush-era policy was the right one morally and scientifically. For President Bush, faith and reason were not at odds. In fact, he believed they were of a piece. There is not a single known cure using embryonic stem cells, but the ethical use of adult stem cells is showing promise.

Stem-cell expert Wesley Smith of the Discovery Institute wrote: "The hype of embryonic stem-cell research, the promise that was so often made that people would be out of their wheelchairs . . . that Uncle Charlie's Parkinson's will soon be cured—has been busted."[7]

In his eleven-minute speech to the country that hot August evening, the president said, "At its core, this issue forces us to confront fundamental questions about the beginning of life and the ends of science."[8] Indeed it did, and in doing so, the president hewed to his core pro-life convictions and proved his character on one of the foundational moral issues of the new century, of which he was the first president.

The Bush policy recognized the inherent relationship between the necessity of medical research and the immutable principle of human dignity. The policy was rooted in a view that any federal funding for the further destruction of human embryos would be prohibited on ethical grounds. The president navigated this storm with alacrity and faith, and his goodwill and natural prudence shone in that speech. The process of getting the message out, and making sure we blanketed the stakeholders, was a life-affirming chapter of my tenure at the White House; and it confirmed for me that, on the questions of the sanctity and dignity of every human life, I was working for the right man. No one could say he made a brash, unthoughtful, snapshot decision. He was deliberate; his internal moral compass guided him, rooted in his faith. There would be no moral obtuseness in defense of human life. It was a tonic and nourishing decision. All Americans saw the national stem-cell debate as an important test for their new president, and George W. Bush did the right thing.

Chapter 7

Faith, Compassion, and Conflict

*The legitimate object of government is to do for a community
of people whatever they need to have done but cannot do at
all, or cannot so well do, for themselves—in their separate, and
individual capacities. In all that the people can individually
do as well for themselves, government ought not to interfere.*
—ABRAHAM LINCOLN[1]

*I pledge our nation to a goal: When we see that
wounded traveler on the road to Jericho,
we will not pass to the other side.*
—GEORGE W. BUSH, FIRST INAUGURAL[2]

Despite the material prosperity America was enjoying when President Bush came to office, the attendant moral and social decay was real. America's social fabric was fraying. Too many marriages ended in divorce; the out-of-wedlock birth rate was high; the sheer destruction of the nuclear American family in some socioeconomic quarters was frightening, as was the increase of gambling addiction, pornography use, and gangs in urban areas. The number of hopelessly drug- and alcohol-addicted Americans was high. The net result was significant levels of poverty, homelessness, a growing prison population, and a general brokenness in the lives of too many Americans. What would the new president say about this? How would the new administration address America's most pressing social problems?

As governor, President Bush was impacted by the work of two important scholars, the University of Texas's Marvin Olasky and the Manhattan Institute's Myron Magnet. Both thought deeply about how civil society, not government, should be empowered to address these pressing social problems. Their books, Olasky's *The Tragedy of American Compassion* and Magnet's *The Dream and the Nightmare*, a social history of the 1960s' Great Society programs, documented and illustrated the deleterious effect of more government involvement in trying to address serious social problems.

In one of his first major speeches after coming to office, President Bush was invited to deliver the May 2001 commencement address at Notre Dame University. The speech is now largely forgotten. It deserves to be remembered. Its historic importance is its direct challenge to President Lyndon Johnson's famous 1964 University of Michigan speech commencing the Great Society's war on poverty. President Bush said repeatedly during his campaign that a new emphasis on faith-based solutions to some of America's most entrenched social problems would be an important element of his domestic agenda. He said one of his priorities, the one closest to his heart, would be a specific directive to knock down institutional barriers in the federal government to the funding of religiously based social programs. Those who kept those walls high erroneously believed there was a constitutional prohibition on the funding of such programs.

In that Notre Dame speech, the president set out the intellectual, constitutional, and policy basis for the creation of the new Faith-Based and Community-Based Office at the White House, and he illustrated what would come to be known as his "compassionate conservative" agenda. Juxtaposing the failure of the Great Society's welfare provisions with a new way forward, rooted in a partnership among faith- and community-based groups with government, the president said that while the Great Society "had noble intentions and some enduring successes . . . the welfare entitlement became an enemy of personal effort and responsibility, turning many recipients into dependents." He said the war on poverty turned "too many citizens into bystanders convinced that compassion had become the work of government alone."[3]

The president believed neither an all-big-government nor a libertarian, hands-off approach to addressing America's most entrenched social decay was the way forward. Instead, he called on the country and new Congress to "revive the spirit of citizenship, to marshal the compassion of our people to meet the continuing needs of our nation." He said he would do this by creating a new partnership between faith and community groups and the federal government. He said he would give the private sector wider latitude to address and resolve some of the pressing needs of the country. It was a practical commitment to compassion, rooted in Judeo-Christian social thought. Government would have a role, he said, but the historic brick wall of discrimination between government grants and contracts to faith-based groups would be eliminated and dismantled.

President Bush believed without religious liberty all the others liberties were not secure either. He favored religious freedom at every level of American life, including the ability of those charities to apply for government funding.

The president made his intentions clear from the outset of the creation of the faith-based office. What he did not want was government funding religion. Rather, he envisioned funding to support the "good works" that religious groups were doing in every community in America to help the poor, the needy, the destitute, the lonely, the orphans, the prisoners, and the widows. In addition, he wanted American taxpayers to be able to deduct their charitable giving, which in turn would create a new pool of nearly $15 billion a year in private funding. Also, he called on corporate America to do its part.

The president's personal faith was the genesis of these policies, a faith that taught him duty to others was more important than self; that serving a neighbor in need gave life deeper meaning and purpose. He said, "The same God who endows us with individual rights also calls us to social obligations."[4] He offered a challenge to the sea of young people before him that day at Notre Dame: "You're the generation that must decide. Will you ratify poverty and division with your apathy? Or will you build a common good with your idealism? Will you be a spectator in the renewal of your country, or a citizen?"[5] The president wanted the rising generation to "build a common good" by working to fight poverty and to battle against the social destruction that had descended on America. In the decade after that speech, a new generation of evangelicals, orthodox Catholics, and conservative and orthodox Jews made helping the poor and desperate a foundational part of the way they saw their faith.

In his presence on multiple occasions, I heard people ask the president what he considered the most important parts of his domestic agenda. He always listed the faith-based program first or second, whether the group he was speaking to or meeting with was a religious group or not. The heart and soul of this new set of initiatives was his Christianity and the role faith played in American history to make people's lives better. But his personal commitment to the faith-based agenda was even deeper and more personal than that. In his thirties he experienced a remarkably difficult struggle against alcohol abuse, which was impacting his marriage and family. He knew from firsthand experience that effective faith-based programs could save lives, marriages, and families. He talked about this openly and frequently on several occasions. When he spoke about it, it always made me appreciate even more the personal strength and fortitude of the First Lady and how she must have coped with his struggle through sheer love. When he overcame alcohol, it strengthened not only his faith in God but also his relationship with Laura. Theirs is a remarkable marriage—strong, loving, God-centered.

I believe Laura Bush is the most graceful, elegant First Lady we have had. Her natural grace and beauty gave the president, and the country, great strength during their eight years in the White House. That same panache succored the president through difficult times as he experienced life-changing renewal. His personal relationship with Jesus Christ, which he referenced in that Iowa Primary debate and which had become the most important relationship in his life, came to impact the way he understood effective, religiously-rooted public policy.

As governor, he came to see how faith-based groups addressed the most serious social needs more efficiently, more cost effectively, and more successfully than government. This is why he wanted to empower successful faith-based groups. Their "effective compassion" made them a terrific tool in the arsenal of battling social and moral decay. For instance, during his years in the Texas governor's office, he witnessed how faith-based groups transformed the lives of prisoners because of the central place of Providence in those programs. He worked closely with Prison Fellowship founder Chuck Colson on a Texas prison project, Innerchange, which significantly reduced recidivism rates and became a model for other states. The goal was to help these prisoners get back their self-worth and dignity, to build a new life beyond prison, and to be so changed by the power of the gospel they would become productive, contributing members of society. The prison model worked in Texas, and the president knew other such models would allow faith and government to work in tandem.

The faith-based and community-based program was formally launched nine days after the president's inauguration, January 29, 2001. I was there for the launch in the glorious Indian Treaty Room in the Eisenhower Building overlooking the White House and South Lawn. We wanted to show that drug addicts, homeless people, the mentally ill, and prisoners were not going to continue to be the sole wards of a secular, soulless state. Instead, they were going to be helped by a new working partnership. The president's remarks that day could not have sounded more different or distinct from President Johnson's forty-one years earlier. "When we see social needs in America, my administration will look first to faith-based programs and community groups, which have proven their power to save and change lives,"[6] he said, surrounded by a tapestry of leaders from faith and community groups to further underscore the partnership between faith and public policy.

The president named University of Pennsylvania Professor John DiIulio to head the new office. The mandate was to lift the bureaucratic barriers stopping or significantly slowing government funding to faith and community groups. This would be accomplished by establishing new offices inside select Cabinet agencies that had a significant role in these areas. A similar announcement was made a few days later at one of the faith-based ministries in Washington that worked well, The Fishing School, which was designed to help at-risk kids. The president personally visited the school to bring attention to how taxpayers could deduct their charitable gifts and benefit places like the school, which were making such a difference in the lives of young Americans in communities large and small across America. I accompanied the president and was smitten by the love and devotion that powered the program.

The former mayor of Indianapolis, Steve Goldsmith, who was named that day as chairman of the Corporation for National Service, and who would also have a significant hand in the new agenda, said, "Government should never fund religion. It can fund the soup, it can fund the shelter, it shouldn't fund the Bibles."[7] This would prove to be a critical and Constitutional distinction in the years ahead.

I had a firsthand understanding of this body of ideas comprising the faith-based and community-based approach since my years as U.S. Senator Dan Coats's press secretary. The senator was the first to launch, at a federal level, just such an approach. In the 1990s he offered a series of bills called "The Project for American Renewal." Like the president's approach, the Project recognized the central role faith played in true, personal transformation. The Project allowed for a role for government partnership as well but never at the expense of the centrality of faith, and always making the government secondary and not primary. Religion was the taproot.

The ideas for the Project grew from a variety of sources, among them from the Catholic body of ideas known as subsidiarity—how the church actually meets its obligations to the poor and the destitute. Also, from the ideas of eminent sociologist Robert Nisbet, whose pioneering research on what has been called the "intermediary institutions"—neighborhoods, fraternal groups, churches, synagogues—comprised healthy civil society in addressing social problems apart from government. These ideas prompted what would always be the main battle over compassionate conservatism: Whether government should have a funding role, or any role at all, in addressing social pathologies. If so, how and to what degree?

A *battle royale* of the first order accompanied the creation of President Bush's faith-based office from its first day. Groups that otherwise would never be in the same room together—liberals, libertarians, Goldwater-era conservatives, and many evangelicals skeptical of using any government funds for faith-based needs—all joined into a formidable phalanx against the office. Liberals did not believe faith-based groups receiving federal funds should be able to retain their unique hiring and firing privileges as ministries. Libertarians felt it was not the role of government to fund faith-based groups of any stripe. Goldwater-era conservatives did not believe government had the capability or the constitutional duties outlined in the president's faith-based agenda. Many evangelicals feared that if faith-based groups received federal monies, their ministries would be opened to government intrusion.

The sentiment expressed by Americans United for the Separation of Church and State was typical of the reaction on the Left. A spokesman said the new office was going to result in "an all-out battle" because "a lot of people see this as one of the biggest violations of church-state separation that we've seen in American history."[8] He was wrong in that analysis because he was wrong about the historic reality of church-state separation. The founders never intended to keep religion out of government but rather feared government's intrusion into religion. The founders were against a federally established church. The safeguards President Bush built into his proposed faith-based legislation carefully recognized and respected those constitutional boundaries and distinctions.

We expected this kind of reaction and formidable opposition. We also knew many of our otherwise most trusted friends and allies would not stand with us on this set of issues. It was not that the faith-based office did not have a constituency. Those who shared the president's view that there was a role for government funding in faith-based work had not been historic partners of conservative presidents.

John Ashcroft—a former governor of Missouri, U.S. senator from that state, and President Bush's first attorney general—knew firsthand how formidable the alliance against a faith-based approach could be. I remember discussing this with one of Ashcroft's senior policy people on the faith-based approach to welfare reform during the famous 1996 debates in Congress. The Ashcroft legislation allowed faith-based groups to compete for federal funding if they were using the money to help the dispossessed prepare for a new job and work. This was called charitable choice. Several state-based lawsuits arose from that legislation. Ashcroft counseled extreme prudence on how we proceeded in our outreach at the White House, which proved invaluable counsel to me. No overpromising, he said, and a scrupulous commitment to the necessary wall between government funding and constitutional restrictions. The Bush approach assiduously respected that bright line.

The biggest battle we faced was over those hiring and firing protections for faith-based groups that would receive federal funds in the president's new legislation. The recurring theme on the Left was that these provisions, which already existed in federal law, were discriminatory. What came into sharp focus immediately was that the Left and their allies on the Hill wanted to shut down the president's faith-based legislative agenda unless those provisions for faith-based groups receiving federal funds were either eliminated or severely restricted.

The president signaled to the Hill that he wanted to work together and was open to a reasonable discussion of these matters but he would not back down on two principles. First, faith-based groups should retain their right to hire and fire along the lines of the doctrinal teachings of their faith. Second, federal funding would flow to the substantive and programming parts of effective programs and ministries that were changing lives for the better but would not flow to any activity related to proselytizing or evangelizing. Having visited numerous faith-based programs, dating from my time in the Senate with Coats, I knew it was actually easy to separate programming funding from proselytizing. Yet the Left, which is often hostile to traditional religion and which wanted to use the faith-based agenda to create a political truncheon against the president, used its strong influence inside the Democratic caucus in Congress to stop the president's legislative initiatives.

My role in the whole faith-based effort was not Hill related. That was DiIulio's and his team's primary task in those years. They worked overtime, day in and day out, through months upon months of Hill visits with members of Congress, meetings with senior staff, phone calls, and other meetings to make the president's case. Yet the Left was uncompromising and put heavy pressure on Democratic members to thwart the Bush agenda. They gummed up the process of reasonable discussion and common sense and succeeded in closing down the president's legislative agenda. Once the legislative battle was over and the smoke cleared, they felt confident they succeeded in killing the faith-based agenda for good, but they were wrong.

The president decided to implement much of the faith- and community-based agenda by executive order, accomplishing with the stroke of a pen much of what Hill liberals and their allies thought they succeeded in closing down or shutting off for good. They had not fully taken stock of the moral convictions of the president. He was not one for turning. Despite the mean-spiritedness and religious bigotry amply displayed by some of the president's opponents, the executive orders allowed the historic bigotry that existed in some of the federal agencies against religious groups to be removed. Effective practitioners of faith-based compassion would now be allowed to apply for federal grants to help those whose need was great. Several cabinet agencies eventually opened a faith-based office. Compassionate conservatism was given a human face despite the storm of criticism and risible constitutional assertions that our founders never intended.

The president made the faith-based office and its themes a major priority during his years in office. He spoke about the successes of faith-based programs annually in his State of the Union Address. He liked to shine the spotlight on programs doing successful work. His push against federal-funding discrimination aimed at religious charities was a constant theme of his presidency. The Bush administration's programs of mentoring the children of prisoners and helping addicts get the treatment they needed impacted numerous lives for the better. Dozens of conferences were held nationwide, all designed to help faith- and community-based groups do their work more efficiently and cost effectively and to reach even more people in need.

The president kept his promise. Religious groups seeking entrée to federal funding would not have to check their principles at the door as they were used to doing. The president, in that initial news conference launching the program, said his administration's new policy would "encourage faith-based and community programs without changing their mission." He said his legislation would "help all in their work to change hearts while keeping a commitment to pluralism." In that Notre Dame speech, which set out the goals and intellectual foundations of this new initiative, the president made another promise, namely that because America had a successful tradition of "accommodating and encouraging religious institutions when they pursue public goals" his new Administration would "expand it to confront some urgent problems."[9] That is precisely what the administration did despite ferocious opposition.

The single most important thing I learned from my own work with the faith-based initiative, however, had nothing to do with the constitutional battles over federal funding, or the related ideological disagreements on the Right and Left over hiring and firing rights for ministries receiving federal funds, or the internecine battles over the proper role of religion in public policy. The crucial thing I learned, and it sort of frightened me at first, is just how vicious some could be toward the president simply because he was willing to stand up and talk publicly about his faith.

Presidents of both parties, from the beginning of our country's history, have spoken out about their religious beliefs and how those beliefs guided them in public life. But George W. Bush was the first contemporary, conservative evangelical president to successfully make it into the Oval Office after the rise of the new Right came of age. All the old and leftover baggage from those cultural battles of the 1970s, 1980s, and 1990s were applied to him with a vengeance, however unfair. Some of the president's opponents almost came unglued when he said he was a praying man; or that American schoolchildren ought to learn about intelligent design; or that morality played a part in the consideration over stem-cell policy; or that his decision to run for president was, in part, a decision made consonant with his Christianity; or that there was a role for religion to play in helping the people DiIulio called "the least, the lost, and the last."

The whole debate over the president's faith-based agenda taught me that any person in public life who dared to step up and speak about his or her faith publicly had to be prepared not only to be ridiculed or criticized; he or she also had to be prepared to experience deep personal animosity. But on this issue, the president refused to put his religion under a bushel. Margaret Thatcher said, "If you set out to be liked, you would be prepared to compromise on anything at any time, and you would achieve nothing."[10] President Bush is a man of great personal warmth and civility, but his first goal in public life was not to be liked. His faith was the center of his life, and if its public explication meant a deep outpouring of loathing and vilification from some, then he was prepared to accept that. His Christian faith, he believed, was relevant to good public policy and from that principle, he would not, and could not waver.

Chapter 8

Lightning Out of a Clear Blue Sky

Freedom is not something to be secured in any one moment of
time. We must struggle to preserve it every day. And freedom
is never more than one generation away from extinction.
                                        —RONALD REAGAN[1]

And what the dead had no speech for, when living,
They can tell you, being dead: the communication
Of the dead is tongued with fire
Beyond the language of the living.
                                        —T. S. ELIOT[2]

September 11, 2001 dawned in Washington as the most beautiful day
of that year and one of the most beautiful days I have ever experienced.
I left my home in Northern Virginia early that morning. The route to work
was always inspiring because of its historic evocations along the way.

The morning of September 11 was almost Edenic, with the clearest
blue skies I had seen in weeks. I arrived earlier than usual at the White
House because we were preparing for an afternoon briefing with the
president that would involve a large group from the American Association
of Christian Schools (AACS), and I wanted to double-check a number
of details. I knew the president would be spending the early part of the

day in Florida and then returning to the White House for our briefing, so I wanted to make sure the last-minute details were set.

Diane Knippers, president of the Institute on Religion and Democracy, and I planned to have a business breakfast that morning, and so as I crossed through Lafayette Park to get to the restaurant, I was particularly taken not only with the beauty of the day but also with the freshness of the air. After such a long, hot summer, it felt great to be outside and to see so many other people enjoying the last gasp of summer, even at that early hour. Diane and I, at one point, joked that we should have held our meeting in the park instead of the restaurant.

On my way back to my office in the Eisenhower Building, I stopped to say hi to a friend who worked in the speechwriting office, but he was out. When I peaked my head inside his office, I noticed his TV was on, set atop a filing cabinet, and that some commotion was going on in a live TV news report, the details of which I did not pay attention to since he was not there. I went back to my office, popped open my computer, and almost in an instant, events began moving rapidly, as if in a blur.

First, I received a call from my public liaison colleague and friend Matt Smith, with whom I worked through four iterations: in the Coats Senate office, in the Bauer campaign, in the Bush campaign, and now in the White House. Matt was overseeing the briefing with the AACS, and he told me the guards were not allowing him to bring people into the White House for the meeting with the president, which puzzled me. I knew the details for the meeting were set and the security clearance was correct for the group. Matt then asked me if I had turned on my TV, and I told him I just gotten back a little while ago and had not turned the set on since I left for breakfast. He said he was hearing buzz at the White House gates that a plane hit the World Trade Center in New York City. I told him that must have been what I was seeing when I briefly stopped into the speechwriting office earlier. Yes, I said, I did see commotion of some kind, but surely whatever hit the building must have been a small plane. Matt said he would phone me back.

Next, my second phone line lit up, and I noticed it was my parents phoning me. Had I seen what was happening in New York, they asked. I told them I had just gotten off the line with a colleague, who heard the same thing and that I was in the process of finding out and I would phone them back. Before I could find the TV remote, my phone rang again.

Now Matt said the guards were asking everyone to leave the White House all together, and foolishly I told him: If a plane has hit a skyscraper in New York, why would we be evacuating the White House? It genuinely never dawned on me that a large passenger plane could have hit the World Trade Center, or any skyscraper, and so the whole thing, from experience, was not computing. Having lived in Washington for many years at that point, I had been evacuated from federal buildings any number of times, and it was always because of false alarms or some unintended mishap resulting in standing on sidewalks and waiting for the all-clear, often for long periods of time. The day ahead was a busy one, and I knew if I left at that moment, the things that needed to be done would quickly pile up. Just then, my parents rang back: They said they heard the plane crash was intentional.

By this time my TV was on, and the horror of what was happening in New York City was unfolding. I couldn't believe what I was seeing and hearing. In this terrible moment I knelt at my desk and said a quick prayer, asking for God's mercy on those in the building and all those terribly impacted in any way in New York. It was an unreal, horrible moment.

Not five minutes later I heard a man in the hallway telling everyone to get out. I opened my door and saw him running through the hallways of the Eisenhower Building. He was sweating from every pore. He told a number of us to leave right away, that this was not a drill, and that we needed to depart as fast as possible. I quickly grabbed my jacket, shut down my computer, and was heading for my office door when my phone rang.

It was Matt Smith. He told me one of the guards nearly threw him over the turnstile in the old 17th Street entrance to the Eisenhower Building, working to evacuate people as fast as possible from the White House. There was no alarm system then, and though panic had not set in, a terrible urgency filled the building. We were like a river of humanity flowing into the checkerboard hallways, going down the winding staircases and out through the 17th Street exit of the White House. When we got outside, it was mass confusion, in complete contradiction to the calm beauty of the city just an hour and a half before. Cars and small delivery vans were rushing up and down 17th Street, not paying attention to any of the traffic lights. There were so many people on the sidewalks no one knew where to stand or where to go.

Amid the chaos around me, I witnessed a strange oasis of calm. It was among the most moving things I have ever witnessed. Some of the people who were to have been part of our White House briefing with the president formed small circles on the street, asking those who were panicked or distressed to join them for a quick moment of prayer for our country. Complete strangers were hugging other people, and I saw a number of people with hands over their mouths in a state of disbelief about what was happening.

As people poured into the streets, the buzz about what was actually occurring had a ricochet effect: Someone said there was a bomb blast and a fire on the Mall. Someone else said the Pentagon was hit. Someone else said a second skyscraper in New York City was hit by another plane. By now every office around the White House was being evacuated, and because of the near pandemonium in the streets, many people did not know where to go or what to do. I was among them. A group of guards on the street urged people to make their way down toward the World Bank and International Monetary Fund a few blocks from the White House; the goal was to clear the perimeter around the White House. But given the buzz about terrorist attacks, people did not want to head in the direction of those two global institutions, so many people scattered elsewhere.

I tried to remain resolute and calm, and then realized I could not get to my car because the White House and the parking lot were now closed indefinitely. I had plenty of friends with offices near the White House, but they were all likely gone as well by now. I tried repeatedly to phone my wife, but the phone lines were dead. Matt Smith and I met up amid the crowds and decided to make our way uptown to the offices of—of all things—*Crisis Magazine*, which was published by the Morley Institute's Deal Hudson, a friend. He was in his office that morning and welcomed us. *Crisis* never owned a television, he said, and since the traffic was by now locked up and immense, he decided to walk to a local store, purchase a TV, and bring it back to the office so we could access news of what was occurring. We decided to stay at the *Crisis* offices for a while and catch our breath. Once Deal got back and we turned on the TV, we were able for the first time to get a fuller and more definitive view of what was actually happening in New York and Washington. It was the first time we learned the Pentagon and the second World Trade Center tower had been hit. It was almost too much to take in.

I tried again throughout the morning to phone Jenny and my parents, but the phone lines were overwhelmed. I knew they would be phoning me as well, but we were unable to connect.

As the morning unfolded, we learned about the president's reaction in Florida after our Chief of Staff Andy Card whispered the news of the attack into his ear during a public event with schoolkids there. We learned that Air Force One was not coming back to Washington for fear of another attack in the Washington metro area. We learned that the vice president and members of the senior staff remained in the White House situation room even as the rest of the White House was emptied.

The horror of seeing the buildings come down while our fellow Americans remained inside, looking out of or jumping from the windows; the news about the plane crashing in Pennsylvania; the reports from the blown-apart Pentagon; the endless footage from the streets of New York—the composite was a horror show on a magnitude almost beyond my comprehension. Several times I excused myself from the office where we were watching TV just to pray and attempt to internalize what was happening. Foremost in my prayers were the families of those who lost their lives in New York, Washington, and Pennsylvania. Amid the confusion, I grew deeply frustrated in my inability to reach my wife and parents on the phone.

After several hours of watching and waiting, the traffic was clearing out a bit, and Deal kindly agreed to drive Matt, me, and three others home. I thought about taking the subway but learned the blue and orange lines, which I would have taken to Alexandria, were closed because they ran through the Pentagon. As we headed home and hit a high point in Northwest Washington, I looked over my shoulder and saw for the first time the black smoke billowing from the Pentagon. I drove past the Pentagon every morning on my way to work and every evening on my way home. The side of the Pentagon closest to the George Washington Parkway was hit, and I had driven by that side of the building the morning of 9-11. The Pentagon, for me, symbolized the ultimate symbol of American strength and freedom. I would later come to befriend a brother in Christ, Brian Birdwell, who was one of few people to survive the terrorist attack in that part of the ring of the Pentagon, and his experience, which he tells in his own gripping book describing how he survived that day and in the weeks following, is nothing short of miraculous.

The normal commute to my home in rush hour from Washington was twenty to thirty minutes or so; on September 11, it took nearly two hours. When I finally arrived home, I was never so thrilled to see my family in all my life. I did not want to let my wife or boys out of my embrace. Our boys were then five and three, and Jenny informed me she was at our son Paul's preschool where one of the teachers' husband was in New York City that day for a meeting at the World Trade Center. We later learned he was fine, by God's grace.

I will never forget the power of President Bush's statement to our country, that "freedom itself" had been attacked. He said: "Pictures of planes flying into buildings, fires burning, huge structures collapsing have

filled us with disbelief, terrible sadness, and a quiet unyielding anger. . . .
America was targeted . . . because we're the brightest beacon for freedom
and opportunity in the world. . . . I ask for your prayers for all those who
grieve. . . . I pray they will be comforted by a power greater than any of
us, spoken through the ages in Psalm 23: 'Even though I walk through the
valley of the shadow of death, I fear no evil for you are with me.'"[3]

By the end of that day, all I wanted to do was be in the presence of my
family, pray for those impacted, and be in touch with family and friends
who so kindly called to make sure we were OK. Coincidentally I had been
reading about the British in London impacted during the Battle of Britain
in World War II. They were buttressed by a singular motto: "Keep calm
and carry on." I could only pray for such fortitude, especially as it became
clearer this was in fact a terrorist attack on American soil, the worst since
Pearl Harbor. Despite the horror of it all, I knew I wanted to be with my
colleagues at the White House the next morning. We prayed as a family
that night, got as much rest as we could, and I rose early, taking the subway
into work, opened now following the attacks.

By mid-morning a skeletal crew had assembled at the White House,
and I received a call from Karl's office, asking me to be part of a small group
gathering in the Eisenhower Building to think about and plan for the next
few days. This was a meeting comprised of the Office of Political Affairs,
White House scheduling, the White House military affairs office, the
First Lady's office, White House Communications, and the White House
Social Office. People were giving serious thought about the president's
schedule—in Washington, New York, and Pennsylvania. During this
meeting I learned the president asked the First Lady and Karen Hughes to
give serious thought to a church service to remember those who lost their
lives. I was asked to design a plan for this service, perhaps at Saint John's
Lafayette Square—the so-called "Church of the Presidents" across the
park from the White House where many presidents worshipped. One of
the early ideas was to have a small, low-key service to remember all those
so terribly impacted by the events of what was even then being called
"9-11." Those two numbers were rapidly entering the American lexicon.
I told my colleagues I was honored to help plan the service and said I would
report back later in the day.

I returned to my office and spoke with a friend of mine, Paul McCain,
who was working at that time in the national headquarters of the Lutheran
Church-Missouri Synod in Saint Louis. He was an expert and scholar on
worship styles, services, and hymnody. In the course of our conversation,
I concluded it would be important to propose a large, national service.

It seemed to me this was one of those key times in the life of our nation where we needed to grieve together publicly, where we needed to express our faith in God and ask for His blessings upon our nation, and where the nation would want to publicly and formally remember those who were the first victims of terrorism in this new era. Above all, it was a time for prayer—for those who lost their lives; for those whose family members were killed or badly injured; for those who gave their lives for other people, whether first responders or passengers on airplanes or otherwise; for wisdom and clarity of mind and purpose for the president; and for those who were working around the clock at Ground Zero, the Pentagon, and in Pennsylvania.

Later that day and working in conjunction with many others as part of a team, I formally recommended the idea of "a service of prayer and remembrance," that we consider using the Washington National Cathedral, and that we work closely with members of the military and others to gloss it with formality as a fitting tribute to this terrible war wound our country was experiencing and mourning. Everyone agreed this was how we should proceed, and I began to outline, in rough draft form, how the service might come together and whom we might include. One of the things that emerged quickly was a desire on the part of some to make it an ecumenical service, including those of various faith traditions, as a reflection of America. I contacted some people I knew at the Cathedral and developed an outstanding working relationship with Tina Mead, who was then the CEO of the Cathedral Foundation. Our planning began in earnest that day, and we worked around the clock.

One of the key questions that emerged immediately was who should deliver the sermon? A number of important names were bandied about, but I felt strongly that, if he would agree to do it, Billy Graham was the right person and perhaps best suited to this most specific funereal moment in our country's history. I knew Franklin, Dr. Graham's son; and working with Matt Smith, we reached out to Franklin, who in turn asked his dad. I was told by a number of people that Billy Graham, whose health had been declining in recent years, was unlikely to make the trip to Washington. But Franklin called us back promptly after speaking with his dad. Dr. Graham agreed to deliver the sermon. Matt worked with a number of administration officials to get clearance of the air space for Dr. Graham's flight into Washington. Following 9-11, Secretary of Transportation Norm Minetta closed down America's air lanes. Dr. Graham was cleared to come to Washington within twenty-four hours. We included a number of religious leaders in the service.

In the service we wanted to highlight two meaningful solos. We wanted just the right person for those tender moments in honor of the deceased. I had been reading a lot about the young, stellar mezzo soprano Denyce Graves, who was getting remarkable reviews nationwide. She happened to be singing at the Kennedy Center during the 9-11 week, so using a contact in the White House Social Office, we reached out to her. She said yes instantly. She would be accompanied by her classical guitar-playing husband. Her solos "America the Beautiful" and "The Lord's Prayer" for the National Cathedral Day of Remembrance were luminous, her voice deep and rich like a viola. Those solos were among the most remarkable elements of the entire service, moving and inspired. Her excellence was of such a high caliber she was introduced to a new national and international audience for the first time. The service was a glory, a gift from God to our nation. The hymns, the beautiful Scripture readings, the elemental sense of remembering reached remarkable emotional heights and honored all those impacted so personally and tragically. The music soared and wafted across the buttresses of the Cathedral during that service as perhaps they have never done before or since. The unity of America that morning was unbreakable.

The highlights of the service, however, were both Dr. Graham's simple yet powerful sermon and President Bush's speech to the nation. I do not think he ever delivered a more effecting, more meaningful, or more timely speech in the whole of his presidency than the September 14 speech at the Cathedral. His sense of resolve, conviction, and justice shone brightly that morning. The net effect of both sermon and speech seemed to touch every chord, twining modernity and the skyscrapers with the eternal and transcendence of heaven. As we listened, we seemed to hear God's providence amid the evil of destruction and death.

Dr. Graham said, "We've always needed God from the very beginning of this nation, but today we need Him especially. We're facing a new kind of enemy. We're involved in a new kind of warfare. And we need the help of the Spirit of God. The Bible's words are our hope: God is our refuge and strength; an ever present help in trouble. Therefore we will not fear, though the earth give way, and the mountains fall into the heart of the sea."

Dr. Graham shared the right words at the moment our nation needed to hear them, but he also evoked the unreal nature of it all and how we were to try to comprehend the depth of it. "Why does God allow evil like this to take place? Perhaps that is what you are asking now. You may even be angry with God. I want to assure you that God understands these feelings that you may have. We've seen on our television, heard on our radio, stories that bring tears to our eyes and make us all feel a sense of anger. But God can be trusted, even when life seems at its darkest."[4]

The president's own speech complemented Dr. Graham's sermon, as if Jerusalem and Athens were in perfect equipoise that morning. "This world [God] created is of moral design. Grief and tragedy and hatred are only for a time. Goodness, remembrance, and love have no end, and the Lord of life holds all who die and all who mourn. . . . It is said that adversity introduces us to ourselves. This is true of a nation as well. In this trial, we have been reminded and the world has seen that our fellow Americans are generous and kind, resourceful and brave." President Bush quoted another war leader that morning, Franklin Roosevelt, saying that America, in all our wounded tragedy, was experiencing "the warm courage of national unity."

A touching, tender moment occurred after the president concluded and returned to his seat in the front pew. His father, President George H. W. Bush, looking straight ahead, leaned over and grabbed his son's arm as if to say, "Well done. I love you. I'm proud of you." It was a great moment. Sitting behind the Bushes were the Clintons, the Carters, and Nancy Reagan. America came together in a way it had not since the World War II era. The centerpiece of the service was prayer, and in a way it was the greatest national day of prayer the country had experienced since the end of the Second World War. By God's grace the spirit of common purpose and national destiny in that 9-14 service seemed boundless even amid the ruin of twisted metal and death of Ground Zero, the Pentagon, and the fields of Pennsylvania. Earlier that week members from both sides of the aisle in Congress materialized on the steps of the U.S. Capitol building to sing "God bless America" together. That unity helped us grieve as a country.

On the fifth anniversary of 9-11, the president and First Lady returned to New York City to visit Ground Zero, where they placed wreathes in pools of water there and attended a service at the historic St. Paul's chapel in Trinity Church, Wall Street. This was the parish George Washington attended after his inauguration at Federal Hall in 1789. It is the oldest public building still being used in New York. The church survived the 9-11 attacks even as buildings around it were crumbling to the ground. I was honored to help design the service for that anniversary occasion too. When the soaring, simple music commenced, so did the tears, the heartache, and the emotion and reality of it all: the buildings, the sirens, the fire, the smoke and ash, but most of all our fallen countrymen.

Those services, and the ones the Bushes attended every year on 9-11 at Saint John's Church on Lafayette Square across from the White House, embodied the best of the Bush presidency. They said something about the person who led the free world in those years: that he is a man of compassion for individuals, a man of prayerfulness, a man of decisiveness, and a man whose staff revered him for his transparency and lack of cant. On special, important occasions during the Bush years, the day always began or ended in church, and this was not by chance. This was a reflection of a man whose faith was the center of his life and his presidency. The president had a special gift of differentiating the genuine from the ersatz. This gift would serve him well in the parlous days ahead for America.

September 11, 2001 began on a beautiful morning. Then, quickly, with no warning, came lightning out of a clear blue sky. It will always be remembered as a tragic day, and in the weeks and months that followed, the president would lead our nation into two wars. The ramifications for the president's foreign and security policy, and the changes those policies wrought here and abroad, were immense. His would be a war presidency. But during that first week of sorrows catapulted by the initial attacks, the president navigated the most traumatic moment of his two terms with ineluctable solemnity, confidence, and resolve.

Chapter 9

Tackling a Tough Task

Next to faith this is the highest art—to be content with the
calling in which God has placed you.
—MARTIN LUTHER[1]

I love people, and I place a premium on friendship and collegiality. In my role in the White House Office of Public Liaison, I would come to see that my love for people was a part of my vocation, and in a way I never could have explained before I went to work for President Bush. Though I had been blessed with a series of professional situations since graduating from Indiana University in 1986, I had never really thought of my professional life in terms of a unique calling. An otherwise quiet and thoughtful priest, though, encouraged me to think of my work at the White House in just that context, and over time I would come to see both the glory and the utility of such a mind-set.

One of the men with whom I became close friends during my time serving President Bush was the chaplain of the House of Representatives, Father Dan Coughlin of Chicago. I am certain we never had a single political discussion, and I have no idea whether he is a man of the Left or the Right. Our time together invariably revolved around discussions concerning faith in public life, the potency of prayer, the mind and will of God, the most effective way to serve those in power, the importance of retreat from the busyness of the world, and perhaps the single most recurring theme of our many wide-ranging discussions—vocation.

Martin Luther famously wrote that vocation was what God intended us to do in life and vocation is not singularly or even uniquely a churchly role or position. It is not the same thing as our profession. Rather, vocation is that sense of being in sync with what Providence intends us to do with our lives. It certainly can be a religious calling. Father Coughlin, for me, will always be the ultimate priest, a man whose heart and mind from a young age was intended to serve others in his priestly vocation. For many others of us, vocation is not only the professional duties we have in life but also an added sense of feeling that what we are doing is the thing God selected for us before time.

In one of our lunches in the Capitol Building, I remember Dan telling me a strong sense of vocation was an utter blessing, that many people went through life never feeling called to any particular thing and that life for them was filled with professional frustration. He told me we were to be humble in our vocation, knowing God was bestowing upon us a gift, and we were to perform our vocation with grace and civility. He also stressed that each and every job has equal value and dignity before God and that the hierarchy of status in Washington and elsewhere was illusory and ephemeral.

Coincidentally, after one of these discussions on vocation, a White House intern asked to see me. He wanted to discuss what he would do with his life after college. Like Hamlet paralyzed by his indecision, my intern felt a grave sense of anxiety and frustration because of lack of clarity about what was the right thing to pursue after graduation. When I suggested he think about his life's work in the context of vocation, he asked me to frame it in the form of a question. I said, "If money were no object, how would you spend your life?"

I told him that in my own life, coming to work at the White House was the daily tackling of a tough task, but despite its rigor, stresses, pressures, and frustrations, there was never a day when I did not think it was the best job in the world. I told him it was the toughest, most difficult thing I had ever done professionally but also the most gratifying. I told him no one is ever fully prepared to serve the president of the United States, no one naturally slips into such a role with ease, but you grow over time in your vocation.

I loved serving the president, but I came to see the manner in which I could best serve him was by developing a multitude of friendships and professional relationships, culled from a wide variety of people in a host of professions both inside the Beltway and far beyond it. Hearing a variety of views from a number of perspectives helped me more accurately reflect back into the White House bloodstream the buzz on the street. It also helped me sharpen and hone my ability to conduct a good meeting, make a good presentation, and deliver an effective speech.

Successful coalition building sprang from a wide variety of activities: from one-on-one meals or meetings; from teleconferences among like-minded people; from reading widely in newspapers, magazines, and influential journals; from getting to know the scholars, authors, and reporters who wrote key stories and essays; from cultivating friendships in think tanks and public policy institutes; from conversing intelligently on timely or cutting-edge thinking; from casting the net widely beyond politics and getting to know cultural shapers and formers in the leading museums, world of arts, letters and humanities; and from getting to know men and women in the military and among the key veterans groups. I made it my business not always to convey the administration agenda but rather to listen, to absorb their information and knowledge, and take every opportunity to ask others their opinion, their views, their "take" on any given issue.

Over time I came to see that training myself to really listen was an art form; that the taking of notes was a sign of respect; that returning an e-mail, phone call, or letter promptly and with substance was part of the good manners and good service the president expected me to render to the American people. I came to the conclusion that everyone deserves to be heard and there is no substitute for forming a friendship cultivated and tended with care and precision through the years.

When I first came to the White House, among the first friendships I was eager to deepen was my friendship with Chuck Colson, the founder and chairman emeritus of Prison Fellowship. He essentially created the Office of Public Liaison at the White House for President Nixon. One day over coffee when he was visiting Washington, he offered me an intriguing idea: Why not reach out to a group of men and women who served as either the director, deputy director, or associate in that same office for other presidents, in other administrations, over the years. Why not spend a little time with them, he suggested. He said I would benefit from their counsel and advice, that I should just sit and listen to how they did their jobs and see what I could learn. I thought this was a brilliant idea, and over the course of the first six months of the new administration, I met with a host of women and men who served in the Office of Public Liaison or its equivalent for six presidents—Nixon, Ford, Carter, Reagan, Bush 41, and Clinton. The insight they offered was breathtakingly good, and I absorbed their war stories like a sponge.

I was intrigued by their sense of candor, transparency, and personal brushes with political history. The Office of Public Liaison is the most retail part of the White House—that is, the office that most routinely works with people with and without a political affiliation and often without a governmental moniker on their resumes. I garnered all kinds of tips—the do's and the don'ts—but above all, I was counseled to reach out proactively to people of influence and power, both in politics and in culture, and not wait for them to contact me or my colleagues. One former deputy director told me it was important "to build up a fire wall." I will never forget that phrase because in a pinch, it would be important to be able to call upon a particular person for help and that a previous relationship would help guide things toward resolution in an otherwise stressful or pressure-filled moment. I garnered all kinds of wisdom during those meetings, and I worked to apply the best of what I heard and learned.

I came to see that the most effective way to serve President Bush and the country was to communicate effectively his agenda to key groups and networks of influencers and opinion shapers, never forgetting that merely speaking to them was not enough. I had to build capacity at many levels by calling on those friendships and relationships to make the case for the agenda and to move it along. In other words, my job was not merely about information sharing; it was knowing precisely whom to call, whom to have coffee with, whom to visit, whom to teleconference with, what group to speak to, and what questions to ask (and what questions to avoid).

My modus vivendi was people and relationships, particularly with like-minded allies but often with men and women of a different political or partisan composition or stripe. It all depended on the issue and how we might do business together. It was all about coalition building— constructing a network of allies and partners working toward a common goal, whether it was new legislation, a new domestic or foreign policy, or an upcoming speech or major address.

I was tasked with communicating and conveying the president's key agenda items with crystal clarity to people of influence, to build relationships that could be leveraged to advance that agenda, to mobilize the right people for action, to build alliances that strengthen and grow through the thicket of political opposition, to organize high-level discussions, to explore principles, and to work out how to influence opinion formers.

Achieving these goals took a wide variety of formats, forums, and venues. For instance, I spoke each week when Congress was in session to the Wednesday gathering of the Paul Weyrich group, a luncheon of the top seventy-five social conservatives in Washington. I would usually speak for five to seven minutes about timely items on the president's agenda and then open it up for questions, answers, comments, and input. The atmosphere was like the prime minister's question time in the House of Commons. Though civil, those Weyrich lunches were a major part of my regular schedule, and I had to study and prepare for each of them because the questions, comments, and concerns were granular and sometimes biting.

Similarly, another group of conservatives—mostly economic and libertarian conservatives—met weekly under the auspices of the Americans for Tax Reform group headed by Grover Norquist. I spoke there each Wednesday as well and, as with the Weyrich lunches, had to prepare for the dodge, parry, and thrust of the weekly repartee and gamut of issues.

Both rooms were filled with allies, friends, and coalition partners, but the comments often differed with the president's agenda, sometimes starkly. Grover and Paul did a superb job of getting to the substance of the issue and effectively worked against personal criticism of the president or his cabinet even when they strongly disagreed. The issues and agenda, though, were fair game. American conservatism, in the best sense, can be barbed and pointed, and I had to prepare for the slings and arrows tossed my way on a variety of issues. Going into either one of those meetings unprepared would be the kiss of death, and more than once I saw the group mix it up with an unprepared member of Congress, or candidate for federal or state office, leaving the presenter almost speechless after his time on the agenda.

Grover's wry and sharp wit and Paul's famously acerbic nature (yet graced with mercy and good humor), made those meetings both intellectually stimulating and timely. Thought and action were of a single piece in those weekly gatherings, and there were no better forums anywhere for the give and exchange of information. The Norquist and Weyrich gatherings were the ultimate in conservative networking and planning. I often brought a guest speaker from the administration to make a timely presentation on some upcoming policy or issue, and I always told my guest to prepare for tough but fair questioning. Over the years Karl Rove, Ben Bernanke, John Bolton, Elaine Chao, and a host of others came to one or both of those meetings.

I made a priority to attend the gamut of center-right meetings, receptions, breakfasts, lunches, and dinners; to be a part of the think tank and cultural worlds; to attend the official or ceremonial goings-on around Washington with regularity. The special emphasis was always on increasing the network, expanding the coalition, deepening the relationships, and widening the circle of support for the president's agenda. In those instances where there was no support, I had to summon ways to convey why the president was doing what he was doing and how and to make sure that even when our opponents disagreed with us we had a rationale and a purpose.

In the world of coalition politics, one school of thought says if a group cannot or won't support you, why waste your time? That view prevails too often. But I found that someone who agreed with the president at least some of the time could be his friend, and for the group or individual who could agree even less than that, I was keen to single out that particular niche where we did agree and to build on that agreement to advance the cause and larger mission.

As the first twenty-four months flew by and we approached our first midterm, I came to see that many professional relationships were fast becoming friendships and that I could do my job for the president better and more effectively the more candid and transparent I could be, rooted in trust. We built permanent coalitions in a variety of policy arenas, but none was more important than the creation and maintenance of a reliable, fixed, outside coalition of like-minded men and women on the critically important issue of the nomination and confirmation of federal judges and Supreme Court nominees.

I sensed early in that first administration we would need to draw from four separate and distinct worlds comprising the center-right judicial and legal worlds: the social conservatives, the Reagan/Goldwater conservatives, the established legal community (both Republican and moderate-to-conservative Democrats), and the growing and important conservative nonprofit sector made up of the world of blogs, think tanks, and various public policy groups. All four of these groups were united in their common view of the founders' vision of the United States Constitution and the application of originalism. All four groups were dubious about the so-called "living constitution" theory—that the Constitution did not have a fixed meaning but its meaning was evolving over time.

A core leadership group of four or five reliable allies who could help mobilize, advocate, and push into the nomination and confirmation process on behalf of the president's nominees was the goal. The toxicity that developed in the U.S. Senate around the prompt and orderly confirmation of judicial nominees became almost legendary, and the Left's counter-goal of gumming up that confirmation process began almost immediately after the president was inaugurated.

I reached out to Jay Sekulow, Chief Counsel for the American Center for Law and Justice; Ed Meese, the seventy-fifth attorney general of the United States under Ronald Reagan and holder of the Ronald Reagan Distinguished Fellow in Public Policy at The Heritage Foundation; C. Boyden Gray, who served as counselor to President George H. W. Bush and an important Washington attorney in his own right; Leonard Leo, who is the executive vice president of the Federalist Society; and Ed Whelan, formerly of the Department of Justice and president of the Ethics and Public Policy Center. This proved to be a masterly team and fully united.

This core group of our coalition and the work they did on behalf of President Bush's nominees was without peer in the history of the American conservative movement. The excellence of their work was nothing short of breathtaking, and the president would not have had the success he did without their help. The building and maintenance of this coalition, and others, was foundational.

Similarly, on veterans' issues, I organized a regularly scheduled breakfast with all the heads of the major veterans service organizations in Washington. We gathered for breakfast quarterly with the express intent of allowing the groups to tell me without varnish what was on their minds. I told them at the beginning of every breakfast that my express purpose in coming to see them was not for me to tell them what the Bush administration was doing—though there were ample occasions when I did that—but to hear from them what they were hearing from their constituents far beyond the echo chamber of the Beltway. I absorbed their information and then conveyed what they shared with me to my colleagues around the White House and throughout the administration and in the agencies, all with the permission of the veterans groups.

I always made a point of leaving the groups with one action item unrelated to the veterans' agenda per se. I asked them to share this particular item with their vast memberships as a way of getting the message out to an otherwise unconventional audience. It might be an item from the faith- and community-based office; it might be a new health-care policy from the Department of Health and Human Services; or it might be something from the Pentagon. This kind of cross-information sharing turned out to work well with all coalitions, and it was a great way to move the president's agenda along in an otherwise counterintuitive manner.

In addition to all the work I did on the outside of the White House gates, I made a point to build relationships with my colleagues inside, and I placed a premium on the collegiality and goodwill I knew were important to the president.

I came to see that while senior aides had the most influence on the president (none more influential than Karl Rove, Condi Rice, Josh Bolten, and the vice president), another group of little-known senior aides played an especially pivotal role in the success of the Bush presidency, none more so than Matthew Scully and John McConnell in speechwriting, whom I mentioned earlier; Pete Wehner in speechwriting and later in the Office of Strategic Initiatives; Pete's deputy and later director of that office, Joel Scanlon; Jeanie Mamo in media affairs; Matt Schlapp in political affairs; Lezlee Westine, Julie Cram, and Rhonda Keenum in public liaison; Barry Jackson and Israel Hernandez, who were Karl's aides de camp; Ruben Barrales in Intergovernmental Affairs; John Bridgeland, Tevi Troy, Karl Zinsmeister, and Jay Lefkowitz in the Domestic Policy Council; and Stuart Bowen and Brett Kavanaugh in the White House Counsel's office and later the Staff Secretary's office. There were many others, too. Their talents, patience, good humor, loyalty, and—above all—commitment to excellence were endless and unstinting.

My colleagues' friendships gave me great joy despite the harried, stressful nature of the White House. In the world of Facebook, My Space, and tweeting, I came to see nothing can replace a person-to-person friendship. These unselfish people gave a rare gift to me, most of them without even knowing it: a sense of shared meaning, mission, and purpose far greater than any material gift they could have given.

The foundation of my work both inside and outside 1600 Pennsylvania Avenue was trusting, strong relationships. The glue that kept those relationships intact was fostering an atmosphere of diplomacy and civility, even when we differed.

Father Coughlin, the House chaplain, whose wisdom allowed me to think of my life in terms of vocation during our lunches and meetings, was right. He said when you are doing something you love, you echo the character of Eric Liddell in the film *Chariots of Fire*, who tells his sister in a powerful, pivotal scene from that film: "When I run, I feel God's pleasure." That is the essence and the nature of vocation: knowing you are in the heart of God's will; doing what you love; and serving a cause, mission, and purpose higher, deeper, and broader than yourself. It is knowing your purpose is in sync with God's will for your life. I felt God's goodness to me time and again, none more profoundly than when I came to that level of trust and friendship in the ennobling work of public service.

Chapter 10

Fortunate Friendships

*Friendship is born at that moment when one person says to
another: "What! You, too? I thought I was the only one."*
—C. S. Lewis[1]

In Washington, D.C., relationships matter. During my time in the White
House, I learned there are many levels of such relationships, and I came
to see there could exist a mutually beneficial professional bonhomie for
advancing President Bush's agenda while also rooted in the noble principles that fuel healthy friendship. These kinds of friendships are easily
misunderstood. That's because so many of them are formed and solidified
through high-pressure, high-stress political situations. Those natural highs
and lows of American politics burnish relationships.

During all my years in Washington, I have been the beneficiary of
some fortune friendships—people who I came to know, love, and trust,
and who have become among the most important friends of my life.
Some of these men and women were colleagues in the Senate, on various
campaigns, in the White House, or in other perches in the administration.
Still others were friends outside politics or public policy all together.

Two towering intellectual friendships of my life were formed long
before I came to the White House. These men actually guided me in
ways more important than I ever would have thought possible in the days
when our friendships were new. I met Russell Kirk, one of the founding
fathers of the American conservative movement in the years after World
War II and the author of the magisterial *The Conservative Mind*, when I

was a junior in high school in 1981. I met William F. Buckley Jr. during my early years working in the U.S. Senate, and ours solidified into a warm friendship almost immediately. His books *God and Man at Yale* and *Up from Liberalism* impacted my life powerfully.

With Russell, a fellow Midwesterner, I developed a friendship by letters, all of his typed personally and neatly and with nary an error, flowing as if each one was written for publication, so lucid and eloquent were they, word upon word. We exchanged letters on and off through the rest of his life, well into the 1990s, and we saw each other whenever he came to Washington, which was at least two times a year on average for lectures and speeches. *The Conservative Mind* had the greatest influence on me of any single book or poem I have ever read, and I eventually came to read all of his books and monographs. His remarkable wife Annette, whom he always referred to as "the beauteous," became an equally cherished friend. After Russell's death, she carried on his legacy in founding The Russell Kirk Center for Cultural Renewal in Michigan with the help of the indispensable Intercollegiate Studies Institute in Wilmington, Delaware, where Russell and Annette's son-in-law Jeffrey Nelson, also a friend, serves as a senior vice president.

Russell changed my life by seeding my intellectual curiosity. I came to see that his external life was much smaller than his internal world, which was large, deep, and wide. He taught me to be wary of ideologues because they got in the way of a good life. He famously said that "ideology is anathema." Conservatism, I came to see, because of the influence of Russell, was not an ideology but instead a way of life. There is no official or unofficial handbook for what constitutes conservatism, and in fact the conservative life is various.

Through all our letters, through our many conversations, through reading his prodigious oeuvre—both fiction and nonfiction (his ghost stories are remarkable)—I came to see I was not exclusively a social conservative, an economic conservative, or a defense/foreign policy/national security conservative. I was a conservative without prefix or suffix, one who believed, with Russell, that "the twentieth-century conservative is concerned, first of all, for the regeneration of spirit and character—with the perennial problem of the inner order of the soul, the restoration of the ethical understanding, and the religious sanction upon which any life worth living is founded. This is conservatism at its highest."[2] When I read those words for the first time in *The Conservative Mind*, I knew I had found a soul mate, even if we did not agree on all things. In fact, I once raised this point with Russell, and he was pleased that in fact we did not agree in all matters. He told me disagreement is a key part of conservatism, that there is no single document or manifesto that guides the conservative but that there are precepts rooted in transcendence, custom, order, and tradition that guide the thinking and faith of those who find wisdom in prescription.

When William F. Buckley Jr. once visited Russell in Kirk's small ancestral Michigan village of Mecosta—Russell liked to refer to that part of Michigan as "the stump country"—and asked him what he did for intellectual companionship there, Russell pointed at the wall of books comprising his library. That is not an inapt description of how Russell's friendship impacted my own public service in the Senate and the White House but especially the latter. Russell showed me it was important to live your ideas, that faith and action go together and not one without the other. He was a commanding public intellectual, deeply respected by men and women of the Left as well as the Right. I remember having lunch with the librarian of Congress, Daniel Boorstin, in the Senate dining room and asking him who had not only most profoundly shaped his intellectual life but effectively challenged it. He told me it was Russell Kirk; he said Russell was one of the most astute thinkers he had ever known. Arthur Schlesinger Jr. also had great respect for Russell, and both men shared a mutually high regard for Tocqueville's *Democracy in America*, among many other things. During my years in the White House, Schlesinger invited me to his Sutton Place apartment and office in New York City. We spoke of Tocqueville, Emerson, FDR, and JFK. But when I told him of my friendship with Dr. Kirk, that is all Schlesinger wanted to talk about for the next half hour.

I remember spending a winter weekend with the Kirks in Mecosta. I drove to their home, which was about five hours from Fort Wayne. When I arrived, I thought it was one of the bleakest days of the year: The skies were grey; the fields and forests were cropless and leafless; and the bitter wind seemed endless. When I came into their village, I did not know precisely where their home was. Annette had said, "Just ask anyone when you arrive," as it was a small village. So I stopped at the first place I found, a kind of combination gas station and gift shop. "Oh, the Kirks. Yes, they live in that haunted house down there," pointing just down the street. I chuckled, but the woman gave me a lame grin as if to say, "Just wait. You'll see what I mean." The Gothic house was indeed a landmark in Mecosta. The original Kirk homestead burned to the ground many years before on Good Friday, but Russell and Annette built a beautiful Italianate home in its place. It was not grandiose or luxurious; but it had a remarkable personality, perfectly capturing its patriarch.

The highlight of my time with the Kirks was when Russell and I took a short walk down a snowy old lane to the former cigar factory that became his library. Thousands of volumes animated the place, but there were two focal points in the room: the desk where Russell did his writing, usually in the dead of night while his family slept, and a large, roaring, crackling fire in the fireplace that in those winter months was rarely extinguished. When we walked in, I felt a sense of serenity and warmth and even peace. So many of the books special in my life were written in that library.

The last time I saw Russell was on his final visit to Washington. We had tea on the rooftop of the old Hotel Washington where he stayed when he was in the city. It was a glorious afternoon, and the terrace where we sat overlooked the White House and the Department of the Treasury. I made a comment about the statue of Alexander Hamilton that stands just behind the Treasury, near to the East Gate of the White House. Russell began to expound on the key chapters of Hamilton's life, the centrality of his role in the Federalist Papers, and was discussing the importance of Hamilton to America's founding as if he, Russell, was literally sitting having tea in the eighteenth century. He was not lecturing or moralizing but rather discussing and evoking in the most remarkable fashion, from his great mind, one of the central characters of all of American history. Russell's comments had a learnedness and vastness of knowledge that astounded me, and yet there was not a scintilla of pedantry in his approach. When I was with him, I always felt a sense of calm which was irretrievable, never fictive. He was a gentle man. He died, surrounded by his wife and four daughters, April 29, 1994.

Russell's friendship, animated by the first postulates of the good life, guided me in practical ways time and again. His was a worldview animated by a realm of noble ideas, mysterious splendor, and the ways God affronted confusion, doubt, and fear. Russell taught me to embrace justice, mystery, and an orderly and stable universe which was God-ordained and true. He showed that literature and civilization matter to the man or woman who chooses public life and that being guided by those central, exciting ideas—truth, beauty, justice, goodness—was a wonderful way to navigate a good and meaningful life. In all of my letters, lunches, dinners, and time with him, he never once raised a political idea or discussion. With Russell there was never a time of punditry or current events. If I made a comment about something in the news, he might express an opinion, but by and large we discussed history, biography, poetry, philosophy, theology, or shared a bit of humor. Russell Kirk's impact on me was indelible. So was Bill Buckley's.

In the 1990s I attended a noontime lecture at The Heritage Foundation, which was just three blocks from the Russell Senate Office Building, my office for nearly a decade. (I began going to The Heritage Foundation in the summer of 1985 when I was an intern for Dan Quayle in the Senate. Heritage hosted lectures and symposia that attracted young conservatives from the Hill and all around Washington. A bevy of authors, thinkers, and policy makers always made for a fortifying hour or so.) After the lecture I was particularly intrigued by an idea raised there. I wrote a letter about it to my friend, the Dartmouth professor and senior editor of *National Review* Jeffrey Hart, to get his perspective. Jeff shared my letter with Bill. I didn't know Jeff shared the letter, and I had never met Buckley. Shortly thereafter, in my postbox in the Senate, I found a letter from Buckley. He told me Jeff shared my letter with him, that he agreed with me on that particular point and would like to discuss it further. He invited me to have dinner with him and members of the *National Review* editorial board (the senior staff at NR) at Buckley's pied-à-terre in New York City.

As a young Senate deputy press secretary, who read virtually everything Bill wrote, watched innumerable *Firing Line* episodes from a young age, and enjoyed his Blackford Oakes fiction series, I was astounded that he was inviting me to dinner at his home based on a letter I sent not to him but to a colleague of his. I accepted the invitation; took the train to New York City two weeks later; and spent one of the most enjoyable evenings of my life with Bill, his wife Pat, and a small coterie of NR editors and other guests at their home at 73rd Street and Park Avenue. I remember walking into their apartment: King Charles Cavalier dogs barking and nipping at my feet; a tuxedoed young butler offering me a drink from a silver tray; Pat Buckley in a flowing white dress, perfumed aplenty; a harpsichord in the entry hall Bill was plucking; brightly colored paintings on every wall, many of them abstracts; and thence into a reddish-orange library for drinks and conversation before dinner.

This was the first real salon I ever joined, and the conversation ranged from that day's *New York Times* editorials to many topics far beyond. Bill had just returned from a sailing trip and was discussing the beauty of Newfoundland with his best friend who was there, Van Galbraith, who would later become a friend of mine through Bill's introduction. Dinner followed, eight of us at a large round table in a small, mirror-filled drawing or ballroom, the dogs omnipresent. The range and scope of that evening flew by as if in a dream. I suppose I have never felt more like an arriviste as I did that night.

I remember the most humbling part of the evening. During dinner Bill went around the table, raised a point or two, and then asked the guests what they thought, encouraging and prompting excellent conversation and humor. I soon realized he was being fairly systematic and eventually would come to me. I rarely feel intimidated, but I was surrounded by people whose work, both journalism and fiction, I read for years and wasn't quite sure I was actually supposed to be there. When Bill got to me, he put me completely at ease. He shared with the group the narrative of my letter that seeded our friendship, and he made me feel welcome in such a way that I intuited, for the first time, his legendary friendship, warmth, and grace. This was a providential gift, I believed in that moment, and the evening was among the most satisfying of my life. After dinner and now in another beautiful room, we had coffee and aperitifs (Bill and two others had a cigar). The longtime publisher of NR, Bill Rusher, was there, and at one point cited from memory a gorgeous poem by A. E. Housman. Near 10:00 p.m. we all said our good-byes. As we were doing so, Bill sat at the harpsichord, plucking a few more keys, and then saw me and his group of guests to the door. "See you again, my friend," he said to me and gently latched the large front door after we departed. The group quickly dispersed in a hale of cabs, but I chose to walk back to my hotel to try to internalize what had just happened. I simply never had an evening like that before and was certain I never would again.

Two weeks later I found another letter in my Senate postbox, again from Bill. When I was in New York for dinner, he asked me in passing if I had ever been on a sailboat. I told him I was born and raised in Northeastern Indiana; that while we had lots of lakes, mostly people had speed boats, fishing boats, pontoons, or small sailboats; and that I had never stepped foot on a sailboat. I knew, of course, of his fame as a sailor but did not think again of our conversation. One of my interns in the Senate was a direct descendant of the father of American football, Walter Camp. He had rowed crew at Yale, Bill's alma mater. My intern told me that "life on the water" was a different kind of life. I never forgot that wonderful phrase but had no idea what he was talking about. Bill asked if I would like to rectify never having been on a sailboat and come to his home in Stamford, Connecticut, for an overnight sail across the Long Island Sound, on a Friday evening in the early fall. Again I was surprised by the invitation and the generosity of it but felt sheepish: I envisioned it would be a party of ten or so people who all sailed, and then there would be me, the landlubber. I knew it was an invitation I could not turn down, so I steeled myself for awkwardness, happily accepted, and set a date with Bill's indefatigable secretary, Frances Bronson.

I boarded the Amtrak on an early Friday afternoon at Washington's Union Station, one of the most beautiful stations on the East Coast. I had only ridden the train two other times in my life and never as far north as Stamford, which is just above New York City and New Rochelle in the larger New York metropolitan area. Frances told me Bill would likely collect me from the Stamford station; and indeed, when I arrived in a light drizzle, Bill was there to meet me in the smallest Ford station wagon I have ever seen. Though fall, the weather was unseasonably warm. I noticed a Catholic Missal was between the gear shaft and the passenger seat, along with plenty of other reading material: a copy of *National Review* that was about ten years old, a dog-eared copy of *The Human Life Review*, a copy of *Commentary* magazine, and a copy of a Patrick O'Brien novel. Bill was wearing khaki pants, a cashmere sweater with the words *National Review* stitched into the upper left side, Sperry topsiders, and an old Greek-style light-blue sailing cap. His casual informality made him seem like a prep-school senior and not a man in his seventies. He extended his hands in a friendship clasp, and we then sped toward Bill and Pat's home on Wallack's Point (the house was salmon colored) with pot upon pot of blooming flowers of the richest color and variety.

When we arrived, despite the rain, many of the home's windows were open, as was the front door, allowing the sea breezes to pour into the house. The view of Long Island Sound fronting the manse, just down the vast front lawn, was beautiful, as was a pool with statuary and beautiful bushes and willow trees. The rain slowed, the clouds were dissipating, and the late afternoon sun was slowly emerging. A beautiful evening was breaking forth, a great night for a sail. I kept waiting for the other sailing guests to arrive, but this turned out to be a phantom concern.

Danny Merritt, who sailed with Bill for many years, dating from his own boyhood friendship with Bill's son Christopher, would sail with us that evening, as would Danny's twelve-year-old son. I asked Bill if it was just the four of us. Yes, just four; it was a hard and fast rule with Bill. Four was the perfect number for his twenty-eight-foot sailboat called *Patito*, he said, and five would be a crowd. The car was quickly loaded with all kinds of gear and provisions (I kept thinking: *All this for an overnight sail?*), and we then went to the Stamford docks, loaded the boat, and proceeded to have one of the most autumnal glorious sails. The wind was just right, and the sails were beautiful against the emerging sunset.

The clouds folded back; the twinkling stars emerged as if on cue; the Manhattan skyline was clearly visible and shining out of the near darkness. The mast, the sails, the retreating clouds, the dark water: There was an intensity bordering on grandeur which was an epiphany and sublime. We sailed across into Oyster Bay ("Fitzgerald and Roosevelt territory," I remember Bill saying), with Bach's music playing during most of our trip across the Sound. The whole evening seemed serendipitous. A sumptuous dinner followed, which was prepared earlier by Bill's chef Julian and reheated by Danny. As dinner commenced, Bach slowly gave way to jazz by the pianist Dick Wellstood, one of Bill's favorite musicians. The evening was now getting chilly, and fresh air was pouring into the boat as we slept that night, with only the sound of waves lapping against the boat during the night. Bliss.

A wonderful breakfast followed, with Bill rising early and the sound of a New York City radio newscaster giving the headlines and the weather. We returned to Stamford by mid-morning; lunched with the Buckleys and other weekend house guests, among them a prominent journalist, a bridge-playing friend of Pat's who grew up in pre-World War II Washington when it was still a sleepy southern city, and Bill's priest Father Kevin. I spent the rest of the day reading and relaxing. We watched a movie that evening in a leopard-rugged music room that doubled as a small theater, and I departed Sunday morning.

As I settled into my Amtrak seat, I realized that over the previous twenty-four hours I had entered a world unto itself and very much unlike my own, a world I had not been part of two days before. It was a unique entrée, animated by books, music, ideas, humor, good food, and joie de vivre, undergirded by Bill's unfailing generosity. Our friendship was really born that weekend and during the short sail. It also dawned on me that during my entire time with Bill he never once raised a political issue. Like my time with Russell, unless I referred to politics or some current public policy issue, the political scene never arose. We shared love for music (classical, jazz, the American songbook), ideas in literature, classic and contemporary movies (Bill referred to them as "flicks"), new and old novels, and the big and various personalities he had known in a remarkable lifetime including movie stars, politicians, writers, and journalists. These were the people and ideas stimulating our friendship, and it had the net effect of widening my world far beyond the Beltway and the life of pure politics. We would see each other twice a year or so in the course of the next twelve years, sailing together at least once a summer and often on a long summer sailing cruise as far north as the Bay of Fundy in Canada, the

Saint John River, much of Nova Scotia, and most of the East Coast, from Blue Hill, Maine, into Penabscot Bay, to visits on Nantucket, Block Island, Martha's Vineyard, and Newport. During those summer sails, I felt a sense of relaxation and insouciance that I have rarely enjoyed since then, or ever.

My friendships with Bill Buckley and Russell Kirk changed my life.

When President Bush came to office in 2001, I got Karl Rove's permission to honor a major conservative annually at the White House. The goal was not only to honor their achievement but also to evoke their role in shaping and molding the cultural and political contours of America through the conservative movement. In the first year we honored Whittaker Chambers, the masterful author of *Witness*; the second year, we honored Russell; the third year, we honored Bill; the fourth year we honored Ronald Reagan; and the fifth year we honored Milton Friedman. We had major speakers at each event—President Bush, Secretary of Defense Don Rumsfeld, Robert Novak, Chuck Colson, Annette Kirk, Michael Reagan, and George Shultz. Both Bill and Milton Friedman were able to speak during the sessions that celebrated their lives, which made those special occasions for the 250 guests in attendance.

The Buckley event was particularly memorable because it was scheduled to coincide with *National Review*'s fiftieth anniversary. The president's remarks were wonderfully done, laced with good humor and wit. He and Bill actually shared a lot in common. Both went to Yale, where they were members of Skull and Bones; Bill's son Christopher worked for the president's father as a speechwriter; both had a common family oil tie to Texas, the president through his dad and Bill through his; and both were well-known families in the East Coast Republican and conservative establishment. There were also important differences too. Bill was a libertarian economically, and the president was not; the president thought the war in Iraq was a necessity, and Bill was opposed even though *National Review* was a strong and consistent supporter of the war.

The world of conservative ideas formed the bridge into most of my closest professional friendships during those years in the Bush White House, and the world of the conservative and libertarian think tanks was a concentrated world indeed. In the think tank world, no friendships were more valuable than the ones with Ed Feulner, Ed Meese, and Bridgett Wagner of The Heritage Foundation. Heritage became the leader of the conservative movement, and their output of empirical research and significant studies was dazzling. Feulner, Heritage's president, is a man of vast experience, sage wisdom, an honest and transparent sounding board, and a principled thinker who knows how Washington really works. His counsel, insight, and sense of fair play helped me time and again, none more so than his willingness to pick up the phone and explain why he and Heritage disagreed with the administration on any number of things. I have already discussed the invaluable input of Meese, who is probably the most beloved and respected single figure in American conservatism now, a true gray eminence, and among the last living and active links to the Reagan governorship and presidency. He is wisdom and virtue personified. Bridgett Wagner is the ultimate coalitions builder inside the conservative movement and works with a perspicacity and efficiency that was astonishingly helpful.

George W. Bush will always be my favorite president. His personal kindnesses and generosity of spirit are unparalleled in my life, and I owe him so much professionally. As a conservative, I most admire two statesmen, Ronald Reagan and Margaret Thatcher. The power of their ideas, the strength of their character, and the wisdom of their governance were remarkable, and I consider one of the great honors of my life to have lived in the same time as these luminaries. Their governing conservatism was of the highest caliber.

When I was working in the White House, I received a call one day from Ed Feulner. We worked closely together, and during one of our occasional breakfast meetings, he asked me whom, other than Reagan, I admired most in political office. I told him Margaret Thatcher. I told Ed that her debating style was singular and that as a young man I learned from her ability to persuade through evidence-based reasoning instead of the use of cheap emotion, so often the fuel of contemporary political debate. Ed agreed, and in his call to me he asked if I would like to join him and a group from Heritage for a dinner with Lady Thatcher, who was coming to the States the following week. I readily accepted and anticipated the pending dinner with great relish. But three days before the dinner, I became violently ill. I was to have been in New York with President Bush the day before the planned Thatcher dinner in Washington, but I had to cancel the trip to New York, unable to leave my sickbed. Not only did I miss a key event with President and Mrs. Bush, but now, I thought, I would miss the dinner with Mrs. Thatcher, an event that surely would be one of the great disappointments of my life. Yet three hours before the dinner and for the first time in three days, my fever lifted, and my stomach ceased its endless summersaults all at once. Jenny pleaded with me to remain in bed, but I showered, shaved, dressed, and drove to the dinner as if I had never been ill.

The evening was a triumph because Lady Thatcher was in prize form despite a history of small strokes. She became the patroness of The Heritage Foundation, and her remarks that evening, though brief, were spot-on and florid in the great Thatcher tradition. It was actually exciting to listen to her defend a certain body of ideas, echoing Walter Bagehot's view that "the essence of Toryism is enjoyment."[3] I spoke with her after the dinner, telling her that, with Reagan, she inspired me to enter political life. "Ronnie inspired all of us. He is a great man. Great," she said, using that word twice. The next time I saw Thatcher was at Reagan's funeral at the Washington National Cathedral. There sat the former British prime minister, along with former Soviet President Mikhail Gorbachev, former Canadian Prime Minster Brian Mulroney, and former President George H. W. Bush. The Bush eulogy was inspired, deeply moving, and personal—a truly humility-laden appreciation. The Thatcher eulogy, which was taped earlier, was equally personal, equally well done but framed by the same dynamism and idea-centric rhetoric that made her, with Churchill, one of the two great prime ministers of the contemporary era. Margaret Thatcher is unique, and we shall not see her like again at 10 Downing Street— intellectually incandescent, and a leader, with Reagan, of a conservative fermentation in the West, rooted in the confidence of liberty. They deserve to be remembered as the two world leaders of the second half of the twentieth century who understood, at the deepest level, the spiritual dimensions of communism and socialism. Their righteous defense of immutable principles gave the so-called "Special Relationship" between America and England a burst of energy but also of elegance, grace, and continuity.

Thatcher, like Reagan, represented a world of ideas connected to action. This bridge of ideas and action was how my professional life was organized in these White House years. None more so than in the world of think tanks and public policy groups.

Herb London and Ken Weinstein of the Hudson Institute were equally gracious at every turn, as was Chris DeMuth, Mike Novak, and Walter Berns at the American Enterprise Institute. Larry Mone and Lindsay Craig at the Manhattan Institute were an oasis in New York City for the best conservative ideas. On the West Coast, John Raisian and the team at the Hoover Institution were always on the White House radar scope, and Hoover economist Ed Lazear ended up with a key economics post in the White House.

The State Policy Network—a coalition of loosely affiliated, state-based, center-right think tanks across the country—has become a force to be reckoned with. Friends at the SPN introduced me to a bevy of other, international free-trade, market-oriented think tanks across the globe, which helped provide yet other avenues to get our message out worldwide.

Also, I developed friendships with the leaders of organizations that reach out to bright, young, smart conservatives: Roger Ream of the Fund for American Studies, Ron Robinson of the Young America's Foundation, Ken Cribb of the Intercollegiate Studies Institute, Morton Blackwell of the Leadership Institute, Tim Echols of TeenPact, and Keith and Maureen Wiebe of the American Association of Christian Schools. These great folks were not always of one accord; most were nonideological; but all of them were good about allowing the Bush administration to share our ideas and policies, and the students were always willing to tell us where they agreed or disagreed. I recognized early on the great importance of reaching the rising generation of young conservatives and always wanted to make sure there was plenty of room for give-and-take.

Through this matrix of think tanks, public policy groups, and organizations uniquely constituted to reach out to young American conservatives and libertarians, I came to see in the first Bush administration the importance of reaching another important group of conservatives. These were the most important conservative magazines and journals comprised of the authors, writers, scholars, wonks, and historians who propounded a certain right of center worldview that battled back against the dominant, regnant liberal domination of the media.

But how to mesh with these worlds? One relationship at a time, building a level of trust and friendship over weeks, months, and years, and always respecting the bright line between my role as liaison and my White House colleagues' media and communications roles. It was a balance and ballast we achieved incrementally. The goal was not to get important people to agree with President Bush. The goal was to open a dialogue, earn the honor of being heard, and having the president's viewpoint thoughtfully considered.

The glue of the American conservative movement is the Madisonian view that our framers created a government of strictly enumerated and restricted powers that give most power to the states and to the American people, not Washington and its permanent, ever-expansive bureaucracy.

I came to see the conservative intellectual and journalistic world as a vibrant place, peopled by talented individuals whose own diversity of opinion, outlook, and styles destroyed the myth that there was anything like unanimity on the American Right. Yet there was a singular devotion among all conservatives to first principles and to the idea of American exceptionalism best exemplified in adherence to and respect for our nation's founding documents, none more so than the Constitution. That idea bound all American conservatism and was the foundation of some of the most fortunate, blessed friendships of my life.

Chapter 11

Jaw-Jaw to War-War

On matters of style, swim with the current.
On matters of principle, stand like a rock.
—THOMAS JEFFERSON[1]

The desk the president used in the Oval Office—the same one used by Franklin Roosevelt, John Kennedy, and Ronald Reagan—was constructed from the wood of a former naval ship, the *USS Resolute,* and given to the United States by Queen Victoria. The name of that desk fit George Bush to a tee; he was resolute by nature and never more so, I would come to see at close range, than in this new war against radical jihadism.

Three weeks after 9-11, on a rare, quiet Friday afternoon—the first quiet afternoon since the day of those terror strikes—I had been at Georgetown University for a meeting, and as I was departing, a friend made an important observation: Isn't it amazing, she said, how much our country has changed not only since 9-11 but also since the president's inaugural speech? I told her so much happened in the previous three weeks that the last thing I thought about was the president's inaugural speech. But I was pleased she made that point because it prompted me to reread the speech and further explore exactly what she meant.

After I returned to the White House, I stole away to my office to reread the speech. She was correct. As I read through that speech, it dawned on me that American peace and prosperity, which flow through those remarks, were jarringly at odds with the daily pictures of Ground Zero and the near-constant stories of horror (and bravery) that continued to splash across the front pages of newspapers and on cable TV day and night. After reading the speech, I felt an intense incongruity between that cold, gladsome inauguration day and the palpable fear now gripping our country.

The first thought I had in finishing the speech that autumn afternoon was that my young sons, now three and five, would probably know only a period of intense international conflict in their boyhoods. Although I could not have known the Iraq and Afghanistan wars were on the horizon, I sensed—as did all Americans—that war seemed increasingly inevitable. Our young country had known the wars inflicted by Wilhelmine Germany, by Nazi Germany and her Axis allies, and by Leninist-Stalinist-Soviet Communism. In my own boyhood I vaguely recalled the end of Vietnam. The Cold War was a defining feature of my young adulthood. But reports of daily bombs and bullets and America at war were no part of my growing up. For most of my childhood, our country had been at relative peace until the Gulf War. But all of that changed. Our country was badly assaulted, and those responsible—directly or indirectly—would feel the full might of the United States. The unity in the country in those weeks and months after the attack was unsurpassed in my lifetime. My parents told me it was equaled in their lifetimes only by the World War II years and its aftermath.

Intense international diplomacy was underway at the United Nations; the Bush-Blair friendship was growing closer and would prove to be as important as the Roosevelt/Churchill, Kennedy/Macmillian, and Reagan/Thatcher relationships. A definitive shift began in the buzz in Washington as recurring questions were raised: Who was responsible for 9-11, and how should America and her allies respond? This was quickly becoming the narrative in Washington and in the international capitols. Working in the White House during this time was intense as I watched, day by day, a two-term Texas governor, under the age of sixty, being transformed from the deliverer of a peace and prosperity inaugural address into a war president. The clash of civilizations narrative was intensifying, and for the first time terms like *jihad* were being bandied about in the common vernacular. The president's daily schedule was now driven almost exclusively by 9-11, and though domestic concerns continued on one track, all the emphasis in and outside the White House was on this new narrative, culminating in a new kind of debate: How much could be jaw-jaw (diplomacy), and how much would be war-war? The president worked overtime to avoid the latter, but at every key turn Saddam and his allies nixed the former. A new kind of enemy was emerging—a totalitarian, radical, fundamentalist Islamism which was patient and well-funded.

The solemnity of the president's decision to take the country into war was a memorable moment in my life and in the lives of my colleagues at the White House. I wanted to be home with Jenny and our sons when the president made his Oval Office announcement on March 19, 2003. As he declared the United States would invade Iraq, everyone who worked for him saw instantly the gravity of his tone and mien physically transform his appearance; both his face and his body language visibly changed. His opening line could not have been bolder: "American and coalition forces are in the early stages of military operations to disarm Iraq, to free its people, and to defend the world from grave danger." That was his pledge and his commitment from which he never wavered. The president understood the nature of Saddam and his henchmen, and he told the nation and the world of his diabolical character, that we faced "an enemy who has no regard for conventions of war or rules of morality." The president said the goal in Iraq was to "remove the threat and restore control of that country to its own people."[2] Those were the twin goals of our invasion of Iraq from the beginning.

No one, save perhaps Theodore Roosevelt, wants to become a war president. The men we elect to our nation's highest office are men who we necessarily want to be reluctant war presidents, rooted in prudence. George W. Bush was a reluctant war president, and that is as it should have been. It is easy to forget that fact now because of the unfair and harsh criticism directed at him and his presidency. But once he made the decision to take the nation to war, he became one of our country's most effective war presidents ever, and it is his single greatest achievement that he kept us from being attacked again after 9-11 on our domestic soil. Only history will record the series of small and large decisions he made to protect our homeland.

During this shift from diplomacy with world leaders and in the United Nations to the actual war footing, I came to observe the real George W. Bush. I witnessed what I believe history will show: the making of an extraordinarily gifted wartime leader. The seed of his leadership gifts were rooted in his clear-eyed ability to see the situation as it really was after 9-11 and not in the way some others may have wanted to see the situation. The president then translated that innate focus into a wartime policy and on to a wartime footing..

Aristotle believed that in order to translate wisdom into a policy that works on behalf of the common good, such wisdom must arise not only from moral excellence but also from a kind of wisdom rooted in common sense. A leader must discern not only what will work in the short term but also what his policy decisions will mean over time and for generations yet unborn. This discernment does not arise from intellect, per se; it arises from character and the prudential judgment one either possesses or doesn't. It is a natural, inborn ballast, and it arises in a particular set of circumstances not of one's choosing. This was George W. Bush's hour for choosing, and he made the right choices. I personally witnessed all the traits that comprise greatness in a leader: resoluteness and steadfastness instead of indecision; independence of analysis and thought; prudence instead of reaction; and what the great Irish statesman Edmund Burke called "moral imagination,"[3] which is the ability to see your way forward informed by an ethical view not tarnished by political considerations.

Yet there was something else about the president I observed time and again, which has not been fully appreciated about him: He was not given to despair or desolation. When bad news rolled into the White House about this or that turn in the war, I would on occasion be with the president for a briefing in the Eisenhower Building, an Oval Office meeting, or a speech he was giving in or around Washington. You learn things about a president not only by listening to him but also by watching how he reacts and responds to others. Like Churchill, President Bush had genuine fortitude in moments of disappointment. The election of 2000 prepared him for confidence in the face of unpredictability, which is faith. The president showed courage, and a fighting spirit arising from the confidence of his initial, well-considered decision to take the nation to war. In Churchill's final speech in the House of Commons as prime minister in 1955, he told his countrymen to "never despair."

President Bush never vacillated, even amid the somber turns and twists of what would become America's long war. Even when his opponents were at their bitterest, he refused to lower himself to their level. The most constant refrain I heard from the president's supporters is that he needed to hit back, to get in the proverbial sandbox and throw some verbal punches. The president preferred to ignore his critics' over-the-top rhetoric but to listen to their substantive disagreements. He was about focusing on the job at hand, which took an enormous reserve of energy and confidence. President Bush took personal responsibility for decisions. He simply refused to blame other people.

Why was this? I came to see—because he talked about it frequently—that the president believed this war was between good and evil, between liberty on one hand and tyranny on the other. He often framed his arguments in terms of justice to the consternation of his critics, many of whom supported the war before they were against it. The president believed in good and evil, in right and wrong, and was comfortable putting things in that perspective. There was no "values-free" foreign or domestic policy in the Bush White House and he saw the war in those terms. The enemies of freedom were evil, and the defenders of liberty were good. Also, he came to believe that destiny and faith went together, that the reason America and her allies would succeed was because we were on the right side of history.

What was the genesis of the president's hopeful nature and outlook on life? I believe it was his personal faith, which also informed how he viewed America. His faith gave me and millions of others great confidence in him. We believed our fate and destiny as a nation were in the hands of a kind and sovereign God who honors righteousness in the life of a nation devoted to justice. President Bush's outlook in this regard was similar to President Reagan's, who also often used his faith to express confidence in the country's future. Both men believed Providence placed a special hand on America and shed His grace on our country while using us to be a beacon of freedom and hope in a beleaguered time in world history.

The role I played in that period after the president's official declaration of war in 2003 was rooted in how we reached out to the major veterans and military organizations, think tanks and public policy groups, and religious and faith-based communities to explain why the president made the war decisions; to convey the purpose and goals behind those decisions; and to build support for the war to the broadest possible cross-section of the American people. Much of our early outreach was rooted in the explanation and practical application of what became known as the "The Bush Doctrine"—the willingness to proactively weaken and destroy those who would undermine or endanger American liberty and sovereignty.

The Office of Public Liaison began a series of activities with individuals and groups to get the message out about the war and the Bush Doctrine. We regularly scheduled teleconferences with the same purpose but designed to reach out to and penetrate a variety of groups and individuals who did not have the time or means to come to Washington. And we helped arrange and coordinate speeches, meetings, briefings, and presentations by administration VIPs with groups and individuals who could act as reliable conduits into various other networks. Other administration agencies had their own efforts too, namely the Pentagon and the State Department. But inside the White House our goal was to be a nexus point of idea and information sharing and to connect with as many venues and forums as we could.

Coalition building, networking, leveraging of relationships—this is why the Office of Public Liaison exists in any White House. The goal is to tap into the broad array of groups and institutions and to get the president's message, agenda, and mission onto as many radar scopes as possible. Every briefing we had at the White House, every speech we helped arrange in Washington or far beyond the Beltway, every teleconference we hosted, every meeting we had, every presentation we helped conduct or schedule, every set of remarks we helped prepare, every discussion group we convened had a "war narrative" component to it. This is part and parcel of how a president becomes a war president, by relying on his aides not only for the best speeches, news conferences, TV appearances, and weekly radio addresses—all highly significant, to be sure—but also for the bevy of intricate, often interlocking human networks constituted and equipped to convey messages and data points.

The president would sometimes join us when Public Liaison was sponsoring a briefing. Articulate, bold, determined: his strength was the ability to convey a vision of freedom and a changed Middle East. Attendees responded enthusiastically to his message not only because of who he was but also because of the way he comported himself. Often he would step into an anteroom before being announced and tell the announcer to "please keep it short." He wanted to maximize his time with the people. In all the briefings we held across seven years—with large groups up to 250, in smaller groups, and held sometimes in the Roosevelt Room near the Oval Office—I never once saw the president arrive with prepared remarks. He spoke extemporaneously, sharing his insights broadly, and then answered fully any questions asked of him with a respectful and humble tone. He was eloquent and convicted.

I was with the president that day in the Roosevelt Room when he used the phrase "bring them on," in reference to America's enemies. The Left saw it as a statement of bravado. I saw it as a statement of confidence in our military to prevail to victory. The president was pilloried for that comment by a number of his opponents, but the American people understood those comments as a passionate defense of our troops' ability to win, that there was no enemy our men and women in the armed forces could not defeat. I was there, too, on a few occasions when he met veterans of the Iraq and Afghanistan wars, some of them missing arms and legs and eyes. Those veterans told the president not only how much they loved

America and were willing to die for her but also that they supported his war time policies and were honored to fight for our security and freedom.

I was present for a large South Lawn event at the White House where we welcomed hundreds of our veterans and their families to thank them personally for their sacrifices. I spoke to dozens of them, asking how they felt about the war and their role in it. The feeling was nearly uniform and categorical: They hated being away from their spouses and families, but they supported the war; they supported what America was doing, and they were proud of their role. They were patriots in the front ranks of the highest caliber who understood the nature of the war we were in and the nature of our enemy, the radical jihadists who meant harm to us and our allies around the world. The veterans I met were consonant with the views expressed years later by retired Marine Colonel Eric Hastings, who cofounded a group called "Warriors and Quietwaters": "I know what it's like to be in combat, and I also know that *semper fi*—always faithful—is more than just a slick motto. You can't just walk off into the sunset. This is an honor contract between Americans and the people who were sent to war in their name. It's about serving your fellow warriors."[4]

When the era of second-guessing the war got underway, laced with acrimony and often rooted not in principled differences but rather in political ones against President Bush in the lead-up to the 2004 presidential election, some of our political leaders began to say the war was lost even as we were making measurable, incremental progress. In the years ahead some politicians who supported the war—seeing the same intelligence President Bush saw and agreeing with him in his assessments until it was no longer in their political interests to do so—began slowly, slyly, craftily to shift their positions. As these shifts were taking place, the president refused on principle to shift with them. I remember in April 2007 listening to Senate Majority Leader Harry Reid assert the Iraq surge was "not accomplishing anything" and that "this war is lost."[5] Another president in another time may have buckled from the pressure or tried to find a political solution. Another president may have caved or become preoccupied with public opinion polls. President Bush did none of these things because he knew the mission was the right mission for the future of our freedom and security.

He made a sound decision to go to war in Afghanistan; he made an equally sound decision to go to war in Iraq. This is not revisionism. He understood, at the most crucial time for America after the horror of 9-11, that America was in a new era, in a new war, and that our enemies meant business. The president knew if we did not reconstitute and reorganize our government and intelligence agencies for this new era, we were choosing the way of destruction of our way of life. I am confident President Bush will be confirmed in his major decisions by history, even though I heard him say on multiple occasions he did not give much thought to his legacy. He said if the historians were still debating the legacy of Washington and Lincoln, then surely they would be debating his legacy too.

Chapter 12

Continuation

We shall not fight our battles alone. There is a just God
Who presides over the destinies of nations.
—PATRICK HENRY[1]

Two clichés were being perpetuated in the lead-up to the 2004 presidential campaign. The first was an assertion that it was clear why America went to war in Afghanistan but unclear why we went to war in Iraq. The second was that President Bush was a morally flawed man, a weak leader, and a man who was not fit for office. It is important for history's sake to explore both these clichés and to show their hollowness and aridity.

President Bush repeatedly addressed why he took the nation to war. He said America's enemies were those who harbored, trained, or funded terrorists. Saddam Hussein's life and reign of terror fit that profile categorically. His record of evil was clear to everyone.

The best intelligence concluded there were weapons of mass destruction (WMD) in Iraq, and leaders in both political parties agreed with that assessment. The intelligence concluded that Saddam intended to begin afresh his WMD programs when the UN sanctions were lifted. Leaders of both political parties agreed with that assessment. There were other things about Saddam everyone agreed on as well. He was a Stalinist, a sadist, a warmonger, and a blood-thirsty fanatic. He had proved his horrific capacity by murdering thousands of his own citizens, including women and children, and invading a sovereign country that impacted the rest of the Middle East. Saddam regularly built alliances for evil purposes with America's enemies and adversaries, and he defied multiple UN resolutions for a decade and would continue to do so indefinitely. These were the facts, despite how revisionists worked overtime to cloud the Bush record. It is almost a moral obligation to make sure the president's record is not occluded, only to be converted into something it was not. Those who supported the war, the president, and our allies did so for substantial reasons. The fall of Baghdad and the trial and death of Saddam were victories of justice. The shock and awe success of our military action was one of the greatest blitzes and invasions in American history—250,000 U.S. troops coupled with 50,000 allied troops brought a swift end to Saddam's twenty-four-year reign of terror and mass brutality.

When WMD were not found, despite the best intelligence reports saying they existed, everyone was surprised and disappointed. The heart of that intelligence was that the man who founded al-Qaeda, Abu Musab al-Zarqawi, was producing WMD in Iraq. The president himself admitted his dismay that the supposed WMD were not located. He said he carried this burden with him every time he thought of it. But going to war was the right decision; and the net result is a better world for the removal of a dictator who used chemical and biological weapons.

Just as the revisionists smeared President Bush's war leadership and decision making, so too did they smear his personal reputation and character. Despite their venal attacks on his integrity, George W. Bush is in fact a man with a great soul whose internal moral compass made him a gifted leader during a deeply fraught time for American security and liberty. He is a man who is comfortable in his own skin and does not need or seek validation from others. In the political class, this makes him unique. His transparency and candor is an attendant gift, not a weakness. He is the same person in private and in public, a rare thing among public men and women. *New York Times* columnist Ross Douthat once referred to him as "a straightforward man of faith." That is exactly who he is whether the cameras are whirring or behind closed doors. This is a refreshing strength.

I witnessed this time and again. For instance, in meetings he was keen for everyone's opinions and all their views. He was respectful to everyone and was expert at give-and-take. But then he decided and when that decision was made, as a member of his staff, you definitely knew the direction you were headed. The president was not a gotcha politician. Tony Blair once said it was "easy to mock that simplicity," and he was right. But a genuine strength flowed from the Bush-style definitiveness, and in that he had much in common with another gifted leader, Margaret Thatcher, who once famously told the president's father not to go wobbly in the Gulf War. That comment would not have been necessary under President Bush's leadership in Iraq or Afghanistan, which is not to say there were not major setbacks; there were indeed.

The 2007 surge was a brilliant shift on President Bush's part and will be historically vindicated not only as the right decision but also as a decision arising from the president's leadership. The success of the surge may have been one of the two or three most important chapters of the entire Bush presidency in foreign policy. The surge was won because President Bush put America on a path to victory with the help of a gifted team he put in place, none greater than General David Petraeus and America's longest serving general in Iraq, General Raymond Odierno. These two generals will be lauded in history.

The surge was won because President Bush made the right decisions at the right time. It took courage—mental, spiritual courage—to make that decision and not to back down when huge numbers of the American and international political and pundit classes were pounding him every day, demanding retreat.

This was coupled with stunning demagoguery regarding other matters related to the war: that the prison at Guantanamo Bay was like a Soviet gulag, which was absurd; or that it had become clear America should pull out of Iraq altogether, the implications of which would have been disastrous for both the Iraqi people and our allies; or that the Bush administration was busy shredding the Constitution in defense of illegal renditions and tribunals that affronted our founding principles, which had no basis in reality; or that the Patriot Act was an attack on America's constitutional prerogatives. The list went on and on, all proven fallacious.

For all the criticism in the 2008 presidential race of how the war was being executed by President Bush, what was the net result three years after a new president came to office? We did not pull out of Guantanamo Bay; our troops remain in Iraq; renditions were seen for the value they provided to prevent more attacks; and there was no push to overturn the Patriot Act. It is easy to forget that Secretary of State Hillary Clinton herself once said it required "a suspension of disbelief"[2] to listen to key congressional testimony of General Petraeus, even though Petraeus was later personally selected by President Obama not only to remain but also to take on newer and wider responsibilities and later become the director of the CIA. In other words, many of the actions of the Obama administration vindicated the hard policy choices of President Bush.

In fact, when he was running for the Democratic presidential nomination, President Obama said the surge failed. He pledged that, if elected, all the American troops should be pulled out of Iraq by March 2008. This is the same president who later said Iraq proved to be a "remarkable chapter." Vice President Biden claimed Iraq as one of the "greatest achievements" of the Obama-Biden administration. The bottom line is President Obama, despite his harsh rhetoric, adopted and continued the Bush war and antiterrorism policies because they were the right ones.

President Bush instinctively knew early on that Islamic extremism was real, that it had to be faced directly and without apology, that we were at war and would be for years to come. His wartime raison d'etre never changed: The absolute security of the United States and the protection of our homeland from another attack was his first constitutional obligation and without peer. He coupled this dedication to security with a message about human liberty. I heard the president say repeatedly, in small, personal gatherings and before large groups, that there was a genuine, inherent human desire to be free, that we had to play to those strengths and not to the lowest common denominator of relativism and defeatism. He knew decline and defeatism in a great country under duress were choices, and they would never be his choices.

I often wondered how his morale remained high, even in the toughest moments of the war, of which there were many. Leaving the Oval Office after a meeting he hosted with the leaders of a major veterans organization, during one of those difficult weeks, I turned to him briefly and said, "Mr. President, I just want you to know I have heard from many people this week who have asked me to tell you they are praying for you and our troops during this time."

"Tim," he said, "that is the most important thing I have heard this week. Please thank them and tell them their prayers mean a lot to me." I believe prayer helped sustain the president during those tough days, and God heard those prayers and gave to the president and our troops supernatural strength and wisdom for the way forward.

The president spoke about the war often, in many settings, but he never apologized for America's, and her allies', posture after 9-11. Yet there always remained about President Bush a kind of equilibrium and humanity about the Muslim world that frankly caused as much criticism from the Right as it did from the Left. What I mean is that the president often went out of his way to demonstrate respect and a sense of honor and equality, and in some instances a willingness to find a way to cooperate and work together. He believed there was a standard for the values and principles of how mankind was to live together. This sense of fair play emanated directly from the president's own faith and sense of hope, and it was the basis for the president's expression of confidence in America and the West. Too often this confidence was willfully mistaken for arrogance, when in fact it was rooted in humility.

When I listened to what seemed like hourly, passionate criticism of the Bush White House and its war decisions, I often felt our critics had somehow forgotten we were in the Middle East with the full support of the United Nations. The anti-Bush rhetoric made it appear we were on a unilateral mission. What were the metrics of international support? Billions of dollars from the international community supporting American leadership in Iraq and Afghanistan; democratic elections were held in Iraq; the new constitution in Iraq was holding; and the Iraqis were determining their own future.

This all led, I think, to the oddest and most disturbing reality of how some of the leading political and pundit critics viewed the war: That while Saddam and his henchmen were given a pass for their flouting of the United Nations, the liberators were routinely vilified, as if the status quo ante, allowing Saddam to stay, was the preferable option.

No small part of the criticism was because of President Bush's strong and categorical support for Israel. This was the reason Prime Minister Ariel Sharon said President Bush was the greatest friend Israel ever had in the Oval Office. He was right. Even though the president was the first to make it official U.S. policy that the goal was a peaceful Palestinian state residing next to a strong and sovereign Israel, the anti-Bush, anti-Israel rhetoric was nonstop, and especially in Europe. President Bush always kept Israel's security concerns uppermost in his mind, and he believed Israel was our greatest ally in the Middle East. When Natan Sharansky came to see the President, the two men had an immediate rapport. This was not dint of fate; they were soul mates on the question of Israel's right to exist and unquestioned security. President Bush surrounded himself with aides who shared his view on Israel, and of course this made the critics angrier still.

Elliott Abrams, who became a good friend early in the first administration, eventually became the president's deputy national security director with a specialty in Middle and Near East policy. He flourished in this role and was instrumental in his assistance and advice to the president.

I had always admired the late Senator Henry "Scoop" Jackson, with whom Elliott worked closely; and Elliott embodied the same high principles and unwavering commitments of that late, great senator. Also, I relied heavily on my colleague in Public Liaison, Tevi Troy, whose outreach to the American Jewish community was singularly well done.

So how does one assess the Bush legacy in foreign and security policy? How does one assess the war and its ramifications for the future of American liberty? How does one think about President Bush as the leader of the free world during eight tough and tumultuous years? You start with the view that no president has enough information, nor does he ever know everything he needs to know before making life and death decisions. All presidents are evaluated based on whether their decisions showed acuity and foresight, and how they were able to convey those decisions to the country. A president's skill in large measure is a function of his experience and his discernment. The realities of making the most difficult decisions anyone this side of eternity could ever make, because they place human life in the precarious balance, are necessarily fraught. Yet I believe the president made these life and death decisions with aplomb, wisdom, sensitivity, and skill. Yes, history provides a unique lens that helps us see with better depth and clarity, but the president's most difficult decisions are already being vindicated and not altered.

Standing in the burning rubble and refuse of Ground Zero shortly after 9-11, he took a bullhorn and told those around him, and around the country, and world, "I want you all to know that America today is on bended knee, in prayer for the people whose lives were lost here, for the workers who work here, for the families who mourn. The nation stands with the good people of New York City and New Jersey and Connecticut as we mourn the loss of thousands of our citizens." A rescue worker nearby shouted, "I can't hear you" to which President Bush replied, "I can hear you! I can hear you! The rest of the world hears you! And the people—and the people who knocked down these buildings will hear all of us soon!"[3]

The world indeed heard from the United States and our allies, under the direction of a leader who meant that the world would remain free, and free from another attack on our own soil, under his watch. The great economist Thomas Sowell once said, "You can always avoid a fight surrendering."[4] The president was a man of great honor, decency, vision, but also action. There was no part of surrender in his DNA. He knew America was free because countless, selfless men and women had died for our freedoms since the founding. He was true to their sacrifice, none more so than to those first victims of terror on 9-11.

Saint Augustine wrote, "Moral character is assessed not by what a man knows but by what he loves."[5] The president's character shone in the terrible shadow of those collapsed buildings; amid the horror and rubble, he never lost the vision or the love for the greatness of America.

The president's foresight and wisdom have been confirmed by history. A decade after 9-11, our country faces an ever greater and escalating threat from a mix of native-born insurgents and the al-Qaeda movement. The writer Kevin Williamson has lucidly said: "We still do not understand all of the implications of our country's confrontation with Islamic radicalism. The trauma of 9-11 has deposited far too much emotional residue upon our thinking."[6]

Perhaps the least appreciated of all President Bush's cabinet members was the former federal judge Michael B. Mukasey. His appointment as attorney general was an achievement because there was no man in America who better understood, from first-hand experience, the depth of evil of radical Islam and its threat to America. Mukasey was the first federal judge to hear major terrorism cases in his New York City courtroom. After the presidency he delivered a Memorial Day speech that put his personal observations into context and reminded his listeners of the depth of courage shown on 9-11. He said that courage should be remembered as "the highest public virtue because . . . courage is the one virtue that guarantees all the others; without it, all the others are useless."[7]

In 2010 a major report was released by former New Jersey Governor Thomas Kean and former Representative Lee Hamilton of Indiana. The thesis of the report is startling: that the radicalization of Muslims in America is growing and not declining. The report says a combination of radicalized American immigrants and homegrown fanatics comprise a terror threat to America that is real and increasing. Western intelligence agencies concur al-Qaeda has a plethora of coalition groups who in turn use a decentralized network of cells to aid terrorists worldwide.

President Bush said we faced not only a war against al-Qaeda but also the growing need to secure American interests in the Near and Middle East for a dangerous new era rooted in multiple threats to our national security. He took America to war for the right reasons at the right time, avoiding the temptation of an era of isolation that could have provoked even greater damage to our country, our liberty, and our way of life. President Bush taught us that in this new threat from radical Islam worldwide, we must not become apologetic, feeble, inhibited, or imbued with doubt about our central mission on the world stage, the promulgation and defense of liberty. This is the Bush legacy. It is a noble legacy.

Chapter 13

Debating the Definition of Marriage

There is no more lovely, friendly, and charming relationship,
communion, or company than a good marriage.
— MARTIN LUTHER[1]

The two revolutions in America with the most lasting impact were probably the America Revolution, which gave us our independence from England, and the Sexual Revolution, which fractured the nuclear family, the contrails of which we are still internalizing as a country, culture, and civilization. The latter revolution was an ethical and social tsunami of the first order, and its impact has been tectonic. This revolution ultimately led to one of the most heady chapters of the Bush administration, George W. Bush's decision to endorse a federal marriage amendment on February 24, 2004. The pathway leading to his announcement was an intellectual and political promontory providing a fascinating portal into how social policy bubbles upward directly to the Oval Office in ways expected and unexpected.

The debate over a federal role in marriage formally began long before the president came to office, dating eight years before, when President Clinton signed the Defense of Marriage Act (DOMA) in 1996. The Republican Congress passed and sent to him a bill that, for the first time, placed into federal law a formal definition of marriage as between one man and one woman. Marriage had always been a state issue. But by the mid-1990s, it was clear federal legislation was needed to protect that definition from the growing lawsuits and various legal mechanisms underway to change that definition, allowing members of the same sex to marry. The House and Senate overwhelmingly passed DOMA.

In the ensuing eight years after President Clinton signed the bill, two important trends emerged. The first and most serious was a series of decisions by activist judges who, despite the clearly stated definitions of marriage set forth in law, sought to redefine marriage allowing same-sex people to marry. The second trend was evidenced in the actions of various state legislators, governors, and local activists who pushed against the federal law with an equal fervor, working in tandem with those judges to change the definition of marriage. Both trends skipped over the democratic process of allowing residents of those states to decide whether they wanted marriage redefined.

The single most important catalyst, without peer, was when the highest court in Massachusetts decided, contra federal law, that same-sex marriage would be legal in that Commonwealth. Four judges on that court imposed on the Bay State a mandate: Beginning in May 2004, same-sex marriage would be legal there, and the residents were not asked their opinion. Conservatives were outraged, but the outrage was not limited to conservative circles. African Americans and Hispanic Americans were equally angered by that ruling, as were any number of Democrats, many of them liberals, who opposed conservatives on almost every other issue but agreed that marriage was unique and deserving of protection. Among those liberals was a little known United States senator from Illinois, Barack Obama, who opposed same-sex marriage.

Massachusetts's judges were not alone in defying federal law that year. Officials in San Francisco began allowing thousands of same-sex couples to marry, even though the California Family Code—approved overwhelmingly by the people of California in a ballot referendum—expressly forbade it. President Bush and the White House staff watched these trends closely and knew the marriage issue would eventually arrive at the front door of 1600 Pennsylvania Avenue. Pushing toward the doorstep were a host of conservatives in the various states who not only looked with dismay at what was happening to marriage in Massachusetts and California but also were working proactively to stop the same thing from happening in their states. This state-by-state effort to protect the institution of marriage in its traditional form was comprised of people who were among the strongest supporters of President Bush, and for the first time I heard the term "values voters" applied to them, united in their opposition to the imposition of same-sex marriage by judicial, gubernatorial, or legislative fiat.

After observing this growing national battle over marriage, I remember telling my White House colleagues that for the first time since 1973, when *Roe v. Wade* was passed by the Supreme Court legalizing abortion in all nine months of pregnancy, that the issue of marriage was becoming co-equal with abortion as *the* two central social issues in American politics. As the attack on marriage gained steam nationwide in 2003, I began to hear daily from conservatives around the country who were urging the president to consider endorsing a federal marriage amendment. In fact, at one point I was hearing from three different, equally influential conservative camps about their version of just such an amendment. I was careful never to comment on any version because it might have appeared the White House supported that particular amendment strategy. That decision had not been made.

As these early discussions took place, one of the central issues emerging was whether a constitutional amendment should also include a provision against civil unions. Some felt if civil unions were not banned along with same-sex marriage, they could eventually become a camel's nose under the tent leading eventually to an attack on the definition of marriage. These people believed legal civil unions would over time soften the legal ground for people of the same sex to marry.

Every time I was asked, I was clear to say the White House did not inject itself into state-based, pro-marriage amendments or state-based efforts. The view was categorical: A state ballot initiative must not have added muscle from the White House. It was not only that the optics would be wrong, but it would allow others to say the Bush White House was pushing for such efforts for political reasons. Karl Rove was clear with me: The White House would not get involved in the states on this issue. He said if the president decided to support a federal marriage amendment, we would then focus our time, attention, and energy on the man for whom we were privileged to work but only after he made such a decision. We did not want to get ahead of the president on the marriage issue.

Thus, I did a lot of listening but was careful not to lend White House support or backing to what was happening in the states, and Karl was later vindicated in this decision. No one could assert the Bush White House was pushing any agenda in the states or working to enact marriage amendments in the states for political or any other reason. We were not unsympathetic to what was happening in those states. But we wanted prudently to recognize the bright lines between state activity and federal activity, and we honored that commitment up to and including the day the president made his decision on how to proceed on the marriage issue. One thing I learned early in observing the whole marriage debate nationwide: Successfully getting marriage amendments on state ballots and getting them passed was no easy task. This was a massively difficult and time-consuming process.

In the whole of 2003 and early 2004, I heard more about marriage than any other issue. I made clear to my White House colleagues that, despite the differing conservative camps' views on possible versions of a federal marriage amendment, everyone in those allied groups was of a piece that there should be an amendment and that time was of the essence.

No groups favored it more strongly than Focus on the Family and its state-based allies comprising the family policy council network, the Family Research Council, Concerned Women for America, Eagle Forum, the Traditional Values Coalition, the Southern Baptist Convention, the Alliance Defense Fund, the American Center for Law and Justice, the American Family Association (AFA), the American Association of Christian Schools, and the National Religious Broadcasters.

They were the core, along with a group formed expressly to defend traditional marriage in the states, the Arlington Group, which had a plethora of allies in the states. These groups formed the nucleus of support for the emerging constitutional amendment, and I was in touch with all of them regularly. They provided a superb framework for thinking about the national ramifications for marriage, and though they were eager for the president to endorse an amendment, they understood the necessity of the thoughtful nature the president was pursuing in coming to a final decision, just as he did in his decision on stem-cell research. On some of the major social questions confronting the Bush administrations—a marriage amendment, stem cells, the faith-based office protections for religious liberty—the president sought wide counsel, wanted lots of input, and in each instance came out with the right decision.

By late 2003 the momentum on marriage was growing rapidly as state after state was putting forth successful, pro-marriage ballot initiatives or state legislation. Almost predictably, opponents of marriage would then file lawsuits against the ballot initiatives or seek to stop legislatures from voting on the pro-marriage bills. It became clear the mechanism of DOMA, which deferred heavily to the states for the protection of marriage but sought to protect marriage's key legal definition, was under direct assault. It was not that it was becoming obsolete because of irrelevance; it

During my first year at the White House, I remember walking from the West Wing to the mansion, through the colonnade next to the Rose Garden, and stopping to view the sheer beauty of the first snowfall of the season across the South Lawn.

Each year, on the anniversary of 9-11, the White House staff would gather with the Bushes for a moment of silence and prayer beneath the Truman balcony.

Next to my own dad, there is no man I admire, love, or respect more than Dan Coats, who I believe is one of the truly great United States Senators of the twentieth century. I worked for him as an intern in the summer of 1986, and then became a part of his U.S. Senate staff during his tenure in the Senate 1988–1998. His wife Marsha was integral to his success as a congressman, U.S. Senator, and later Ambassador to Germany during the Bush Administration.

My greatest mentor outside politics, and outside Washington, during the Bush White House years was Chuck Colson. His counsel, insight, and advice became the foundation for our treasured friendship. President of Focus on the Family, Jim Daly, is emerging as one of the leaders of the new generation of evangelicals in America. Jim's humility, integrity, and humor make him the right man to lead Focus in this new century.

I am a member of the Young America's Foundation Board of Governors, which oversees Ronald Reagan's ranch in Santa Barbara. I speak annually to their national gathering of college students at George Washington University.

I have spoken on many college and university campuses during my professional life, including at Cedarville College in Ohio, where I was privileged to be the Commencement Day speaker in 2004.

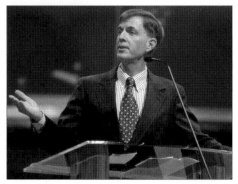

The Conservative Political Action Conference (CPAC) is the largest annual gathering of conservatives in the United States, numbering about ten thousand people. I have attended CPAC each year for the last twenty years, and in 2011 moderated a panel on the future of the pro-life movement.

I was privileged to speak on President Bush's behalf to the gala dinner of the Victims of Communism Memorial organized by the historian Lee Edwards. It was the last Washington dinner that my friend Bill Buckley attended before his death. Also at our table that evening was the former Attorney General in the Reagan Administration, Edwin Meese III, and Edwin J. Feulner, Jr., the president of The Heritage Foundation, both of whom became good friends during my years at the White House.

One of the great things about working for President Bush is that he always gave everyone an equal opportunity to weigh in, which was a gesture of respect. Before a briefing at the White House, I often spent a few minutes with him going through any last minute questions he might have had. Blake Gottesman was his indispensable aide de camp whose sense of humor was a hallmark.

One of the highlights during my time at the White House was the evening party commemorating the Abraham Lincoln Bicentennial. The Bushes shared a great moment with Jenny and our boys Tim and Paul after the ceremony in the Blue Room.

The greatest honor a president can show a White House guest is to welcome him or her into the Oval Office for a personal meeting.

The Rose Garden on a sunny day was a thing of splendor, and I remember sharing a light moment with the president before he prepared to deliver a set of remarks in the garden on one of the most beautiful days of the year.

President Ronald Reagan came to Washington to dedicate the Republican Senatorial Committee building named for him, and I met him by happenstance and enjoyed a brief chat.

With Ronald Reagan, there is no one I hold in higher regard in public life than Lady Margaret Thatcher. I believe that she and Winston Churchill were the two greatest prime ministers of the twentieth century. After her years in Downing Street, she became the Patroness of The Heritage Foundation, where I am a Senior Fellow. Heritage's president Ed Feulner invited me to a dinner in her honor in 2006.

The first time I met Lady Thatcher was during a Mont Pelerin Society gathering in London. She delivered an eloquent, powerful speech about the future of liberty in the West.

Shaking hands with President Richard Nixon. President Nixon returned to Capitol Hill only a handful of times after he resigned. On one of those occasions, in the early 1990s, I met him in Republican Leader Bob Dole's (R-KS) suite of offices.

American religious leaders met with President Bush regularly, and Archbishop Demetrios's visit was made all the more special when the First Lady joined us.

Queen Elizabeth II, Prince Phillip, and the Bushes enjoyed a lively East Room event during the royal visit, and the president's white tie and tails gave the evening a regal cast.

A group of prominent conservatives met with the president in the Roosevelt Room, across the hallway from the Oval Office. That meeting included Michael Novak, James Dobson, Kenneth Cribb, Alan Sears, Gary Bauer, Jay Sekulow, and Chuck Colson.

One of the highlights of my time at the White House was the day the president honored Bill Buckley on the 50th anniversary of *National Review*. After the Eisenhower Building ceremony, the president invited Bill and his wife Pat to lunch in the White House.

Karl Rove was given an Honorary Doctorate from Liberty University and was the commencement speaker before his departure from the White House. Before the speech, both Dr. Jack Graham, the president of the Southern Baptist convention, and Jonathan Falwell, who would succeed his father as senior pastor at Thomas Road Baptist Church in Lynchburg, joined us in the Green Room.

There is no military man of my generation who I venerate, honor, and respect more than General David Petreaus. The general will be remembered as having led the successful Iraq surge and the allied coalition in Afghanistan.

Our first Chief of Staff at the White House was Andy Card, a man everyone loved and respected. When he left the White House, there was an air of real sadness because Andy had united the staff in a singular manner, person by person.

One of the highlights of the 9-11 "Service of Prayer and Remembrance" at the Washington National Cathedral after the terrorist attacks was having Billy Graham deliver the sermon. Members of other faith traditions comprised a powerful, impactful service for America.

Supreme Court Justice Samuel Alito has already made an indelible imprint on the court. The coalition that worked together to confirm him became a closely-bonded group of men and women Leonard Leo of the Federalist Society was a leader of that coalition.

One of the greatest moments of my time working for President Bush was being part of the team that helped successfully confirm Chief Justice of the United States John Roberts. Jenny and I saw him again five years later during a dinner at the Supreme Court.

The White House team that worked on the nomination of John Roberts to the Supreme Court was a united, talented group led by Ed Gillespie and former U.S. Senator Fred Thompson.

The team that worked on the Alito nomination gathered in the Roosevelt Room to watch the Senate vote. When the confirmation was assured, everyone applauded, and my former boss, U.S. Senator Dan Coats, standing behind the president, who had played such a pivotal role on the Hill in helping to get Alito nominated, was pleased. Steve Schmidt (second from left), who oversaw the Alito nomination team, did a great job.

The Bushes at the groundbreaking ceremony of the George W. Bush Presidential Center in Dallas.

It was an honor and privilege to be invited to the groundbreaking ceremony for the George W. Bush Presidential Center in Dallas on the campus of Southern Methodist University. It was a great day, and the largest reunion of the alumni of the Bush-Cheney Administration since 2008. The president gave a well-received speech.

Senator Jim DeMint (R-SC) was one of the leaders of the historic Tea Party movement in 2009 and 2010. I believe the Tea Party is the most important political movement in the United States in the last decade, and DeMint showed courage and persistence leading to the conservative gains in the 2010 midterm elections.

Karl Rove and I spent a few minutes together reliving two presidential campaigns as Karl prepared to leave the White House. Our life-long friendship was sealed in those years.

was becoming obsolete because the Left found a successful way to thwart Congress's clear intent, brushing aside the law's federalist foundation. Everyone, on both sides of the marriage debate, knew DOMA would eventually be knocked down in a courtroom, opening the floodgates against marriage unless the Constitution itself was amended to preserve the definition of marriage. State by state legislative and ballot efforts, however, continued apace.

The DOMA law was supported as the right strategy by the overwhelmingly majority of American conservatives; we always felt states should have maximum power in the realm of marriage. But we were warily coming to the conclusion this was one of those rare times when the Constitution needed to be amended to protect the most vital institution in America, traditional marriage, which we believe underlays the healthy formation of the American family. Federalism was the essential guiding conservative principle, the Madisonian view that amending the Constitution should be done only with prudence and great reluctance when all other avenues have been exhausted. I knew from my interactions with the president how strongly he felt about marriage because I heard him often refer to it as "a sacred institution."

President Bush was coming to the conclusion that while DOMA was good legislation, it was not strong enough to prevail against the phalanx of legal, gubernatorial, and legislative activists seeking to change the definition of marriage. Also, he knew if he endorsed a federal marriage amendment, it would be the only time he ever officially supported a change to the Constitution. Vice President Cheney supported a new right for people of the same sex to marry if they chose and said so in the 2000 vice presidential debate with Senator Joseph Lieberman. Some key conservatives and libertarians agreed with Cheney, among them the prominent Washington lawyer Ted Olson, who in later years would argue against California's Proposition 8 allowing only traditional marriage in that state.

By January 2004 the president was putting the final touches on his policy decision, and at the end of February, he formally endorsed a constitutional amendment banning marriage between people of the same sex. He recounted the history of DOMA; he illustrated how officials in Massachusetts, California, and New Mexico decided to thwart federal law and said that unless a process for amending the Constitution was formally put in place, it was likely activist courts would continue attacking marriage. In his remarks endorsing a federal marriage amendment on February 25, 2004, the president gave a philosophical defense of marriage, making clear his decision was not rooted in a practical political calculus or upon a utilitarian model. Rather he said, from history and from his faith, he came to see marriage in a unique and special light deserving constitutional protection.

"After more than two centuries of American jurisprudence and millennia of human experience, a few judges and local authorities are presuming to change the most fundamental institution of civilization. Their actions have created confusion on an issue that requires clarity." He said judges legislating from the bench "have left the people with one recourse. If we're to prevent the meaning of marriage from being changed forever, our nation must enact a constitutional amendment to protect marriage in America." Prophetically, he made the point that if successful efforts to amend the Constitution were not made, "attempts to redefine marriage in a single state or city could have serious consequences throughout the country."[2] That is precisely what has happened.

To fellow conservatives who continued to say DOMA was the best route for defending marriage, the president wanted to explain why that was a faulty strategy and why DOMA essentially lost its salience as a way to defend marriage. "Yet there is no assurance that the Defense of Marriage Act will not itself be struck down by activist courts [and] . . . furthermore, even if the Defense of Marriage Act is upheld, the law does not protect marriage within any state or city." In other words, in an era of crusading judges, a constitutional amendment could ultimately defend marriage.

The president explained he did not come to his decision "lightly" but believed the protection and "preservation of marriage rises to this level of national importance." Why? Because, he said, "the union of a man and woman is the most enduring human institution, honored and encouraged in all cultures and by every religious faith. Ages of experience have taught humanity that the commitment of a husband and wife to love and to serve one another promotes the welfare of children and the stability of society. Marriage cannot be severed from its cultural, religious, and natural roots without weakening the good influence of society. Government, by recognizing and protecting marriage, serves the interests of all."[3]

He called upon Congress to pass the amendment and to send the amendment to the states for their collective ratification. He reconfirmed that America's commitment to personal liberty did "not require the redefinition of one of our most basic social institutions," and said, "There is no contradiction between these responsibilities." Before concluding his statement, he made a rather remarkable personal pledge: that in the marriage debate, the nation would "match strong convictions with kindness and good will and decency," and the president never wavered from that promise despite the harshness and bitterness directed at him and those who disagreed with his policy decision on the protection of marriage between a man and a woman.

The impact of the president's decision was significant. Those working in the states on behalf of marriage knew they had a great ally and champion in the Oval Office; the Congress was no longer in the dark about how strongly the president felt about the importance of the marriage issue; and the legal, political, academic, and media debate and discussion that ensued throughout 2004, and directly into the presidential election that November, was huge. The values voters felt emboldened to create a state infrastructure that could be tilled for a possible ratification process.

After the president made his announcement, there was buzz he decided to endorse the amendment to shore up his conservative base of support but especially the evangelical base. That is untrue. The one element of the conservative base that remained most constant in its support for the president were both American evangelicals and members of the American military, especially young military families. When many others were abandoning the president, the evangelicals, conservative Catholics, and military families stuck with him. They knew they had a friend, ally, and kindred spirit in the president who, on the major social issues they cared about, always got it right. The fact that evangelicals or members of the military would ever consider switching their support to John Kerry—one of fourteen U.S. senators to have opposed DOMA in 1996—or sit out the presidential election in 2004 was preposterous even before President Bush endorsed a federal amendment. When he came out in support of the amendment, it was a confirmation of what the values voters already believed about him.

Another false assumption is that the president, in endorsing the amendment, somehow telegraphed that such an endorsement would come at a cost for those who were uneasy about amending the Constitution. The president, like the American people, was cautious about making any changes to the Constitution; but they, like the president, were made uneasy by judges who were chipping away at the rights of the people to determine the definition of marriage. People were coming to see that if judges were willing to usurp their rights on marriage, they were willing to usurp their rights on other issues too.

The president did not make this decision to placate his base; nor was his decision a cynical political move, as some suggested at the time. He concluded that there was more than ample evidence that judges and others were moving, posthaste, to change the definitions of marriage, and he has been proven right in light of recent history. The president's decision had broad appeal and broad support, but it was not an attempt to pick up pro-life or Reagan Democrats, whether it had that net effect or not. It was part of President Bush's achievement that he was not a panderer; he made major decisions rooted in principle over potential political appeal. The public was overwhelmingly with the president on the marriage issue, from both parties.

A significant part of the marriage debate, however, lingered throughout 2004 as an undertow to the president's remarks. Because the proposed constitutional amendment was silent on civil unions, what was the president's view on that issue? He made clear in his White House announcement on marriage, in a little-remembered part of his formal statement, that state legislatures should be "free to make their own choices in defining legal arrangements other than marriage." Also, in an interview with ABC's Charlie Gibson in November before the election, the president stressed, "I don't think we should deny people rights to a civil union, a legal arrangement, if that's what a state chooses to do."[4] The president concluded the national debate should be about marriage and its legal definition and should not spill over into a debate on civil unions.

George W. Bush's decision to endorse, encourage, and defend a constitutional amendment defending marriage as "the most fundamental institution of civilization" was, along with his stem-cell policy decision and his signing of the ban on partial birth abortion, among the most consequential decisions on social policy of his eight years in office. The president believed, with the overwhelming majority of Americans, that children were best raised in a marriage comprised of a mom and a dad who were committed to a lifelong monogamous relationship and which had a sacred foundation.

A month before he formally endorsed the amendment, he referred to the family in a now forgotten but eloquent line from his January 2004 state of the union address, as among the "unseen pillars of civilization." That was not a clever turn of phrase. That little line flowed from both his faith and his own family experiences of being raised by parents whose love and commitment to each other provided a remarkable fulcrum and shelter of love, compassion, and stability for his sisters and brothers. I once observed, at close range, the president with his mother and father, and I have rarely observed such love of family—natural warmth and closeness, a special, genuine love expressed so freely among son and parents. Experience taught him marriage was not only worth preserving but was foundational without peer, rooted in a complementarian view of the two sexes. The president's parents celebrated their 66th wedding anniversary in January 2011.

Chapter 14

Getting Out the Values Voters

*Sure, they might want lower taxes and smaller government,
too; but they also want to return to an era in which their
own traditional values were reflected in the TV shows they
watched, the movies they went to, the education that their
kids received in public schools paid for by their tax dollars.
They do not want to see what they cherish most in the world
held up to ridicule, especially when the ridicule is presented
in attractively packaged forms that are designed especially to
appeal to their own kids. They resent what they perceive as the
indoctrination and brainwashing of the next generation.
They feel that their own deeply held "traditional American
values" are under attack—and they are right.*

—LEE HARRIS[1]

The centrality of the "values voters" to George W. Bush's two presidential victories is huge. Historically the values voters will be studied more closely because of just how decisive we were in both those elections but especially in 2004, where American evangelicals comprised about 40 percent of President Bush's total vote.

The term "values voters" was coined in 2004, but we were alive and well, if without a label, in the 2000 election. The values voters, by whatever title we may have had, came to trust President Bush in that December 1999 Iowa Republican Primary debate when the GOP candidates were

126

asked who their favorite philosopher was. George W. Bush said, "Christ, because He changed my heart." There was an audible but low gasp in the green room where I was standing watching that debate, as if he had made a gaffe. But he did not make a gaffe; he answered honestly, and those six words began building a bridge of goodwill that lasted his entire presidency and beyond.

The values voters are the most important base of the Republican Party, the foundational, conservative core of men and women who will be the last ones standing even when everyone else has run for the tall grass, the ones who continued to support President Bush. Our conservatism is to preserve the Constitution and the Declaration of Independence; to uphold the Judeo-Christian foundations of the country's moral core; and to herald the sanctity of every human life, the sanctity of marriage, and the defense of religious liberty. In short, the values voters are motivated by our love of God and country and all that is best about the virtuous nature of the United States of America. We believe America is exceptional, and our politics are motivated by that central belief. The exemplary nature of America is, we believe, rooted in its Judeo-Christian founding and in the providential underpinning that produced our Constitution and Declaration. In President Bush we found a soul mate on the issues we cared about most.

Values voters are the voters during campaigns who plant yard signs, go door-to-door with leaflets, lead the largest "get out the vote" efforts across the country (even in cities, counties, and districts already thought to be "lost" by the political classes), listen to conservative talk radio, pray for America regularly, and continue to believe the founding of America was a transcendent moment in all of world history where Providence chose America to be the leader for freedom.

Values voters believe patriotism is a duty because ours is a country worth defending, and most values voters' eyes still well up when we hear the "Star Spangled Banner" playing or sung in almost any setting.

Values voters respect the different roles between church and state, and we believe government should stay out of religion even while religion needs to be in the public life of the country, consistent with the founding fathers' embrace of religion as not only true but also necessary for the proper, healthy functioning of a country, culture, and civilization. Values voters believe with the founders that we cannot have liberty without virtue and that virtue is rooted in the Judeo-Christian tradition of America.

Values voters believe in the morality of the Ten Commandments and in the Sermon on the Mount. We believe these principles are as true today as they were when God gave the commandments to Moses on Mount Sinai and when Jesus delivered the greatest sermon in the history of the world in Palestine, defending the meek and the powerless. This Judeo-Christian moral code, we believe, is the standard for right and wrong, good and evil; and we are comfortable with distinctions on ethical questions. Yet while we value and uphold the law, we believe strongly in grace, mercy, and forgiveness because we understand that human nature is flawed and fallen, and there are no perfect people except One, Jesus Christ. We believe it is our duty to forgive.

Values voters believe in being engaged in every facet of American political life; we believe it is our civic duty to serve in the military, serve in political office, direct or serve in political campaigns, serve in public policy roles, and otherwise be engaged in the public square. Contemporary values voters emerged in the 1970s from a subculture of separatism from American public life. We were called the New Right because—in addition to our defense of low taxes, less regulation, limited government, and a strong national defense, which we believed was consistent with the United States Constitution—we also believed that traditional values, the heart of what made our country exceptional, were under assault in the halls of Congress, in the Supreme Court, in international institutions, in Hollywood, and in much of the media.

The hallmark narrative of the values voters is that we see truth, reason, and our faith as one piece; we reject relativism that denies truth and which has become, all too often, the animating principle of so many of America's most prominent thinkers and politicians. We believe a kind of post-Christian secularism is trying to drive us out of the public square. Too often our faith is reduced to bigotry or a triviality by opponents, when in fact our views are just the opposite. The so-called "new atheists" have been particularly aggressive, promulgating an anti-Christian narrative that defies the tolerance that is their mantra. When the late U.S. Senator Daniel Patrick Moynihan wrote in 1993 we were living in a cultural moment that was "defining deviancy down," values voters knew instantly what he meant because we believe there had always been a benchmark of conduct now being redefined and reformed, and necessary stigmas on certain behavior were being loosed or crushed.

The spark for the rise of the New Right was not the legalization of abortion, hippies and yippies, the battle against the Equal Rights Amendment, the drug culture, campus activism, or even the earliest chapters of the sexual revolution, although all of these things, and others, in time would contribute to the creation of the values voters. The spark was when the Supreme Court ruled that prayer in public schools was unconstitutional, even though it had been legal for all of American history. Evangelical men and women, who were never involved in American politics or political life and whose own history favored being separate from the public square, began to wake up en masse as they saw their rights and their beliefs being eroded without anyone asking them their opinion or seeking their view. The brunt of the sexual, cultural, and moral revolution would prove a comprehensive assault.

Thirty years after the New Right was born, with a host of other issues put into the mix, none more important or serious than the slow but steady disintegration of the nuclear family in all economic and race categories, the values voters were coming into their own, born concurrent to the first Bush administration in a torrent of political activism across the country rooted primarily in the fight to preserve marriage between a man and a woman. The values voters eventually adopted the mantra of life, marriage, and religious liberty as the three most important issues of the twenty-first century in social policy, comprising what became known as a "worldview," a way of life rooted in these immutable first principles. These three issues, informed by our faith, formed the nucleus of how we viewed domestic public policy and those we elected to the highest offices of our land. Some version of all three of these issues concretized into the 2000 and 2004 presidential races between George W. Bush and Al Gore in the former and against John Kerry in the latter. These issues were later codified into a document called *The Manhattan Declaration*.

There is a misnomer which I am eager to address, the charge that values voters only care about domestic policy. This is not the case. We care deeply about the whole range of international issues too, and if we are asked in national polling about what issues concern us most, we are as apt to answer terrorism, or the situation in the Middle East, as we are about other issues. Values voters care deeply about HIV/AIDS in sub-Saharan Africa; international sex trafficking, which has become pervasive and growing; basic religious liberties and human rights in foreign countries; and other issues of conscience, like slavery, that get too little attention on the world stage. Not a few values voters-style groups have offices at the United Nations, and we are active in a host of ministries and foundations worldwide.

Also, values voters are, in significant ways, acculturated and reflective of what average Americans believe. Our kids go to public schools; we travel nationally and internationally; and we watch the same TV programs and movies as other people. In other words, the starkness of differences in the way we live and work is overstated. But it is our principal commitment to a set of immutable values that distinguish us, and about those we are civil, diplomatic, but unapologetic.

Ultimately values voters believe in Saint Augustine's view of the two kingdoms, the city of God (heaven) and the city of man (earth). We believe we are citizens of both kingdoms simultaneously but that our ultimate allegiance is to the kingdom of God because we are just passing through this limited time on earth. In part, this explains why so many in the political class misunderstand us; they do not understand this meshing of faith and politics. The net result is that social conservatism in America remains a mystery to many Republicans and Democrats alike. That is because our agenda is not the same as their political agendas, and we are not just another special interest group. Our ultimate motivations are rooted in the heart and soul of the intact, protected nuclear family. This is because we believe strong marriages and families are God's design for mankind.

Because we believe this, we continue to articulate a way of life that is in fact vital for the continued cultural and economic vitality of America. Our desire is that broken families will fall in love again; that policies promoted and passed into law at the city, state, and federal level will not further damage or erode the family unit; that the best social science will always be in accord with healthy, intact families and biblical morality; that such moral strength gives our country the best outcome for the healthy growth and prosperity of children.

This is also the heart and soul of why most social conservatives are fiscal conservatives. We believe a moral case is to be made for the free enterprise system. Even the greatest philosopher of capitalism, Adam Smith, in his little-known book on the "moral sentiments," believed a people's strong moral and ethical moorings lead not only to a healthy society but also a prosperous one. Smith showed there is a direct connection between strong ethics and a strong marketplace. Values voters concur because we believe in the direct connection and correlation between healthy, stable families and healthy, stable economies. We believe any separation between economic and values issues is bad policy and flawed logic.

Alas, America is suffering from a historic familial brokenness that is disillusioning. One of the best and yet saddest examples of this is the increasing number of American kids who live in poverty, the root cause of which is, in the words of The Heritage Foundation's Robert Rector, "the collapse of marriage."[2] Thousands of other examples from social science are equally devastating: increasing delinquency rates in public schools;

shockingly high drop-out rates in schools; drug, alcohol, gambling, and pornography addiction; increases in domestic and spousal abuse; and gang membership. Phyllis Schlafly has written compellingly about the impact on our country of this social and moral decay. "A great deal of the government spending is going for the daily support of people who have had babies without getting married. And that is a very costly and unfortunate thing. It's really the main reason for the budget and spending being at such high levels. We need to address that as both a cultural problem and a fiscal problem."[3] Ultimately a weakened family structure is the root cause.

Social science confirms the consequences for a society where family, marriage, and parental breakdown are too often the norm. Unprecedented numbers of children are growing up without fathers. Our students' grades in math and English are falling while the number of Americans seeking treatment for drug addiction is rising. The federal government has spent sixteen trillion dollars on welfare programs since 1964. A record number of Americans live in poverty.

Among the rising generation of Americans, we are seeing two new trends: less marriage and more cohabitation. Both are widely and socially acceptable, and in the latter form the ramifications for children born out of wedlock will be significant if present trends continue. In 2009 for the first time in American history, the number of young Americans who are not or who have never married was higher than the percentage who are married.

To raise these concerns in American public life, however, leads not to a desire to better understand and address them. Instead, for those who speak out, there is a consequence to pay. There is, in the words of scholar Patrick Hynes, "a demonization campaign . . . to marginalize conservative Christians from public life."[4] Terms like *theocrats* has been bandied about, and as Hynes shows, even Howard Dean, the former head of the Democratic National Committee and a former governor of Vermont, once "threatened to use the IRS to silence them."[5] The values voters have done precisely what Hynes says we have done: been "the true defender of our nation's political tradition"[6] by operating fully within our constitutional rights. The name-calling has pulled down the level and seriousness of debate in our country over important, foundational issues.

In both 2000 and 2004, values voters sought to change the direction of the Clinton-Gore years, and in many important ways we did. We found in George W. Bush the most pro-life, pro-family, pro-marriage president since Ronald Reagan. The president shared our faith and belief in the Judeo-Christian worldview, expressing itself in a compassionate conservatism in which we continue to believe. The primary help for orphans, widows, prisoners, and the homeless continues to come from the heart of the work the values voters do around the country, day in and day out.

This is consistent with the vision of our evangelical, Catholic, and Jewish forbearers, who held a biblical worldview, and who in other centuries led the efforts to abolish the slave trades in England and America; who promoted education for girls and women; who pushed for suffrage rights for women; who reformed the prisons, motivated by the belief in the dignity and worth of every person, even those incarcerated; who worked to end racism in the South and the North long before the Civil War because of racism's inherent metaphysical inequality; who founded the most important colleges and universities in America; who founded the most important hospitals and medical facilities in America; who powered the civil rights movement; and who worked to promote a country that makes room for the innocent preborn, which is the major civil rights issue of our present era at a time when more than half of all babies with Down syndrome are aborted. This is the history of the values voters in America. Our ranks are growing, powered by moral politics informed by our faith.

President Ronald Reagan said, "Democracy is less a system of government than it is a system to keep government limited, unintrusive: A system of constraints on power to keep politics and government secondary to the important things in life, the true sources of value found only in family and faith."[7] If there is a better sentence to capture or describe that segment of American voters called "values voters," I am unsure what it could be. Striking the proper balance between the role of government on the one hand, and the country's private, civil life on the other, is the fuel that fires those of us who are conservatives.

Values voters believe the virtues of courage, wisdom, prudence, and temperance are indispensable to a good human life, the building blocks of morality. We believe the greatest, richest legacy a child can inherit is a loving and stable family life, and we lament deeply the decline of both moral and intellectual standards, none more so than the plague of fatherlessess, which may well be our most pressing domestic problem. Perhaps we need to restigmatize out-of-wedlock births. Our largest overall public policy concern is what the ultimate impact of this collapse of the ethical and moral foundations of America will mean for the next generation of Americans and for the core of our society—the intact, nuclear family.

This deterioration of the social sector is one of the major issues of our time, even as the number of single-family households increases year by year. These are the principles values voters brought with us to the 2000 and 2004 presidential campaigns.

Values voters overwhelmingly believe there could not have been a starker, more remarkable contrast among the three men running for the Oval Office in those years than there was among President Bush, Vice President Gore, and Senator Kerry, despite the obvious and important similarities. While they were all Ivy League graduates—products of famous prep schools and in the Gore-Bush comparison, sons of famous politicians—the contrast in substance on the issues and personal styles were huge factors to the average values voter. The records of two of the most liberal senators in the contemporary era provided ample fodder for comparison with the record of George W. Bush's tenure as the twice-elected governor of Texas. For instance, while Gore and Kerry had been, in their long careers, variously pro-life and pro-choice, both had finally become reliable votes and voices against innocent, preborn life. President Bush never wavered on this issue and showed a consistency that telegraphed reliability.

The case of Al Gore is the best example. As a young member of the House of Representatives, he was eloquently and consistently pro-life. The aging, established Gore was just the opposite. The formerly pro-life congressmen became a pro-choice senator and vice president. To values voters this seemed incongruous. If he could flip on that issue, what other issue or issues would he be willing to flip on? Values voters paid attention to his record and concluded that any man who could so passionately defend human life at one stage in his career, only to spout the reliable, anti-life rhetoric at another part of his career and with such abandon seemed to be a man with a political agenda and was perhaps untrustworthy.

Substantively on social issues, Gore and Kerry seemed kind of like the same man. This was especially true stylistically. During the debates in 2000, Al Gore seemed to have the right answers for his point of view, but the more values voters saw of him, the more unlikable to us he appeared. When he was asked questions unrelated to the issues of politics, he did not seem authentic. Oddly, during the debates with President Bush leading up to the 2000 presidential election, his body language telegraphed hostility and aggressiveness to President Bush. I remember watching the first Bush-Gore debate with my colleagues in the Austin Bush-Cheney presidential headquarters. Every time Al Gore seemed bothered or annoyed, he stepped toward President Bush in a way a bully might on a playground. He seemed to lack confidence in himself, and his body language in those debates sometimes seemed like he was trying to show us how tough he was. The debates of 2000 were a huge net-plus for George W. Bush even though many of the best pundits said it was Al Gore's strong point.

In the 2004 campaign, by contrast, three odd moments for John Kerry captured the attention of values voters. All three made Kerry seem like an out-of-sync and out-of-touch candidate. Each of these three snapshots underscored a man who seemed to live apart from most of the rest of the country and especially from many values voters.

The first snapshot was when Kerry visited a famous cheesesteak restaurant in Philadelphia. Part of the buzz in the air during the campaign was that Kerry was a little stuffy, and so his campaign wanted to put him in situations to show him as more of an everyman. The cheesesteak locale, in theory, should have been the perfect opportunity to mix with the average Joe and Josephine, to order a sandwich, sit down, and have a Coke. But when Kerry materialized in the line, asking for Swiss cheese on his cheesesteak, it was like watching the curtain come down. Swiss cheese on a cheesesteak sandwich, in Philly? It was, as they say in Hollywood, "a moment."

The second moment was during the summer of 2004, when many Americans were vacationing in national parks, at a local lake, at Disney World, or at some other amusement park or campground. This is where President Clinton sometimes got it right: He chose to vacation in national parks because he knew it was reflective of the average American experience, at least in the main. But not Kerry. During an exhausting, otherwise crazy-busy time on the campaign trail, he decided to take a little time off but not to go to a park or a lake or an amusement park or a campground but rather for an afternoon of windsurfing—back and forth, hither and yon—providing an image for the ages. Again, the wrong note was hit.

The third moment, and perhaps most damaging, came when John Kerry gave his acceptance speech at the Democratic National Convention in the summer of 2004. There are few actually painful moments during almost any acceptance speech in the whole of contemporary presidential politics, but Kerry provided one. Even now I wince when I think of it. Much of the buzz dominating the campaign was that Kerry, upon returning to America after Vietnam, was somewhat cavalier about his service. The contrast between that era of his life and his present desire to become the commander in chief of the most powerful military in the history of the world was a little breathtaking. The patriotic undertow of values voters was keenly attenuated on this particular issue. So when Kerry stepped up to the podium to deliver his speech, put his fingers to his eyebrows with a quick-snap salute, and said, "John Kerry, reporting for duty," values voters did not know what to think. My own dad, a veteran, turned to me and said, "Did he really say what we think he just said?" This seemed to capture cynicism.

In sum, both in the 2000 and in the 2004 campaigns, Al Gore and John Kerry not only opposed the issues values voters believed were most central in American political life, especially the sanctity of life, but in almost every conceivable manner held a worldview starkly different from ours. While we were religious, they were mostly secular and sometimes unable to muster the words to share even a modicum of their faith. Where we believed in and defended the sanctity of human life, they retreated into rhetoric about "choice" and "reproductive freedom," the triple-crown words of the pro-abortion forces in America. While we believed in marriage between one man and one woman for a lifetime and as the best environment for the raising of kids, they could never seem just to defend the nuclear family. While we believed patriotism and love of country were good and noble, they could never just say America was a great and exceptional country without qualifiers about other foreign countries and cultures.

Values voters believed both Gore and Kerry were, by and large, transnational globalists who could not seem to find identity in any one community or neighborhood. When Al Gore lost his own home state of Tennessee to George W. Bush in 2000, it appeared a shock to many folks, but it did not surprise values voters who valued home and a sense of belonging and place and who believed Gore was most comfortable either in Washington or with other global elites on the coasts or in other international locales. At the same time the values voters were never in doubt that Texas was home for George W. Bush, that he did not need to be president to feel validated, and that after his presidency he would happily return to the Lone Star State.

Values voters paid close attention to another optics issue in both the 2000 and 2004 campaigns, which has gotten virtually no attention. This is the relationship between the husband and wife running for the most important and the most visible spot on the world stage.

One thing values voters loved and admired about President and Laura Bush was their obvious love for each other and their compatibility. When you see them together, you know they were meant to be together. They complete each other, like President and Nancy Reagan, like President and Rosalyn Carter, and like the president's own parents, President George H. W. and Barbara Bush. Americans like it when the first family has connectedness that is real, transparent, and loving. Laura and George W. Bush just go together, and it is wonderful to see them together, as I often did, in private settings. They are the same in private as they are in public— able verbally to poke and prod each other in a loving, playful manner; able to joke about each other's flaws and strengths but always confirming their love and need for each other; able to tenderly hug or kiss each other in a way that was respectful and appropriate but sincerely felt. The president's love of family—and most especially his wonderful and tender relationships with his "girls," as he always called his daughters—was real. Jenny and I were invited to an annual White House Christmas party, where we spent a little time with the Bushes getting our photos snapped and having small talk, but on two occasions we were invited to the Bush's White House residence, and each time the natural grace of the first family was beautiful to witness.

On the first occasion, following an East Room event in celebration of Abraham Lincoln's bicentennial, the Bushes invited their guests upstairs to see the Lincoln Bedroom and the original Gettysburg Address, which is on permanent display there. The hour was late; the president's schedule the next day was punishingly busy; and yet the Bushes opened up the residence, graciously spending time with us, and importantly, interacting with each other, showing us they were having a good time together. We were in their home, and they made us feel welcomed and appreciated. Togetherness was key for them and never one without the other.

On the second occasion, in 2007, the Bushes and the Cheneys invited all the members of the White House team who had been on staff since the first day of the first administration to dine together in the White House residence. In addition to the remarkable reception and dinner, the Bushes opened up their home, allowing us to visit the president's personal office (the furniture there was used by President Grant), the beautiful Queen's Bedroom, and other treasures. The personal photos around the residence were of the girls and other members of the Bush family. And as exciting as it was to see the rooms, the furniture, the paintings, the history of it all, what touched Jenny and me most deeply was the loving interaction of the Bushes. They were not afraid to hold hands, to share an occasional wink or glance or joke, and the net effect was two strong but winsome personalities who shared humor, warmth, and a genuine sense of shared mission and purpose that permeated our small dinner party.

Their loyalty to staff, personal gratitude, and love and regard for each other were real. I believe this respect and honor were rooted in their mutual faith in Christ. That mutuality extended outward to their love and compassion for other people. It was a wonderful, heartening thing to witness in a president of the United States the validation and concern for his wife in the company of others. He never missed an opportunity to share his love and gratitude for Laura. During that dinner party I understood his famous capacity for friendship with the same people over many years. The president fostered personal goodwill because he was loyal and true and made the formation of strong relationships a core of his being. His relationship with God seemed to form the basis of his relationships with everyone else, most especially Laura. Values voters appreciated this about the Bushes.

While values voters appreciated the president's willingness to speak out about his faith and the importance of prayer in his life, there remains a misperception, in this regard, about the Bush presidency. The perception is that the president, unlike all his predecessors, was distinctly or uniquely outspoken about that faith. This is not the case from evidence or from history. A remarkable book *God and the Founders: Madison, Washington and Jefferson* deserves to be better known than it is. It abundantly documents that almost every one of our forty-four presidents came from a religious tradition; that they spoke often about their faith; and that in significant ways many of them were actually more outspoken than President Bush not only about their own faith but also about the relationship between faith and the public life of America.

Values voters concluded as early as 2000 that George W. Bush was a man of integrity and not turpitude. When they invested their votes in the president, they believed it was a moral act with consequence. His public demeanor was the furthest thing possible from a cloying, mawkish sentimentality or condescension when it came to faith and public life. If he had a piece de resistance, it is that in an age of burn-down-the-house politics, he was civil, respectful, and unwilling to defame his political or cultural opponents. There is no president in the contemporary era who did more to advance life, marriage, and religious liberty than George W. Bush, and that is why, through two hard-fought presidential campaigns, values voters prayed for him daily, stood by him, and continue to maintain a reservoir of goodwill for him.

Chapter 15

Hail and Farewell to the Chief

The Constitution is not a living organism.
It's a legal document.
—Justice Antonin Scalia[1]

To see things as they are, to estimate them aright,
and to act accordingly, is to be wise.
—Chief Justice of the United States John Jay[2]

One of the most memorable nights I had during my time in the White House came on Saturday, September 3, 2005, just after 10:30 p.m. About fifteen or twenties minutes after going to bed, I was jolted awake when the phone rang. No one likes to get a call late at night, and there is always concern that a family member or friend is calling with bad news.

In this instance it was a friend of mine highly regarded in Washington legal circles. His call would provide the opening moments to one of the most momentous chapters in the whole of the Bush presidency.

He was phoning to tell me Chief Justice William Rehnquist died within the last hour or so. He followed with a comment I will never forget: "The President is about to make one of the most important decisions of his life." I offered my sympathy to my friend, who was among the closest friends of the late chief justice. I asked my wife, Jenny, to check the TV networks and the Internet to see if there was news yet of the chief's passing, thinking perhaps I missed the announcement before going to bed.

But when I came back on the line, my friend said he called me as a courtesy because he thought the president would want to know at once—a sentiment I shared. He said he did not know when the announcement of the chief's death would be made at the Supreme Court, but being public spirited and a great patriot, he was keen that the president know as soon as possible.

Knowing only those details, I thanked him, got a number where I could phone him back if necessary, and proceeded to phone Karl Rove, whom I thought would want to let the president know posthaste.

Rehnquist was a giant of the court; one of the most important legal conservatives in the history of the United States; one of the few men who could actually be considered a peer, intellectually and otherwise, with the likes of John Jay, John Marshall, and other greats; and who was an important historian of the Supreme Court in his own right. This would be a huge vacancy to fill and probably the most important nomination of the entire Bush presidency. For me it illustrated that all the time spent away from my family during the 2000 presidential campaign had been worth it because we now had a president who would faithfully nominate to the court a man or woman who was faithful to the framers' vision of jurisprudence.

Elections have consequences, none more so in the American presidency than choosing who gets nominated to the Supreme Court, one of the most important domestic decisions any president makes. This is because whoever sits as one of the nine justices on that illustrious, powerful court shapes, molds, and impacts the lives of untold millions of Americans. In the case of choosing Rehnquist's successor, the stakes could not have been higher for the whole of the Bush legacy. And with that call from my friend, I knew I would be working as part of a team at the White House during a historic chapter of the Bush presidency. My friend was right: George W. Bush, in deciding who would take the place of William Rehnquist, would be making one of the most important decisions not only of his presidency but of his life.

It is easy now to forget the judicial and political jujitsu and sheer dynamism in late 2005 and early 2006 that comprised the Bush presidency's Supreme Court nomination process. There have been few years of more importance in the contemporary history of our country for the future direction of the high court than the one commencing in the autumn of 2005 and culminating in February 2006.

Rehnquist, who served as chief justice of the United States for nineteen years, died two months after Justice Sandra Day O'Connor announced her retirement. The speculation in Washington had always been that Justice John Paul Stevens, in his mid-eighties at the time, not O'Connor, would be the next justice to retire. But O'Connor decided to step down because of the Alzheimer's disease afflicting her husband.

President Bush nominated fifty-year-old John Roberts for the O'Connor seat well before Rehnquist's death. Roberts served as a Supreme Court clerk for Rehnquist and considered the chief his mentor. President Bush was so confident Roberts was among the most stellar judges and legal minds in the country—he was serving on the D.C. Circuit Court of Appeals, which is considered the nation's second highest court—that naming him to that first Supreme Court vacancy was viewed as a validation of merit.

Roberts, who had been an attorney serving in both the Reagan and George H. W. Bush administrations, was well known in all elite legal circles, but especially in Washington, where he began his legal career. He had a well-earned reputation as one of the smartest and fairest conservative jurists in the country. The speculation had been high for years that he would one day get a Supreme Court nod, and as O'Connor's replacement, he seemed the right choice. So when Rehnquist's seat suddenly came open, President Bush made a historically noteworthy decision: He decided to renominate Roberts to the Rehnquist seat, which would make him the new chief—reopening the O'Connor vacancy even though her seat came available first. At that point, in another twist, she decided to remain on the court until her successor was confirmed by the United States Senate.

The expected *sturm und drang* of Supreme Court nominations became standard operating procedure dating from the attacks on President Reagan's Supreme Court nominee Judge Robert H. Bork by the late U.S. Senator Ted Kennedy, and extending to the equally horrific attacks on Justice Clarence Thomas. This same harshness was now applied with equal fervor to John Roberts immediately after he was nominated. Despite his acknowledged brilliance and remarkable record as a lawyer and judge at such a young age, the early assault on his qualifications and character were furious.

Immediately after Roberts was nominated, a Supreme Court judicial coalition began to meet to plot out strategy and tactics to support the nominee in a variety of ways. Even though it had been eight years since a

Republican president last nominated a Supreme Court justice—President Clinton last nominated the liberals Steven Breyer and Ruth Bader Ginsburg to the court in the 1990s—conservatives remembered well the vicious attacks on Bork and Thomas and were now well-schooled and ready in how the Left and its allies worked. The coalition studied their tactics and strategies and the resulting impact they had made on those two nominations. Senator Kennedy quickly emerged as the chief opponent of Roberts, but this time conservatives were prepared. Our allies fired back with the same determination, refusing to allow any of the unsubstantiated attacks on Roberts to go unanswered, and the coalition's effort paid off.

Whenever Kennedy or one of his Senate Judiciary Committee allies unfairly or harshly attacked Roberts, the coalition used every channel of old and new media to put out a balanced, factual, evidence-based response, even to the smallest detail. Applying James Q. Wilson's broken-window theory on crime to Supreme Court nominations—Wilson said crime was reduced overall when law enforcement authorities paid attention to the most minor of crimes because paying attention to the small ones signaled to potential criminals that no crime, however large or small, would go unpunished—the judicial coalition answered every single attack with specificity and granularity. The coalition's goal was to make sure that the attacking senators, the American people, and the media would not be in the dark about unsubstantiated charges or cheap shots.

The coalition's methods worked powerfully. A measurable gap between the Democrats on the Judiciary Committee and their liberal allies was widening even as the Roberts Senate hearings got underway. Whereas during the Bork and Thomas hearings the Democrats and their coalition partners were of a piece, driving the national agenda and dialogue, they were thwarted during the Roberts' nomination because the judicial coalition and its effective efforts prevailed inside the Beltway and across the country. The coalition set a new standard of excellence in that first Supreme Court nomination battle on behalf of President Bush and John Roberts. Leonard Leo, Jay Sekulow, Ed Whelan, Edwin Meese III, and Boyden Gray did a superb job, as did countless allies in the field: Ann Corkery, Gary Marx, Wendy Long, Curt Levey, Barbara Ledeen, Kay Daly, Alan Sears, and a host of others.

But the coalition's success could not have achieved what it did without the unflappable nominee whose hearing process was the smoothest one since Justice Antonin Scalia was nominated by Ronald Reagan. Scalia had garnered a unanimous vote in the Senate—probably the last time that will ever happen. Even a candidate as stellar as Roberts could not hope to attain unanimity because of the toxicity of the Supreme Court nomination process now, founded and fueled by the Democrats in those poisonous battles over Bork. But Roberts did well, with the Senate voting 78 to 22 to confirm him. The Democrats split their votes, dividing evenly 22 for and 22 against, a gap that showed not only Roberts's singularity as a potentially great justice but also the outstanding work of the coalition on his behalf. All fifty-five Republicans gave him their yes votes, which was a victory for President Bush. The White House nomination team was brilliant in its communication, policy, political, and legislative apparatus. All the pistons were firing, and the White House cylinders moved in sync, moving along a great nominee while marginalizing the opposition despite its fierceness and its well-funded operation. My White House colleagues in the Counsel's, legislative, and communications offices deserve the lion's share of the credit for the success of Roberts's nomination and vote, none more so than Ed Gillespie, who led our team.

The Democrats, by contrast, looked weak. For what seemed like purely political reasons, several of the people who were then expected to run for the presidency opposed Roberts, grandstanding against him despite his judicial record and temperament, most notably Senator Hillary Rodham Clinton, Senator Joe Biden, and Senator Evan Bayh.

The gap between the Democrats in the Senate and their staunchest judicial supporters stunned everyone; this was a historically important divide. Never in contemporary American political history had so many Democrats, half those serving in the Senate, broken with their activist allies on a Supreme Court nomination. Why could Kennedy not keep the Left on the same page against Roberts? Despite their best efforts, which were heavily financed and heavily coordinated by wealthy liberals, the Left could not overcome the conservative coalition and its proactive, unremitting activities. The Left predicted and promised a punishing fight to the finish against Roberts, and yet their less than effective efforts let down the Democratic Party's liberal base. The Left pushed and prodded Kennedy and his Senate colleagues to employ a Bork-style withering opposition, but although the rhetoric was white hot at certain turns, it did not result in keeping the Senate Democrats together on that final vote. The conservative coalition reached out across the country and kept the constituents of Democratic senators apprised of what was really happening in the Senate Judiciary Committee hearings, parsing the rhetoric and revealing the truth. For instance, every time a Democratic senator held a news conference or did a radio and TV interview, the coalition measured what was said and, if necessary, put out a rejoinder. News conferences and radio and TV interviews were done, where necessary, to counter what a senator or activist said or charged. The coalition matched them one for one. Every time the Left went on talk radio, the president's supporters went on talk radio; every time the Left went on cable TV, our supporters went on cable TV; every time they put out ads against John Roberts, the coalition followed suit. The conservative coalition was unwilling to allow itself to be put on the defensive. It worked.

Kennedy would never find it in himself to congratulate Roberts or to stand down in his criticism, for which he had built a reputation in the Senate. Kennedy said Roberts had not been candid enough during his nomination hearings and with his colleagues, and the senator pushed and prodded Roberts on abortion, assisted suicide, and civil rights, among other issues. Kennedy later said, rather oddly, "I hope I am proved wrong about John Roberts. I have been proved wrong before."[3] What he meant is he also formerly opposed Republican nominees who turned out to share his own views on abortion and other issues.

The most important thing that happened during the Roberts nomination, however, is that Roberts himself hit a grand slam in his Senate hearings; it was as if he prepared an exact text to every question he was asked, so intellectually alive had he proven during the questioning. Any first-, second-, or third-year law student would benefit from reading those transcripts. Roberts was a marvel to listen to and to observe. I sat in on one of the two hearings and was dazzled by the depth and substance of his reasoning, as was the entire judiciary committee, who voted 13 to 5 for him, with three Democrats joining the majority. In that moment, when the committee voted, the allies of the Democrats knew it was all over for them and that Roberts would probably take his place as the seventeenth chief justice of the United States.

Only one part of the Roberts hearings puzzled me. The Democrats routinely attacked the nominee for his Catholicism, even though the two main critics, Chairman Patrick Leahy and Senator Dick Durbin, were Catholics. Leahy was expert at forwarding the view, left over from the John Kennedy days, that a man of faith would allow his religion to impact his decisions on the court. Roberts adopted a Kennedy narrative, that his faith would have no impact on his decisions. The Left continued to demand that personal faith is OK as long as it is kept private and within the four walls of home. Ironically, Leahy would end up voting for Roberts.

It was and remains a sad reality of our national political life that any man or woman of faith is expected to cloak that faith to satisfy what Pope Benedict has called an "aggressive secularism."[4]

In addition to Roberts's outstanding performance in the hearings, the coalition's great efforts nationwide, and the extraordinary work of my Bush White House colleagues, a fourth factor made the nomination a success: the cooperation between the White House and the Republicans on the Senate Judiciary Committee. The president had a short list of potential nominees ready to go when an opening came up; he announced Roberts as his choice expeditiously, allowing the nomination and confirmation process to happen in a way that, when the Court opened its new term on the first Monday in October 2005, John Roberts was at the helm without missing a beat. Republican members of the Senate Judiciary Committee liked the swiftness but also the substantive nature of how the White House was prepared, and it allowed them and their staffs to work more efficiently on substance without getting caught up in a timing lag or trying to figure out potential pitfalls with the nominee. They could concentrate on the kind of logistical, tactical, and strategic planning always necessary for a successful if not always smooth confirmation process, a process that never just happens.

The Roberts nomination and confirmation were among the signal achievements of George W. Bush's entire presidency. White House colleagues gathered in the Roosevelt Room to watch the Senate vote. As the vote totals clicked into place, excitement and gratitude mounted for John Roberts, his wife Jane, their two children, and for President Bush. The room had a great sense of camaraderie and goodwill. It was a nice touch that the Roberts and the president lunched together that day.

When a president nominates a Supreme Court candidate, it is overwhelmingly the thing that preoccupies the whole of the White House rhythm and tempo, and everyone on the staff knows a Supreme Court nomination is the most important domestic legacy any president will leave. That is a heady reality that motivates everyone toward excellence. There are no short days at the White House during the nomination process, no weekends, and with the 24-7-52 nature of the media, no breaks or lapses are allowed. Hairpin curves in messaging can and do happen, and everyone who is playing a part has to know how to work together. The nomination process bonded those of us who worked so closely together on the Roberts nomination. By God's grace, we accomplished that heavy-lift. The president's choice of Roberts will impact the direction of the country for years to come because Roberts is young.

Three hours after the Senate voted to confirm him, we were in the East Room for the swearing-in. "There is no way to repay the confidence you have shown in me, other than to do the best job I possibly can do,"

Roberts said to President Bush during that White House ceremony. "And I will try to do that every day."[5] The ceremony took place on September 29, 2005. President Bush offered simple but powerful remarks, saying, "What Daniel Webster termed 'the miracle of the Constitution' is not something that happens every generation. But every generation in its turn must accept the responsibility of supporting and defending the Constitution and bearing true faith and allegiance to it."[6] These remarks underscored a major part of the president's achievement: The Constitution was not a living, breathing document open to change and transformation with every fad and style of a new era but rather had a fixed meaning rooted in immutable principles.

He was giving voice to an originalist interpretation of the Constitution he shared, broadly, with Rehnquist, Scalia, Thomas, and now Roberts. The president knew the gravity and historic importance of the Roberts era on the cusp of commencing the following Monday as the new Court term got underway. The president found a worthy successor to Rehnquist, and despite the natural transition between the two leaders, the continuity and stability the president desired and prized would be attained by the affable and accomplished Roberts. It seems to me Rehnquist himself would have been thrilled with the Roberts choice.

Yet as the Roberts era prepared to step off—the president said Roberts was "a man with an astute mind and a kind heart"[7]—there was a new and growing buzz at the White House. The president and all of us who worked on Supreme Court nominations knew the pending, second Supreme Court nomination was, in its own way, probably going to be as or more momentous than the Roberts nomination for a single reason: That historic gap between Democrats voting for and against Roberts meant the Democrats' own liberal base would demand a more fiery nomination battle the second time around, regardless of who the nominee would be. Everyone on both sides of the political aisle knew O'Connor was often a key, swing vote in major 5 to 4 decisions. This only lent more fuel to the fire of the next nomination. This gap among the Democrats would continue to be a huge factor.

But only the president himself could have known there would be a second reason for an uber-contentious *battle royale* in that second nomination: He was preparing to nominate a candidate who, unlike Roberts, did not share a national profile in elite legal circles or come from the accomplished conservative legal milieu that made any Supreme Court nomination and confirmation process among fellow Republicans and conservatives smoother. These two factors—differences with natural opponents and differences with allies—would prove huge bookends in the second Bush nominee to our nation's highest court.

The president suggested he would probably choose a woman or a minority for the O'Connor seat, and he said during the Roberts hearing he was looking for diversity on the high court. So Washington was abuzz that he might choose an African American or a Hispanic, and everyone knew his great friend and lawyer Alberto Gonzales, whom he had nominated as chief justice of the Texas Supreme Court and later White House Counsel, was probably a leading nominee even though some conservatives opposed him on matters dating from his time in Texas. I knew Al well, and we had worked together on multiple projects during our time in the White House. He was a man of accomplishment and character and among the White House staff had a reputation for keeping his own close counsel in the best tradition of judges. He was among the most affable, kind, inquisitive men in the West Wing and a family man who put a premium on his relationship with his wife and kids.

So as the new chief justice prepared to take his seat at that famous horseshoe-shaped bench in the glistening white-marbled Supreme Court, all of Washington, indeed all of America, turned their attention now to the single question: Who would take the place of the first woman on the Supreme Court? How would George W. Bush continue to keep his campaign promise of choosing nominees in the mold of Thomas and Scalia and now Roberts, men who placed an originalist view of the Constitution at the center of their reasoning and not a jurisprudence of empathy that defined the Left? The next chapter of the Bush presidency's Supreme Court legacy would be fraught with heartache, vitriol, puzzlement, and intrigue, yet in the end the result was not only another stellar nominee but a stellar achievement for George W. Bush's legacy.

Chapter 16

Trying to Sell What
Nobody Would Buy

*How you think when you lose determines how long
it will be until you win.*

—G. K. Chesterton[1]

During all my years in the Bush White House, there was no one I had higher professional or personal regard for than Harriet Miers. She was a person of enormous accomplishment across a variety of fields, and yet she was most known among our administration colleagues for her personal humility, loyalty, and singular ability to get things done in a substantial, thorough manner. She was popular in the West Wing for her ability and desire to remain in the shadows, and in a host of ways, most of which will never be known to anyone, she personally reached out to people who were at a professional or personal nadir, showing them love, help, and generosity of soul. Also, she was such an important part of George W. Bush's success that he considered her indispensable and among his closest ring of confidants and advisors.

My friendship with Harriet was rooted in two things, one incidental and one central. The incidental thing is that we were both, in our DNA, early risers and liked to begin our workdays at the White House as the sun rose. She would drive her car into the White House gates almost exactly at the time I was arriving on most mornings, and she would park next to the canopy on West Executive Drive, directly beside the entry of the West Wing on the ground floor.

Sometimes we waved at each other, not needing to say a thing. She held three of the most important jobs among the West Wing senior team: staff secretary, which oversees the paper flow to the president, a foundational job indeed; deputy chief of staff; and eventually White House Counsel, which was held by both Al Gonzales and Fred Fielding, who served in a similar capacity in the Reagan administration. This was a huge trajectory upward for her, and she earned it. She was often the last one out the door at night and the first into the office the next morning. Her energy level was astounding, and she did it all with verve and a great heart.

The most important thing we had in common was our Christianity. She served in important capacities in her church in Texas, and though known as one of the most important lawyers in Texas, she was equally known in some circles for the passion she had in her faith. This she had in common with the president. I deeply admired the fact that she did not keep her faith under a bushel but rather was joyous and outspoken about it.

When Harriet was nominated by President Bush to succeed O'Connor, it would be an overstatement to say my colleagues were entirely surprised, mostly for the reasons I mentioned above. We all knew how highly regarded she was by the president and for excellent reasons. But because the Roberts nomination went so smoothly, rooted in his being well-known in high legal circles and among key Republican and conservative VIPs, many people thought the president would choose not to shift gears, choosing someone with a similar profile as Roberts—a federal judge with long experience on the bench, someone known as a constitutional expert. So when the president chose to go in a different direction, with the success of the Roberts nomination still fresh in everyone's mind, almost everyone on the outside of 1600 Pennsylvania Avenue was stunned, or nearly so.

Yet the president's reasoning was clear. Harriet was a gifted, competent, hardworking, tireless friend and aide dating to his first run for the Texas governorship. She proved her mettle time and again at key turning points in the president's professional success. He had supreme confidence in her—in fact, as much or more confidence than others who comprised a strong bench of colleagues from Texas who came with him to the White House. He believed she would make an outstanding member of the Supreme Court—bringing to that august body the same ability, achievement, and temperament, which was important to George W. Bush in all his most significant nominations administration-wide.

Early in the morning on October 3, 2005, Karl Rove called me and Matt Smith, my White House friend and colleague, to his office, asking us to shut the door and prepare to get some important news. He told us Harriet would be named as the president's Supreme Court nominee later that day, that it was highly confidential, and that he wanted to know the reaction of our allies and friends as soon as we had a good read. I was probably more baffled than some of my colleagues by the news of the pending nomination, which had nothing to do with Harriet and everything to do with John Roberts. Some background is in order here.

The White House Supreme Court nomination team, which clearly was running on all cylinders and congealed during the Roberts hearings, was held together by a particular model of success: the profile of the recent nominee. That profile formed how we worked in our collective duties—communications, media, coalition building, and working with the Hill. Harriet's profile was so dissimilar from Roberts's that everyone on the White House team knew that we would collectively and quickly have to recalibrate our nomination model. We would have to shift from working with a well-known, highly regarded sitting federal judge who was the mentee of Chief Justice Rehnquist—a man so versatile on the Constitution that even his most ardent opponents were regaled and even dazzled by his legal knowledge, resulting in awe—to a profile of a highly accomplished lawyer, public servant, and presidential confidante who was by and large virtually unknown outside Texas or apart from her association with the president. The White House team knew the president's second Supreme Court nominee, Harriet or anyone else, would be immediately compared to Roberts, his having set the bar and standard incomparably high. The unstated reality was that any nominee not seen as Roberts's almost exact peer had the potential to bring on a backlash the size of a political tsunami not only among the president's harshest opponents but also among his strongest allies.

One other key narrative was at work here, apart from John Roberts or Harriet Miers. Because of my portfolio at the White House, I worked closely with a number of the legal groups who comprised a network of conservative institutions known for their intellectual sophistication, credibility, heft, and gravitas. With the rise of the conservative movement also came the attendant rise of the conservative legal culture, and it operated at a high level indeed, holding up Madison and the other framers as the standard bearers in all matters relating to the Constitution and the Supreme Court. They had expectations that men and women of the highest intellectual and experiential caliber would be nominated to the highest court in the land, men and women of the Rehnquist, Scalia, and Roberts model.

So after Karl gave Matt and me the news on Harriet's pending nomination, we began preparing an outreach plan just as we had with John Roberts, but our planning was as different as night and day. The major difference is that, when we reached out on John Roberts, almost all of our natural allies knew who he was, worked with him in the Reagan or George H. W. Bush administrations, served with him on law panels at gatherings, or were familiar with his work on the D.C. Circuit Court of Appeals. That whole record of achievement and familiarity helped bridge our successful coalition efforts because the coalition knew Roberts as a fellow conservative, even if he was never political per se. Our outreach efforts with Harriet would not or could not match that because most of our allies knew only her political appointments inside the Bush administration; and even then, for all her distinguished job titles and personal story, she only occasionally did outreach to the conservative establishment because it was not her duty. As a Supreme Court nominee, by protocol, she could not reach out to potential coalition allies now, only to senators and their staffs.

The same sense of being an unknown quantity pervaded Capitol Hill too, but that was true of Roberts also with one significant difference. When the White House legislative team began its round of Hill visits with Roberts, senior staff on the Hill may not have known him, but they could always refer to his record of jurisprudence as a high-profile, successful federal judge, to his work as a clerk at the Supreme Court, or to his resume as a young lawyer in previous presidential administrations. Harriet's resume was different but not less accomplished. Although she was never a judge, her background was impressive. She was the first woman to become a law partner in a major Texas firm; she became the president of another major Texas law firm; she was the first woman to serve as the president of the State Bar of Texas; she was a member of the Dallas City Council; and she headed the Texas Lottery Commission, inheriting an agency in a mess which she cleaned up. Hers was a significant resume and yet with no bench experience, no record of scholarly constitutional work, and being largely unknown in Washington, lacking almost any history senators on either side of the aisle could immediately latch onto with the exception of important details largely from her professional life in Texas, everyone knew the nomination process was going to be tough. For these reasons, the White House and the Hill knew those one-on-one meetings with individual senators would be far more important than the Roberts meetings because she would be going into those meetings as a bit of a blank slate.

Between the Roberts nomination and the Miers nomination, lots of senators, Republican party officials, public policy types, and legal elites weighed in with the White House, asking the president to choose a nominee who was of the Roberts profile and who shared his well-regarded conservative jurisprudence. They knew that, at age fifty, Roberts would be putting his stamp on the high court for years to come and would welcome a compatriot and like-minded fellow justice. The court had been bending in a rightward fashion, and the replacement of O'Connor, as a key swing vote in many 5 to 4 decisions, was in this sense more important than the Rehnquist-to-Roberts exchange because while Roberts would be one conservative replacing another conservative, the second Bush nominee could be a conservative replacing a moderate to liberal member of the court. Ironically, Harriet was part of the White House team that selected Roberts, and so all these arguments were well known to her.

On that early October morning, with Harriet at his side, President Bush welcomed the national media to the Oval Office to formally announce her as Justice O'Connor's replacement. I knew, for many of my fellow conservatives, this would be their first news of the new nominee, so I braced for the reaction. I knew, within minutes of the president's announcement concluding, I would hear from a number of people and be able to gauge accurately their first-blush take on her nomination just as I had with Roberts, where the reaction was overwhelmingly, categorically positive, bordering on the euphoric. Ironically, the last justice to be nominated for the Supreme Court with no experience on the bench was William Rehnquist, when President Nixon nominated him in 1972. President Reagan elevated Rehnquist to chief justice in 1986.

In his announcement of Miers, the president made three key points: That Harriet had devoted her life to the law; that she would not be an activist justice—no legislating from the bench, which was reassuring to the conservative base; and that of all the people he had been considering, she was a standout and the right replacement for O'Connor. Following the president's announcement, Harriet gave a wonderful set of remarks, stressing again that she would adhere strictly to the Constitution and rule in sync with "the founders' vision of the court."[2]

The reaction to the Miers nomination was quick and mostly warmly welcomed on the Left. This did not help with the conservative base, which was at first puzzled by the president's choice. For instance, while Senator Schumer (D–NY) voted against John Roberts, saying he was probably out of the mainstream, he initially favored the Miers nomination, saying that, contra his Roberts confirmation vote, "Today is a day, I guess of some hope—there's hope that Harriet Miers is a mainstream nominee."[3] Reading between the lines, what Senator Schumer meant was, unlike John Roberts, whom he supposed was pro-life, Harriet's views were beyond speculation on that issue, so she was initially acceptable to him, in his eyes a net plus for her. This was based purely on his own speculation without any proof of her view of abortion or the Roe decision. But what this all really signaled is that, unlike the initial reaction to John Roberts, whose conservative judicial philosophy was well known from his time of service on the federal bench, most of the Hill conversations would go immediately to this ideological litmus test of whether she was or was not a closet moderate like O'Connor.

Harriet kept getting accolades from liberals who knew nothing about her but were averse to saying anything negative out of the box. For instance, Senator Harry Reid (D–NV) said he was pleased she had no judicial experience because he felt the court needed someone who did not come from the world of the federal courts. Senator Lincoln Chafee (R–RI) said he would consider opposing anyone who was similar to Roberts and left open the door that Harriet might be that kind of nominee. The lack of definition was prompting those on the Left to give early, favorable reports, but those on the Right were naturally skeptical, not because they initially opposed her, but in light of Roberts, conservatives wanted the same or similar kinds of reassurances, which could not be provided other than the early commitment to strict constructionism and a favorable endorsement from the president himself. The president once said Harriet was "a pit bull in size 6 shoes."[4] She was tough indeed, and that is part of what we in the White House loved about her. But what she was facing was not about being tough or weak; rather, it was about the Left-Right matrix that was quickly building into an unfavorable crescendo on the Right. It was among the saddest, most personally difficult parts of my White House tenure because I held Harriet in such high regard. At the same time, what was potentially coming at her on the Hill and elsewhere was the roughest waters possible in Washington.

Karl and I reached out early and often to our conservative allies who were outstanding on Roberts and on a host of other judicial nominations. We shared everything we possibly could including, over and over again, the president's and Harriet's personal commitment to originalism and not legislating from the bench, someone who would be faithful to the Constitution, faithful to the founders' intents and principles, faithful to applying the laws strictly. We could never share how she might rule on any case and would never have speculated in that regard, just as we never could have done with John Roberts. But our allies could not find a way to engage the grassroots, and that was the mechanism so important in the Roberts nomination. It was not that our friends disliked Harriet, or were disbelieving about what the president or Harriet said in their initial Oval Office statements. It was, in part, that too many former Republican presidents made nominations to the court, promising constitutional faithfulness, only to see nominees move steadily to the Left. Without that rock-solid foundation of past experience on which to judge Harriet, the conservative movement would not embrace her completely. The movement simply had to have a reliable record on which to base their support, a trail of personal and professional relationships, or a network of fellow conservatives who might help reassure them of her constitutional bona fides. But the conservative judicial coalition's lack of enthusiastic support was not the death knell of the nomination. By and large it was the neutral to negative feedback the White House was getting from the meetings with the senators, particularly those who were otherwise reliable allies of the White House and conservatives on almost all other matters relating to legal concerns and nominations. This is where the distress signals were damaging. The net result is conservative pundits and media began to come out in almost categorical opposition to her nomination.

Conservative senators, despite the buzz at the time, were not looking for reassurance on abortion, affirmative action, or other social policies. They understood Supreme Court nominees could not tell senators how they might or might not vote on issues likely to come before the court. Rather, they were uneasy about a lack of a clear and concise judicial philosophy in her background they could point to with reassurance. Recurring criticism after those meetings on Capitol Hill was consistent: vagueness, no judicial record, and a general uneasiness about the nomination in light of their strong support for Roberts. In sum, they were uneasy about being supportive. It was not that senators feared another Sandra Day O'Connor, as much as many of them disagreed with her on key issues and rulings; it was that they did not want another David Souter, one of the few nominees who made it onto the court with virtually no record at all on social issues. The reaction of conservative senators unwilling to support her spilled into the media rapidly and dented the nomination in ways that looked increasingly irreparable.

The opposite was true on the Left. That initial good will from the likes of Schumer, Reid, and Chafee was shifting to a new, hostile demand for a look at some of Harriet's personal White House papers relating to other issues during her time serving the president, which was an outrageous demand—a demand the president could never and would never fulfill. It was not as if she served in a long-ago administration whose concerns were now part of history; instead, the senators were eager to go on a fishing expedition, and this was a line the president would not and could not cross. The combination of the Left's demands for papers and the Right's unwillingness to support her nomination resulted in implosion. The combination of uneasiness on the Right and hostility on the Left was now unmistakable nearly three weeks after her nomination, and on October 27, 2005, she decided to stand down and withdraw her nomination. The often visceral criticism of her was wrenching. I could only imagine how deeply her heart was hurting. This was among the most momentous professional chapters of her life, and the gale-force winds of Washington caught her in their midst through literally no fault of her own.

She wrote to the president that her nomination had become a "burden," and the relentless Senate requests for documents would be seemingly unending. The Miers Supreme Court chapter of the Bush administration's history is now little recalled, but it was in fact the first major catalyst prompting a serious discussion of the constitutional question of separation of powers, a debate that would grow during the remaining years of the Bush administration. Was it really the case she could not be considered for a seat on the Supreme Court unless she surrendered White House documents to the Democrats? That was precisely the case they were making, and the net effect is that it was a request not only the Bush White House could never fulfill but also one any administration in such a situation, from either political party, could never fulfill. It was an immutable constitutional principle, and Senate Democrats were asking her to step over that line. Meanwhile, and almost categorically, conservatives said they were eager to start again, to get a new nominee. Many of the president's closest allies and friends, in and out of the Senate, also desired a redo, calling for a strict constructionist with a record to prove it, someone closer to the Roberts profile.

Harriet Miers' decision to withdraw her nomination was an act of courage and humility, rooted in her principled view of life and vocation. I was in touch with her during that difficult time, and I saw a faith and trust lacking any bitterness or resentment. She returned to the White House Counsel's office and was part of the team that helped the president select the next Supreme Court nominee, a highly regarded jurist from New Jersey whose great personal loves in life were his wife, his kids, and the Philadelphia Phillies.

The contrast between the president's third choice to fill the O'Connor vacancy and the Miers interlude, which had just concluded, was striking and immediate. On October 31, 2005, just four days after Miers stepped down, Karl called me early in the morning to tell me the president was preparing to make his announcement that morning. He told me "your folks" would love the choice for all the right reasons, and just after eight o'clock that morning I snapped on my TV at the White House and watched the president nominate Samuel Alito Jr., a federal appeals court judge, to become the next justice of the Supreme Court, a man fully in sync with the new chief justice and whose own record as a sitting federal judge with fifteen years on the bench in the U.S. Court of Appeals for the Third Circuit won plaudits in all the right political quarters. Alito was well known and highly regarded in conservative and Republican legal circles and in fact had been speculated on as a possible nominee since the previous July when O'Connor announced her retirement.

And so, from the first, Alito was cheered by conservatives and hissed by liberals, which was a marked contrast from the day Harriet was nominated, when liberals by and large were uncritical and conservatives by and large were skeptical. The liberal groups believed from the start they had found a nominee whose conservative record on social issues was worthy of their scathing attacks, and they were chomping at the bit to get started in their quest to tear him down in the way they did Bork and Thomas. Because Alito served on the federal bench for so long, there was a paper trail that both sides knew would be a factor in the pending hearings. The Left wasted no time. By the end of that first day, the AFL-CIO, Pro-Choice America, People for the American Way, the Alliance for Justice, MoveOn.org, the Leadership Conference on Civil Rights, and others blasted the president's nominee on everything from his federalist judicial philosophy to his defense of religious liberty. I remember reading those statements; these people were actually suggesting Alito was a bigot and a zealot. Both the People for the American Way and the Alliance for Justice called for a "massive national effort" to stop Alito from going onto the Supreme Court.

But the more everyone learned about Alito, the more we learned he was not only unlike those odd cartoons drawn by his opponents but also unlike Harriet Miers and John Roberts. Although both men were Catholics, and Harriet an evangelical, the fifty-five-year-old Alito was a first-generation American; his father was an Italian immigrant, and he grew up in Trenton. This gave Alito a unique perspective and appeal and made his rise from a working-class background to a Princeton undergraduate degree and a

Yale Law School degree all the more compelling and appealing. This was a self-made man with a decidedly intellectual bent and yet deeply humble despite those gifts.

His rapid rise to an appellate seat—via service as a U.S. attorney in New Jersey, as an assistant to the United States solicitor general, and as a deputy assistant to the attorney general at the Department of Justice in the mid-1980s—gave him a certain gravitas. President George H. W. Bush nominated him for a seat on the Third Circuit in 1990, and he was confirmed unanimously in the U.S. Senate, which was controlled by the Democrats that year.

Unlike Roberts, who exuded supreme confidence and polish, Alito's appeal was more gritty and cerebral; there was no arrogance in him, despite the many comparisons made between him and Justice Antonin Scalia, and his quiet intellectualism gave him immediate standing with everyone. He had argued twelve cases before the Supreme Court and a host of cases in other federal courts. The first time I met him, what struck me was his modesty and natural graciousness. You would never know you were in the same room with a man of such capacity unless someone else told you. This was refreshing, and it was not difficult to see why, in a few short years, he became not only a great federal judge but also an accomplished American who personified the kind of meritocracy that is at the heart of the greatness of our country. This is the kind of man we all wanted to see rise. The Left was offended by his jurisprudence.

The president, in making the announcement first thing in the morning in the corridor connecting the State Dining Room to the East Room, was quick to point out that Alito had "more prior judicial experience than any Supreme Court nominee in more than seventy years."[5] This line was designed to reassure the Right and to put the Left on notice: Alito was a talented, experienced federal judge who spent ample amounts of his professional life at the legal bar and would require no learning curve; he was a natural. He would make a great addition to that august body, the president said. And so with his wife Martha-Ann and two grown kids looking on, he accepted the nomination from President Bush and shared with the nation in those first remarks a great memory.

Just after the president announced Alito as his pick, the judge stepped to the microphone and recalled being in his thirties, arguing his first case before the Supreme Court; he said when he stepped to the lectern in the massive, marbled courtroom, amid those deep red velvet curtains and all its history, he felt a "sense of awe." And endearingly, he mentioned the first question he received from the Court was from the woman he was being nominated to replace, Justice O'Connor. He said the justice sensed he was a rookie, so "made sure that the first question that I was asked was a kind one."[6] That was a nice touch and utterly natural on Alito's part. He made clear he had a demonstrable judicial philosophy: "Federal judges have the duty to interpret the Constitution and the laws faithfully and fairly, to protect the constitutional rights of all Americans, and to do these things with care and with restraint, always keeping in mind the limited role that the courts play in our constitutional system."[7]

The more he spoke, the more methodical he appeared, but it was that modicum of modesty and genuineness that came through more strongly than ever. You could see why he and the president hit it off from the first. The president offered the job to Alito just an hour before, in the Oval Office, and so the fast-track nature of it all was a bit of a blur. The president, who was naturally compassionate even in the toughest circumstance like the one about to get underway, personally warned the Alito children about the pending brutality of the nomination fight, saying the process could be tough on their dad, but they should pay no attention to it. The president knew of what he spoke; as the son of a president, he endured the slings and arrows hurdled at his father during President George H. W. Bush's presidency and unsuccessful reelection bid. This would prove prescient advise and counsel to the Alito family and turned out to be exactly the case: The day-after-day chomping and chewing of Alito would be grinding and unfair and result in Mrs. Alito's tears of hurt for her husband at one of the nomination hearings in the Senate Hart Office Building just a block from the court.

If I had to pick a word that describes how the judicial coalition responded to the Alito nomination that day, it would be *euphoric*. In fact, the center-right coalition of conservatives and Republicans was thrilled beyond a doubt at the president's choice—almost everyone knew of Alito and his outstanding originalist record—and the battle was enjoined from the moment of the formal announcement and nomination. One ally, Jordan Lorence of the Alliance Defense Fund, was quoted in the *New York Times*, "The difference from after the Miers nomination was like being at a morgue versus being at a combination of a wedding reception, Super Bowl party, and bar mitzvah."[8] It is tempting to say that is an overstatement, but it precisely reflects how the conservative base felt about Alito, and the support for him, from the first, was deep and broad.

As if on cue, the liberals and the Democrats began to pounce with a fury. Senator Patrick Leahy (D–VT) came out of the box immediately, accusing President Bush of a "needlessly provocative nomination" in a quest to appease conservatives. Not to be outdone, Senator Ted Kennedy (D–MA) said the Alito pick was done "out of weakness rather than strength," and he was deeply bothered that so many conservatives had come out so strongly in support of Alito. He said conservatives were "shouting from the mountain tops for this Alito,"[9] and Kennedy said he wanted to know precisely why, so deeply disturbed was he. Senators Schumer (D–NY) and Reid (D–NV), who on that first day Miers was nominated wanted to take a wait-and-see approach because they felt they owed it to her out of fairness, showed no such fairness, or should I say justice, concerning Alito. They both took off the proverbial boxing gloves, with Reid calling Alito a "radical" and expressing anger that Alito was both white and a man.

It is tempting to conclude, at one remove, that Leahy had a point when he said the White House was seeking appeasement after the previous nomination of Harriet Miers. But that was not the case. Alito was on everyone's short list, inside and outside the White House, from the beginning of the Bush administration, so he was the next logical choice. If anything, the Alito nomination, after the Miers chapter, was counterintuitive. The buzz was the president might now look for a kind of O'Connor clone—a woman or minority who had been a federal judge, who had a center-right judicial philosophy like hers, and perhaps be forced to choose anyone but a white, conservative, religious male in the mold of Roberts and Rehnquist. Despite the politically correct expectations, the president chose well and, in doing so, stoked the fires of the Left, both on the Hill and among the Democrats' outside judicial allies, for a nomination fight that would make the Roberts and Miers battles look like child's play.

In part, that is what happened. Within a few days of the Alito nomination, the then-ranking Republican on the Senate Judiciary Committee, Senator Arlen Specter (R–PA), said he feared the possibility of a filibuster because of Alito's pro-life record. Specter was categorically pro-choice and knew O'Connor's possible replacement could move the court from a reliable pro-abortion vote to a more pro-life sensibility. One of the top pro-abortion groups in the country, NARAL, issued a statement saying if Alito made it onto the Supreme Court he would "eviscerate the core protections for women's freedom guaranteed by *Roe v. Wade*." Euphemistically, "women's freedom" means the snuffing the life from an innocent, unborn baby.

The pro-choice senators and their pro-choice allies like Kennedy and Leahy were concerned about two cases in Alito's background. The first was the famous *Planned Parenthood v. Casey* decision in 1991, a case that struck down a Pennsylvania statute requiring spouses to be notified before a pregnant woman aborted her fetus, a case later overturned by the Supreme Court, and in the process affirming *Roe v. Wade*. Alito dissented. In a case in 2000, he favored an exception to a New Jersey partial-birth abortion statute if the mother's life was endangered. He said the Supreme Court required such an exception.

It wasn't only the pro-life issue that rankled the Left, though. It was also Alito's defense of religion in the public square. He wrote an opinion that upheld a Jersey City statute allowing the display of menorahs and nativity scenes. This ruling was proof-positive to the Left he was a religious zealot who, if he made it to the Supreme Court, would probably lower that invisible wall between church and state, a ridiculous charge on its face.

There were plenty of other issues in the mix too: Second Amendment gun protections; and questions of affirmative action. Guns, race relations, and religion in public life—all these were important, significant issues to be sure; and in each case Alito ruled as an originalist and not from emotion or politics. But none of these issues, on the emotive judicial scale, rose to the level of abortion. For the Left this was the single most important issue without peer because if Alito made it onto the court, they reasoned, the O'Connor pro-choice position would be replaced. On this issue the Left attacked unmercilessly, unendingly, and unwaveringly through November and December 2005.

As the new year dawned, both sides were fully engaged in either full opposition or full defense of Alito. A group called Progress for America launched an advertising and Internet campaign in defense of Alito, which was a counterweight to similar efforts on the Left. Meanwhile the pro-Alito judicial coalition worked overtime, with the same granularity, preciseness, effectiveness, and singleness of purpose it showed in its defense of the Roberts nomination, continually punching back at the spurious charges. One of the leaders of the judicial coalition, Jay Sekulow, the president of the American Center for Law and Justice, said a "slugfest" was underway and he was right, none more so than on the right-to-life issue. The *New York Times* editorial page targeted four Republican pro-abortion senators in particular—Senators Snowe and Collins of Maine, Senator Chafee of Rhode Island, and Senator Specter of Pennsylvania. The *Times* warned them that, as pro-abortion senators, they had a duty to oppose Alito, and they could not consider themselves pro-abortion unless they voted against him under all circumstances.

Countering this, in part, was my former boss in the U.S. Senate, Dan Coats, who was asked by the White House to act as Alito's "Sherpa" in the Senate. The name derives from a real Sherpa, someone who leads others in mountainous or difficult terrain. This is a great Senate tradition, that when you have a major nominee, you ask a well-respected VIP to help introduce the nominee to other senators and to help guide the nominee through an otherwise byzantine and often confusing confirmation process. Coats is highly regarded, and for all the ideological toxicity over Alito, the senator did a great job in those personal, one-on-one meetings with each senator to help rough out sharp edges.

The Alito hearings proved rancorous, and the slugfest Sekulow predicted came to pass. The attacks and counterattacks among the Left and Right were pointed, and the judicial coalition did superbly at every turn. Alito's fifteen-year paper trail proved to be the most difficult hurdle, and whenever his record showed a conflict with the Left's worldview, calamitous criticism followed. I never spoke with the Alito family about how this impacted them, but it must have been devastating and deeply painful. The hyperbole against Alito was over the top, and its net effect on Democratic senators was real and measurable. The possibility of a Democratic split on the Alito nomination, as was the case with Roberts, evaporated because of these vicious attacks; and the final vote ended up being one of the most partisan I ever witnessed in my time in Washington. In fact, in the century of Supreme Court votes before the Alito vote, only one was closer, the vote over Clarence Thomas in 1991. Yet Alito prevailed, 58 to 42, in a nearly party-line vote.

Despite the well-funded and unending onslaught to demonize Alito, they failed, even though the goal was either to prevent a vote on him altogether or to defeat him outright in the final vote tally. Both proved hollow and ultimately failed on a number of fronts. The judicial coalition and conservative allies helped prevent the Left from being successful in reaching its goals. The coalition did such a great job inside the Beltway, and far beyond, by once again answering every single charge against Alito, countering every small and large criticism, and making sure no attack, no matter how seemingly inconsequential, received a counterattack. This is what Sekulow meant by a slugfest. The opposition failed to prevent Alito from going onto the court but not from a lack of trying. Their opposition was ferocious and consistent.

There was some buzz about a possible Alito filibuster because of his pro-life record, and this proved to be true. The filibuster was taken seriously because of the Gang of Fourteen in the Senate, that group of seven Democrats and seven Republicans who wanted to act as a kind of internal brake on any judicial nominee over whom they had qualms or concerns. Senator Leahy, the ranking senior Democrat on the Senate Judiciary Committee, actually voted to filibuster Alito's nomination even after the Gang essentially decided not to consider doing so. Leahy also consistently and routinely refused to schedule hearings on President Bush's judicial nominees, despite their outstanding credentials and despite the strong support many of them had from their own state's senators. The eventual attempt at the filibuster fizzled when only twenty-five senators voted to prolong the debate. The anti-Alito forces were incensed that the Senate leadership and the majority of the Democrats in the Senate would not agree to a filibuster. They charged the Democrats with throwing in the towel on Alito. The head of the Leadership on Civil Rights said the Democrats "caved."

Also, despite the urgings of the cacophony of other liberal voices, three key Republican pro-choice senators—Snowe and Collins of Maine and Specter of Pennsylvania—voted for Alito. The only Republican to vote against him was Senator Chafee of Rhode Island, who ended up losing his next Senate election. Unlike in the Roberts vote, there was really no big gap among Democrats in the Alito vote. Only four Democrats supported him while forty others and one independent voted against him. The last man to vote was eighty-eight-year-old Robert Byrd of West Virginia, who with cane in hand, gave Alito a thumbs-up. For all the justified conservative criticism of Senator Specter over the years, he almost always did a good job as the senior-most Republican on the Senate Judiciary Committee during the Bush years, moving the president's district, appellate, and finally Supreme Court nominations along to victory.

One of the realities of the Alito nomination, now easily forgotten but worth remembering, is the political math of the Senate during the Alito confirmation battle: In 2004, when President Bush was reelected, voters also gave control of the Senate to the Republicans, who comprised fifty-five of the seats there. This was not a large margin, but in the case of the Alito nomination, it proved decisive. Without those extra votes, Alito might not have made it onto the Court.

The Roberts and Alito victories were also victories for the conservative movement, which vowed after the 1987 treatment and rejection of Judge Bork that we would never again allow the Left to define the terms of the debate.

The Alito vote was a hard-fought but sweet victory; and as with Roberts, the White House judicial team gathered in the Roosevelt Room across from the Oval Office with Alito to watch the vote on TV. We all cheered when we reached 51 votes, knowing Alito would now be the 110th justice of the Supreme Court. It was particularly wonderful to be there not only with the president, the Alitos, and my White House colleagues—we had all become close through both the Roberts and Alito nomination battles—but also with Dan Coats, who did a great job in his efforts to help shepherd Alito through the Senate process. Steve Schmidt— who, like Ed Gillespie during the Roberts nomination, headed our White House Alito team—did a brilliant job.

On two occasions, with a group of colleagues, I spent a good amount of time getting to know the new justice. I found him inspiring and civil, never putting on airs. He spoke of his parents with such honor and respect, and he particularly admired his mom, an accomplished school principal in New Jersey. I learned he received a ROTC military commission and served three months on active duty in 1975 in the shadow of the Vietnam War. He always beamed when his wife and kids were around, confirming that his faith and family were central to his life.

Less than two hours after the Senate vote, in a private ceremony at the Supreme Court, Alito was sworn in as the 110th justice of the Supreme Court. He took the oath from Chief Justice John Roberts; the men had known each other for many years, dating from their time together working as young lawyers in the Reagan administration. Alito was fifty-five years old, four years older than Roberts.

In the small space of four months, George W. Bush put his presidential impress onto the nation's highest court. A few hours after the swearing-in, President Bush delivered his annual State of the Union Address with Justice Alito sitting alongside his fellow members of the Court. It was one of the highlights of my time in the White House. The timing of it all was serendipitous. There are no four people in American public life who I hold in higher regard that Chief Justice Roberts, and Justices Scalia, Thomas, and Alito. They form a historically-important, legally-originalist quartet. For many conservatives, Scalia is an intellectual powerhouse. With the poet John Webster, Scalia seem always able to see "the skull beneath the skin."

Repeatedly during the 2000 campaign, President Bush made a promise when asked about the Supreme Court. He said if he were elected and if he had the opportunity as president to make nominations to the court, his models would be Justices Scalia and Thomas. He knew the danger to the Constitution and to the Court the progressive mentality foisted upon America, legislators in black robes who trusted an empathy standard more than a constitutional one. As early as 1915, the progressive intellectual Herbert Croly, the *bête noire* of the Right, said the mission was to "liberate democracy from the bondage of the law."[10] George W. Bush's jurisprudence was precisely the opposite view. He believed the law was instructive. He said he wanted nominees who would strictly interpret the Constitution and laws and not legislate from the bench. The president said he wanted nominees who would respect precedent, who had impeccable character and integrity, and who were fair-minded. He kept his promise; he made good on his pledge. The battles to confirm John Roberts and Samuel Alito to the high court were arguably George W. Bush's greatest and most long-lasting domestic achievements and ones that would impact millions of Americans for years to come.

Chapter 17

The President and the Pope

Building a culture of life requires more than law;
it requires changing hearts. And as we reach out to others
and find common ground, we can see the glimmerings
of a new America on a far shore.
—GEORGE W. BUSH[1]

Abortion is advocated only by persons
who have themselves been born.
—RONALD REAGAN[2]

One of the major constituencies my colleague Matt Smith and I were responsible for in the Bush White House was America's Catholic communities. There are forty-four million Catholics in America. The irony of my being a Lutheran was rarely lost on anyone in this regard, but the friendships and relationships I forged with Catholics were among the highlights of my time with President Bush. I came to see the Catholic church as the single most important institution in the world advocating and defending the sacredness of all human life, the sanctity of marriage, the dignity faith confers on the human condition, and perhaps most importantly, the centrality of the traditional family, first among equals of those "unseen pillars of civilization" President Bush referenced in his January 20, 2004, State of the Union message. Although the president was not Catholic, he had a Catholic sensibility, and he brought his own personal faith to bear upon the way he thought about, discussed, and promulgated the most important foreign and domestic policies in his eight years in office.

During his first and second terms, I often arranged for many of America's leading cardinals, archbishops, bishops, and Catholic laymen and women to meet and form working relationships with President Bush, gathering either at the White House or while the president was traveling. Although there was great theological and political diversity among the prelates and others, the president did not apply a litmus test on how those friendships developed, and they commenced immediately upon his arrival in the White House. In fact, the first major private dinner party President and Mrs. Bush attended after coming to office in 2001 was a gathering I was asked to arrange at the Maryland residence of the cardinal archbishop of Washington, Theodore McCarrick. It was the first presidential motorcade I rode in, and I naively asked a member of the Secret Service if we could possibly make it to the dinner on time, all the way to Hyattsville, Maryland, given the fact it was rush hour and we were to be at the cardinal's home in less than a half hour. His response to me: "You're new here, aren't you?"

I explained I was, and within ten minutes we were zipping out of the South Lawn gates at the White House, whirling through the city streets of Washington, and whipping around the Beltway, going seventy miles per hour or so, with all the traffic stopped. We arrived at the cardinal's Maryland home exactly on time, almost to the minute. That same Secret Service Agent made a point of asking me, once we arrived, "Well, what did you think?"

The evening went beautifully, and one of the narratives of the dinner conversation was the development of a relationship with Pope John Paul II and the Holy See. The president said he deeply admired the holy father. The cardinal told me after the dinner he felt the president and the pope would get along "famously" if and when they were to meet. Little did McCarrick or anyone know that, even though the Pope was ailing, President Bush would make a point to meet and spend important time with the aging pontiff three times before his death, twice at the Vatican and once at his summer home in the hills outside Rome.

Although eighty-one-year-old Pope John Paul II's health was beginning to fail early in the days of the first Bush administration, the president succeeded in forging not only a meaningful relationship with the holy father but also an important friendship. The generational contrast between the two was striking: One of them was the new, young leader of the free world with the demands of the international arena awaiting him, while the other man was the old, wise, most-traveled pope of all time, the most visible and influential leader of the world of Christendom. The heart of their relationship was their mutual love for Jesus Christ, but the soul of their relationship was the practical working-out of how that faith was evidenced in domestic and foreign policy. Both of them brought a deep, ethical sensibility to how they thought about all matters.

Both were orthodox Christians to be sure—one in the form of the American Methodist low-church tradition—(I believe the president was the ultimate mere Christian, in C. S. Lewis's words) while the other personified the liturgical, sacramental, confessional tradition. But both were deeply interested in orthopraxis as well—the doing of the Word, faith in action. For both men this was foundational to their religion, that faith without works was a deadened faith. Both the president and the pope believed it was important to have a vibrant faith applied to real people living in real situations with real consequences. Both men were energetic heads of state, loved people, and understood well the bright dividing lines between the role of the church and the role of the state, Athens and Jerusalem, but not one without the other.

Their friendship commenced on July 23, 2001, almost exactly six months to the day after the president's inauguration, when the president, the First Lady, and their daughter Barbara traveled to the pope's summer residence, Castel Gandolfo, in the spectacular Alban Hills near Rome. Everyone wore black, and the First Lady and Barbara covered their hair with black lace mantillas. The pope greeted the first family warmly, spent a little time in small talk, and then retreated to a private meeting with the president. This turned out to be anything but just another lighthearted initial chat.

That first meeting between the two was wide-ranging and heavy on foreign policy matters. The public portion of the meeting touched on a host of timely and controversial fronts—the death penalty, the impact of globalization on poor countries, the new White House faith-based office, and basic human and religious rights around the world. But their discussion on another topic helped shape and mold the president's larger thinking on a major social issue coming down the pike rapidly—stem-cell research. The president's first conversation with the holy father turned out to be one of his most important discussions on that subject ever, and it took place almost exactly a month before the president made a final decision about the direction of that pending new policy. The pope's input and counsel helped give shape to that summer stem-cell speech to the nation I discussed in an earlier chapter.

During that first meeting, the pope was decidedly uninterested in a mere photo op and a handshake. He was eager to do business with the president, knowing he had a compatriot who shared his passion for the sanctity of every human life. The pontiff told the president, "A free and virtuous society, which America aspires to be, must reject practices that devalue and violate human life at any state from conception until natural death. . . . Experience is already showing how a tragic coarsening of consciences accompanies the assault on innocent human life in the world, leading to accommodation and acquiescence in the face of other related evils."[3] The pope's concerns were well founded: If taxpayer research was allowed on human embryos, a natural pathway to human cloning would open. "In defending the right to life in law, America can show a world the path to a truly humane future in which man remains the master, not the product of his technology,"[4] the pope said that day.

His admonition had an important impact on the president because the holy father knew the president had a major decision to make about whether taxpayer dollars should continue to be used to destroy human embryos for research purposes. American Catholics, with whom I was in touch on a daily basis, were following the development of this policy closely. The president welcomed the pope's weighing in on this matter. The pontiff was unequivocal in all his comments to the president, and none more so than on stem-cell research; he clearly wanted to make the most of his time in this first meeting with the president, and the president felt precisely the same way about his time with the pope, whose own bold moral statements matched the manner in which the president himself liked to speak. The two men knew they could do business dating from that first meeting, and their respect for each other was rooted in that initial gathering.

But a related issue was also hanging over that meeting. The Pope and the Vatican Curia knew the president had reinstituted the so-called "Mexico City Agreement" as his first official act as president. This was a policy blocking American taxpayer funding of groups who performed or lobbied for abortions overseas. The Vatican strongly supported the president in that policy, as had the American Catholic hierarchy. The sanctity and dignity of every human life were the bond and undercurrent between the president and the pope. The pontiff confirmed these common views when he called upon all Americans to continue "to draw on its heritage and resources to help build a world in which each member of the human family can flourish and live in a manner worthy of his or her innate dignity."[5] From the start of his presidency, the Vatican knew it had a great ally in President Bush on the host of pro-life, pro-family, pro-marriage issues across the next eight years.

Also that day, the president took the opportunity to single out the pope as one of the greatest opponents of tyranny in the twentieth century. "You have urged men and women of goodwill to take to their knees before God and stand unafraid of tyrants. . . . This has added greatly to the momentum of freedom in our time,"[6] he said, foreshadowing a major award the president would confer upon the pope in the years to come for his role in destroying Soviet communism in Eastern Europe. Those remarks also foreshadowed the Bush administration's fulsome pro-freedom, pro-democracy, pro-dissident, pro-international religious liberty, and pro-human rights agenda for which the president would take enormous criticism in the years ahead, most notably after he made those themes a centerpiece of his second inaugural address.

For all the camaraderie that day, the two men did not agree about everything, to be sure, and in fact disagreed strongly on one large matter. The pontiff spoke diplomatically and civilly but unapologetically in opposition to the death penalty. He asked the president to "reject practices that devalue and violate human life" in that regard. The president authorized more than one hundred fifty executions during his time as governor of Texas. The president did not believe abortion and execution were of a piece on the life continuum and continued to disagree on this issue with the Vatican during his time in office. Still, the exchange between the two was not harsh, and the meeting concluded on a note of goodwill.

It had been a great meeting, a fortuitous exchange of views, and seeds planted on one of the major moral issues of our time, embryonic stem-cell research as a bridge to cloning. The president, who was not easily awed by meeting anyone, was in fact awed by meeting Pope John Paul II during that first meeting and more than in any other meeting of his presidency. He said he was "honored to be in the presence of the holy father. . . . It was a moment that I was looking forward to because of his profound impact on the world. I'm not poetic enough to describe what it's like to be in his presence, nor was I surprised to hear his strong, consistent message. One of the things about the Catholic Church I admire—it's a church that stands on consistent and solid principle."[7] President Bush knew he just spent time with, and was influenced by, one of the greatest men of the twentieth century, a man of moral stature equal to the likes of Billy Graham, whom the president knew well and who impacted his life deeply. I consider it one of the honors of my life to have lived in the same era as the pope, Billy Graham, Mother Teresa, Elie Wiesel, Vaclav Havel, and Alexander Solzhenitsyn.

Afterwards the Bushes stepped out onto a balcony at Castel Gandolfo and shared a breathtaking view across Lake Albano. Just before they left, the pope offered a beautiful blessing upon the Bushes and the United States, asking God to grant "wisdom, strength, and peace."

Two specific things about that initial meeting validated the president's deep personal respect and honor for the pope. Instead of always referring to the pontiff as "your Holiness," he also referred to him as "sir." The president believed he was in the presence of a great man, and he used the term *sir* out of love and high regard. Also, as the two men proceeded into the palace's throne room for their private meeting, the pope took the president's hand and personally escorted him. This was, in reverse, an equal sign of respect and favor for the leader of the free world, an outward sign of love and honor.

Although I was not present for that initial meeting in Rome, I received an excellent debrief from those who were, which I promptly conveyed to others around the United States. The reaction was warm and effusive because people knew the meeting deepened and solidified the sense in the American Catholic Church that it had a president who shared their views on foundational issues and principles. They also knew both the president and his White House team had genuine and enormous respect for the aging pontiff who was even then winding down one of the most influential papacies in history. John Paul II was the first non-Roman pope in 450 years, a widely traveled and beloved pontiff who made interacting with real people around the globe a hallmark of his tenure, the first pope to have visited the White House (with President Carter), and a man fluent in eight languages.

The pope and the president would meet two more times during the course of the Bush presidency—in May 2002, during a weeklong European tour in which the president also visited Germany, Russia, France, and Italy; and again in June 2004, when at the Vatican the president presented the pontiff with the Medal of Freedom, the highest civilian award a president can confer on anyone. Presenting that medal was one of the great moments of the Bush presidency because it validated the president's regard for the pope's global grasp and legacy. The Vatican ceremony that day was as simple and elegant as the president's citation, celebrating a man whose "principled stand for peace and freedom has inspired millions and helped to topple communism and tyranny." The president artfully referred to Pope John Paul II as "this son of Poland" in conferring the honor; and the pope's humble reply, never mentioning himself or his remarkable achievement, was equally simple and elegant: "May the desire for freedom, peace, a more humane world symbolized by this medal inspire men and women of goodwill in every time and place."[8] The underlying reality of that third and last meeting was that the holy father's health had become paper-thin fragile, his locked facial features in marked contrast to the young and physically vibrant pontiff the world remembers so well.

A mere ten months later the president and Mrs. Bush would return to Rome, this time for the holy father's funeral. On that occasion the president kindly invited me to join him and the White House entourage, and it was among the most memorable trips of my tenure at the White House. Our delegation included the president's father, President Clinton, and Secretary of State Condi Rice. Although Pope John Paul II was warmly welcomed to the Carter White House for his first famous 1979 visit as the new pontiff, the first time any pope had visited the White House, President Carter did not attend his funeral. The Bush White House hoped he would join the delegation, but President Carter chose to stand down, and President Ford, then ninety-one, was in poor health and unable to join. During his lifetime the pope visited the United States five times and met with all five of the presidents serving during his pontificate.

President Bush was the first sitting president ever to attend the funeral mass of a pope, and it affirmed just how important the president felt his relationship with the pope had become. They were men who saw so much of the world in the same light and expressly on the issues of the dignity of human life, the sacredness of marriage, and the easy expression of faith in public life.

Upon learning of the pope's death, the president issued a moving tribute to his deceased friend, calling him "a great man" who led "a remarkable life, a person who stood for freedom and human dignity." The president said he would remember the pope "as a clear thinker who was like a rock. And tides of moral relativism kind of washed around him, but he stood strong as a rock. And that's . . . one of the reasons why millions came to admire and love him."[9] Later the president said his attendance at the funeral strengthened his faith and that his being in Rome for the funeral would be, for him, "one of the highlights of my presidency."

Having been in Rome with the president for the funeral, I know firsthand why he made those comments. As the city swelled to millions upon millions of people from around the world, pouring in from every continent and every country, there were no major disruptions or disputes.

A veil of holiness seemed to filter down and envelope the Eternal City in a way everyone who attended the funeral felt and witnessed—long lines but no fighting; people everywhere but no sharp elbows or personal hostilities; the death of a great man who felt and expressed strong views on otherwise controversial issues and yet no major protests. I have rarely felt or experienced a greater sense of personal peace and even joy I felt those two days in Rome.

The president described the funeral as "majestic," and that is precisely what it was like: soaring music; a luminous, elegiac homily delivered by then Cardinal Ratzinger, who would go on to become the next pope; and a beatific service both sublime and inspired, the first Latin Mass the president ever attended.

During those two days the president hosted a reception at the American embassy for the American cardinals who were in Rome for the funeral, and the spirit of diplomacy and goodwill in that reception was wonderful to witness. The cardinals expressed repeatedly how pleased and honored they were the president decided to attend and with him presidents Clinton and George H. W. Bush. The president got to know many of the cardinals well during his presidency. Those friendships were further solidified and deepened during that gathering at the embassy in Rome.

But it was the president's attendance at the pope's wake, kneeling near the pontiff's simple casket, upon his arrival in Rome, that most deeply touched him and the White House entourage. "Alone isn't the right word, because I was aware of other people, but felt much more in touch with a spirit. I really did. I was very much—felt peace there and was prayerful,"[10] the president said. This scene, of an American president kneeling at the Vatican out of respect for the life of Pope John Paul II, was a great image and symbol. Both the president and the pope seemed to meet and find connection at the foot of the cross, and both knew the power and efficacy of prayer in quiet moments.

President Bush was asked about the pope's physical struggles and how that was evidenced in his life. "It is a clear example of Christ's influence in a person's life that he maintained such a kind of hopeful, optimistic, clear point of view amidst struggles—in his case, physical struggles. And that's—a lot of Christians gain strength and confidence from seeing His Holiness in the last stages of his life."[11] The president identified the nobility of the aging and infirmed and in the pope's own virtue amid physical struggle. These comments sprang from the president's faith.

Pope John Paul II's funeral may have been the largest in history, and the president's attendance caused him to reflect on those remarkable days in Rome.

"Besides the pomp and the majesty and the colors, there was a spirit that was an integral part of the ceremony. For me, the spirit was also at the wake. I think a walk of faith constantly confronts doubt, as faith becomes more mature. And you constantly confront, you know, questions. My faith is strong. The Bible talks about you've got to constantly stay in touch with the Word of God in order to help you on the walk. But the Lord works in mysterious ways, and during all our life's journeys we're enabled to see the Lord at work if our eyes are open and our hearts are open. And today—you can analyze and you can look at the coffin being held, with the sun shining on it, anyway you want. I happen to feel it was a special moment that was part of a special ceremony for a special person. And it helped strengthen my faith."[12]

The speculation was running high in Rome during the funeral as to who might succeed John Paul II. Before leaving the city, the great Catholic thinker and scholar Michael Novak, who was also a guest of the president's for the trip to the funeral and who became a friend during that trip, and I were dining outside near the Trevi Fountain. I asked him rather casually who in the present College of Cardinals he thought might be the next pope. Without hesitating, Michael said, "Ratzinger." Knowing of the German cardinal's reputation as both a serious intellectual and the chief enforcer of doctrine, I asked Michael how that might play on the larger world stage.

"We would do well with him," said Michael, in his tender manner. And his prediction would prove spot-on. The president met Cardinal Ratzinger at Pope John Paul II's funeral for the first time, and he was shortly thereafter elected in a conclave to become the new pontiff. On April 25, 2005, Cardinal Ratzinger, now Benedict XVI, was installed in a beautiful mass attended by the president's brother, Jeb, a Catholic convert.

The First Lady and daughter Barbara had a brief audience with the new pope in February 2006, but he and the president met formally for the first time on June 17, 2007, at the Vatican, amid heavy protests of the visit, the reaction to the war now being strongly felt in all of Europe. The meeting was warm, friendly, and diplomatic, a half hour together in the Pope's Apostolic Palace Library near the courtyard of San Damaso in the middle of Vatican City. The pope presented a beautiful gift to the president, a first-edition autobiography by the most prominent American

Catholic among the founding fathers, John Carroll of Baltimore, who was also the first bishop of the United States.

The pope expressed his concerns about the fate of Christians living in Iraq, and the president reassured the pope that the Iraqi constitution would specifically safeguard Christians living in that troubled country. Despite serious concerns and differences over the war, the Holy See found several reasons to celebrate the president's record, none more so than on the question of human life. The Vatican's Cardinal secretary of state Tarcisio Bertone said, "The current president has particularly distinguished himself in regard to some positive initiatives in defense of life from conception,"[13] and the Holy See routinely let it be known the Bush record found great accord at the Vatican on a variety of fronts—in the president's view that life begins at conception; his policy affirming the withdrawal of taxpayer funding for abortions in foreign countries; his refusal to allow taxpayer funded embryonic stem-cell research; his pro-marriage policies; his opposition to same-sex marriage; and his creation and leadership of the President's Emergency Plan for AIDS Relief, known as PEPFAR, which made President Bush a hero in much of Africa.

During that trip the president invited the new pontiff to come to the United States; and on April 17, 2008, his eighty-first birthday, the pope made his first American visit and was hosted by the Bushes on a brilliantly sunny spring morning for a festive South Lawn ceremony. This was only the second time in history a pope has visited the White House. Both the president and Pope Benedict XVI delivered two of the most memorable speeches on faith and public life ever delivered by a major political and religious figure in Washington in the same setting. The narrative of both speeches was that America was a model nation—a place where strong religious belief existed comfortably, side by side, with secular life. About fourteen thousand Americans poured into the White House grounds to hear those speeches and to attend the ceremony, replete with a 21-gun salute, the singing of "The Lord's Prayer" by soprano Kathleen Battle, and the singing of "Happy Birthday to You" to the octogenarian pontiff. The biggest roars of approval came when the president turned to the pope and said the American people "need your message that all life is sacred," and when the president, borrowing one of the pontiff's signature lines, also said the American people needed to hear his "message to reject this dictatorship of relativism." The president said the pope's beliefs were consonant with America's founding fathers' view that we could not have freedom without virtue.

The president said: "Here in America, you'll find a nation that welcomes the role of faith in the public square. When our founders declared our nation's independence, they rested their case on an appeal to the 'laws of nature and of nature's God.'"[14]

In reply, the pontiff said, "Democracy can only flourish, as your founding fathers realized, when political leaders and those whom they represent are guided by truth." The pope repeated a central point he made in another meeting with the American cardinals and bishops upon his arrival in Washington: "Any tendency to treat religion as a private matter must be resisted."

Planning for the pope's South Lawn visit was among the last major assignments I had before leaving the White House. I was part of a team that met for weeks, orchestrating a grand and colorful welcoming of the pontiff. In addition to being the head of the global Roman Catholic community, the pope was also a head of state. The formality, the colors, the beauty of that regal gathering on the South Lawn at the White House were glorious. A new relationship between the president and another older pope was commencing and would prove strong. Still their friendship would not, could not, equal that of President Bush and Pope John Paul II's friendship. The latter were soul mates in a real sense, dating from their first meeting on that glorious day at Castel Gandolfo. The chemistry had been just right from the start. When President Bush said, upon learning of the pope's death, that he was a man "humble, wise, and fearless," he meant what he said from the heart. His personal regard for John Paul II was probably higher than for any other world leader of the Bush presidency, their worldviews rooted deeply in the ancient faith that was the lifeblood of each. Yet in his new relationship with Pope Benedict XVI, he found a kindred, conservative spirit who shared his convictions that the secularization of life could ultimately impinge on the freedoms that were the taproot of American confidence and greatness—no freedom without moral excellence and personal responsibility.

Chapter 18

The Days Are Long,
but the Years Are Short

*Modern formulations are necessary even in defense of very
ancient truths. Not because of any alleged anachronism in
the old ideas—the Beatitudes remain the essential statement
of the Western code—but because the idiom of life is always
changing, and we need to say things in such a way as to get
inside the vibrations of modern life.*
—WILLIAM F. BUCKLEY JR.[1]

During my years in Washington, I have come to see a recurring, sad-
dening pattern afflicting people in high-caliber jobs. All too often I
have found myself in rooms at long, oak tables with people whose personal
lives are crumbling even as their professional lives are thriving. The disconnect is jarring. These gifted people are often charged with being part of
a process making major decisions impacting millions of lives, even as their
own lives are coming apart at the seams. One wonders: *If their own lives
are shattered, or soon to be in meltdown, how can they be the ones in charge,
or part of a process that impacts so many other lives?*

I have been particularly concerned with how the natural stresses and
strains of political life impact those newly married, or married with kids,
because it is common in Washington to observe a significant imbalance
between those who are married or married with kids, and those who have
never been married, or who are divorced or separated. Those who are
married or married with kids are almost always significantly outnumbered

by those who are neither. This is generally true around Washington but especially among the governing and political classes. I have come from many Capitol Hill meetings hearing someone say, "The twenty-year-olds are running the country" because twenty-somethings are prominent there.

The so-called millennials first came onto my radar scope as colleagues on the first Bush campaign in Austin and then again in the political and cultural ethos of Washington as the administration was commencing in 2001. This rising generation is pouring into Washington now more than ever, and they are not only impacting but changing the culture of the city in ways worth watching. Their influence will increase in both parties in the years ahead and eventually will have a significant influence on major policy decisions in a way each new generation does.

I became personally reminded of this when I worked in the White House. If there is a place of harder working, more dedicated people, I am unaware of where it could be. Every White House, Democratic and Republican alike, is staffed with some of the most talented, energetic, dynamic people on the globe. I remember leaving several meetings at the White House with a single thought: *Those are some of the smartest people I will ever meet in my life.* The whole idea of America's shift from a semi-aristocracy in our founding era to a meritocracy in the twenty-first century has certainly been achieved in much of professional Washington. Every race, every background, every income level, every hardship overcome, every step up the professional ladder of success and renown seems present in the worlds of politics and government, media, military, the foundations, and the firms that comprise contemporary Washington. The youth factor is huge inside the Beltway and undergirds the vigor of the city.

Everyone seems to be from somewhere else, having converged on Washington. Every morning a city of under one million residents swells to multiple millions, as the panoply of worldviews and agendas come over the bridges, through the tunnels, on the trains and subways, comprising endless traffic patterns to office buildings and row houses humming with people working to advance a cause, an idea, a mission. Busyness is the watchword. It is not unusual in the least to work for years on the same floor, or in the same building, as another person and not know who they are or what they do. It is common in Washington to have every intention of seeing someone who works a few blocks away, only to see them when you arrive at a conference or an engagement half a continent (or world) away.

Washington is a big small town, built on relationships of common need or purpose, comprised of extroverts, and a city that loves to socialize, strategize, engage, and make plans. Yet the human element, despite an era of technology and communication rivaling the revolution of the Gutenberg, remains foundational; and at its core Washington is a city built not on paper or ideas but on relationships, many of them burnished under the most intense pressure and through many professional iterations across multiple years. The bonding process in sports happens when a team, against the odds, sees its way through to a successful season, often reaching the heights in a championship or tournament victory.

In Washington that same paradigm applies: It might be a victory in a House or Senate race; it might be a major scoop in old or new media. The ultimate bonding and lifetime of collegiality comes in that process of the successful campaign for the White House. For many, that bonding is deepened even further during a hard-fought, reelection victory for the nation's highest office. Those who have been through that process together form a relatively small group of alumni from any era; and once congealed, those memories and relationships remain for a lifetime. The emphasis on the professional is the thing in Washington, and the supreme satisfaction of such professional success can be a subterfuge for the things in life that really matter, the things that really count. This is the disconnect of which I speak.

I learned this firsthand during a party near the end of the Bush Administration. Jenny and I were invited to a dinner and dance in Glen Echo, Maryland, to say good-bye to former colleagues a few days before the Bushes flew back to Texas. The Bushes came by the party and offered heartfelt thanks to everyone who had been a part of the White House team during all or some of those eight years. When he departed the stage with folks still clapping, I turned to a former colleague of mine and asked how his family was doing. Through the din of applause, I heard him say, "Not well."

I thought I hadn't heard him properly. To such a question, one always expects the standard "doing well, thanks." So I asked again. Indeed, he told me the preceding two years put a huge strain on his marriage, and he knew of others experiencing the same problems. He told me he and his wife never felt more distant, that he loved her and vice versa, and that the best thing about the administration ending was that he would be putting a renewed emphasis on his marriage. The marriage survived, but he later told me his marriage could not have borne another month. This is not rare in politics and government, and our conversation that evening meant a lot to me for a singular reason.

When I really think about it and honestly assess those nearly eight years I spent in the White House, I can only conclude the stress, strains, pressures, and demands are real and deceptive; they become a way of life. There exists a kind of unrelenting, unending gerbil's wheel. Even when you work hard to build in space to think and unwind, it is difficult for even the most disciplined person. For most of America, the idea of a weekend now seems distant; this is just as true in Washington. I remember another former colleague confessing to me one Monday morning she was eager to get back to work "to recover from the weekend" when she worked two twelve-hour days. Work and private time too often blend.

In Washington it is common to mix and mingle one's social life with work. In part, this is because you mix into the swirl of people who are already social by nature. By giving them lots of new and interesting people to meet—often in dynamic and intriguing situations (i.e., a great dinner party, an interesting cultural event such as a new exhibition opening at a gallery, or a lecture or talk by a famous scholar or expert)—the net effect can be a kind of human catnip, an elixir that becomes a way of life. These are not bad in the least; in fact, it is because of these things Washington is often a unique and attractive subculture in which to live and work. But this dynamism can push couples and families apart instead of bringing them together. It is a way of life in Washington, and in other major urban areas, to attend social events where a husband and wife, who would normally be together in most contexts, are apart and where, ironically, the other spouse is not only not there but actually at another function all together.

This social reality of life in Washington reflects the enormous affluence, education levels, and mission/purpose/drive that animate the city, perhaps now as much or more than ever. This matrix is potentially tough not only on marriages and family life but also on the increasingly large numbers of young people in their twenties and thirties moving to Washington who are often so busy with their professional lives—and with the attendant social obligations that can often go hand in hand with their lives—that dating, courting, and preparing for marriage are put off to older and older ages, if ever. This is not unique to Washington, but it is central to how our capital city operates, and so the net effect is a city with lots of unmarried young people who are in positions of significant influence and power but who do not necessarily have a personal stake in the traditional nuclear family one way or the other. This underscores specifically and particularly what life in my own family was like during my time serving President Bush.

Working in the White House, I missed baseball games, Cub Scout meetings, soccer matches, and other functions with our elementary-aged sons. I could not have done what I did professionally without Jenny, who in many contexts was both dad and mom. In fact, I owe her nothing short of everything for what she did. My love for Jenny is endless, rooted in our love for Christ, and expressed above all in a shared vision for what is important: Our sons, our families, our friends. She is my anchor and confidante, my sounding board, the love of my life. Our shared humor is the bridge, and we are a team. We love each other at a deep level because we grew up together. We aren't perfect, but we are perfect for each other. Her love is my all. She did an amazing job, under stressful and pressure-filled circumstances, and there is no adequate way to say thanks. Every man or woman in politics with young children owes everything to their spouses because of the oftentimes dramatic and unrelenting strains put on marriages and families as a result of life in the public square as I have described it above. This did not make us unique, and it did not make us victims. Our choices had consequences, and almost every family with kids we knew in Washington who were involved in politics or government shared our challenges.

We knew what we were getting into; we discussed it routinely and fulsomely on a number of occasions; we agreed that, for both of us, my time at the White House was a shared sense of vocation, that to do the job excellently, the primary focus and attention had to be given to our sons so that each of us could have peace of mind. As a result, Jenny made the decision to remain home full-time with our boys and routinely missed most of the receptions, luncheons, and dinners that were a natural extension of my working in the White House and particularly in the Office of Public Liaison which is, by its design, an office of outreach and social engagement. We always attended major White House functions together, and in fact, those became some of the most memorable moments of our lives in twenty years of marriage. The Bushes fully understood the impact working in the White House had on kids and worked to accommodate families where and when possible, which meant so much to us.

On a number of occasions, the President and Mrs. Bush graciously allowed us to include our sons, and this was one of the most pro-family sidebars of the Bush White House. They encouraged family involvement in a host of ways during those years. Our boys remember with the warmest memories the White House Easter Egg rolls (often in the rain); the annual White House Fourth of July South Lawn party and fireworks (always hot, humid, thrilling); Christmas tours at the White House; T-ball games on the South Lawn beneath the giant oaks and elms; and seeing movies in the White House theater. These were certainly privileged times, which we did not take for granted. They illustrated the Bushes understood the centrality of family time.

Jenny and I share a common worldview; we are united in our faith, which is central to our marriage and home life; our political, social, and cultural views grew from that faith. But our agreement—and now that our boys are teens, I see the wisdom in that agreement—was that unless Jenny needed to be with me, she chose to be with the boys, and I fully and gratefully supported that view. I came to see our agreement was the right decision for us and, above all, for our sons. Our decisions had real consequences.

During one of the White House receptions, a friend came up to me; and, realizing how full my days were and how often I was away from home, he said to me, "Just remember, Tim, this is all exciting, but while the days are long, the years are short." This hit me in the gut. He was talking about the unique dynamic of the White House and the fleeting nature of it all. His sentence reminded me, dramatically, that I missed a lot of key moments with my wife and kids in those years because of my job, and it prompted the question: Was the sacrifice worth it? This underscored the constant pressures on family life in the nation's capital and particularly on the nuclear family, which was the minority in Washington then and now. This was not a theory in our home; it was a daily, lived reality.

I remember being on Capitol Hill for an early morning meeting in early 2006 and was on my way back to the office a little after 9:00 a.m., walking toward Union Station through the Senate park just behind the Russell Senate Office Building where I worked for Senator Coats for a decade. As I was preparing to cross Columbus Circle on my way to the Metro stop inside Union Station, I saw what appeared to be a proverbial sea of twenty-somethings flooding toward me, up out of the subway, as if a human wall. It struck me that all or most of them were heading to their jobs in the Senate. Some were texting; some had earphones in; most had loaded-down backpacks or briefcases. They formed the nucleus of the staffs around some of the most powerful men and women in the United States. They were Republicans and Democrats, liberals and conservatives; all young, bright; all eager to change the country and the world; almost all of them on the upward professional trajectory of Washington; and all part of that unique, young elite who were the next generation of leaders. I wondered how many of them were grounded in the traditional patterns of family, marriage, and parenting.

I didn't conclude they were opposed to those principles, only that they, or at least a significant number of them, probably did not spring from that sociology in their own lives. This is the future of America, but particularly urban America, which has such a dramatic and perhaps outsized impact on the direction of our culture.

The millennials, those between the ages of eighteen and twenty-nine, are now the largest of the definable generations, larger even than the baby boomers, numbering about eighty million Americans, born after 1980. They are digitally "native" versus those of us who are digitally "immigrant" or pre-Internet era. They are Americans, to be sure, but they also inhabit another country called Facebook and My Space, which is a subculture with its own unique sense of community and place. They are called "mediavores" because theirs is both a visual and an aural reality.

They are globally-directed and rights-oriented. Having a social conscience is foundational to them. Helping others, making a difference, dedicating their lives to a cause and mission larger than themselves—these are the values of the millennials. They are a generation of iPhones, iPads, and endless texting. They have been surrounded by helicopter parents. Many are trophy kids: Everyone gets one, whether you have won or lost your season in soccer or baseball. Significantly, they are controversy-adverse and mostly nonideological. Most of them have known only war; they are generally pro-life, and in this instance far more than their parents' generation; many have never spoken on a phone with a wall cord; they have no memory of Ronald Reagan.

The dramatic impact these millennials are having, and will have, on Washington and our nation will be amazing to watch. I am particularly interested in how their worldviews will impact our nation's capital and the public policies flowing from there like rivers. Will they help fight for the first principles built on faith and families? This question recurs in my own thinking. If the idea of traditional values is, in the main, a million miles apart from their own daily experiences; if this rising generation has lived through high divorce rates and high rates of out-of-wedlock births as the norm in America, it begs an important question: How will these lived experiences actually impact the public policies these same young men and women are so centrally a part of in the culture-shaping, culture-forming roles they have in the echelons of influence on Capitol Hill, the White House, and across Washington?

This question reminds me that politics, public policy, and the law are all downstream from culture. Culture is preeminent. This is worth thinking about as our country steps off into the second decade of this new century. How will their own home lives impact the central institutions that have been the foundations upon which America's greatness was built?

Chapter 19

To Revitalize America, Remoralize the Family

The foundation of national morality must be laid in private families. . . . How is it possible that Children can have any just Sense of the sacred Obligations of Morality and Religion if, from their earliest Infancy, they learn their Mothers live in habitual infidelity to their fathers, and their fathers in as constant Infidelity to their Mothers?
—JOHN ADAMS (1781)[1]

Tradition means giving votes to the most obscure of all classes, our ancestors. It is the democracy of the dead. Tradition refuses to submit to the small and arrogant oligarchy of those who happen to be walking about.
—G. K. CHESTERTON[2]

The late U.S. Senator Daniel Patrick Moynihan of New York was among the most thoughtful liberals of our time. He came to see the hollowness of Great Society liberalism; he often spoke Right while voting Left. "The central conservative truth," he once said, "is that it is culture, not politics, that determines the success of a society. The central liberal truth is that politics can change a culture and save it from itself."[3]

Are we conservatives focused like a laser beam on the culture? Or have we succumbed to the trap of preoccupying ourselves with politics as the answer to our most pressing social concerns?

Moynihan was correct in saying conservatives believe politics has definitive limits. It does, and we push beyond those limits at our peril. The high degree of prowess liberals ascribe to politics is an article of faith, not really a truth. Culture in fact is preeminent. Conservatives must always remember that politics is downstream from culture and not the other way around.

This is the reality, yet too much of the Left and Right presume that the most pressing problems of our time can best be addressed through politics. The reasoning goes something like this: "If we could just get the right political calculus into place, if we could just elect the right men and women to office, then we could begin to right the listing ship of state and the fate of our country."

This is a miscalculation of the first order. If we are not careful—regardless of how any election turns out—the net result will be millions of disappointed, disillusioned Americans who are being encouraged to put their faith in politics as "answers" to the "problems" that most concern us in twenty-first century American life. Such a faith can never deliver because politics cannot adequately or fully address or resolve the most pressing moral and cultural concerns facing us.

It is not that politics is unimportant. Quite the opposite: Politics is both useful and central, and conservatives and Christians need to be more involved than ever in the civic life of our country. The first duty of Christian citizenship is to vote, and we have never needed men and women of faith more actively engaged in American civic and political life than now. Edmund Burke used the term "moral imagination" for that transcendent sense of how citizens might view, engage, and impact their country, culture, and civilization. Such moral imagination is lacking in our public square, and this is a vacuum men and women of faith are uniquely equipped to fill.

But in our lifetime we have seen the net result of the overextension and overpromise of what politics can achieve. American evangelicals by and large remained outside the political arena until Jimmy Carter emerged, our first contemporary evangelical president. He gave reason for millions of men and women of faith to give the political system a fresh look. When he called himself a "born-again Christian," evangelicals knew what he meant, even if many Americans had not the slightest idea.

Carter succeeded in bringing evangelicals into politics in the election of 1976. But when many evangelicals measured Carter's rhetoric versus the reality of his policy promises, as well as how the suffering economy never seemed to get better, they became quickly discouraged and made a historic pivot to another political possibility.

When Ronald Reagan famously told the National Religious Broadcasters during the heat of the 1980 campaign that, although they could not endorse him, he endorsed them, Reagan tapped into a deeply discouraged evangelical base. He welcomed them into the Republican fold, and the New Right changed the political landscape for the next thirty years and more. Traditional-values voters became the mainstay of the GOP, as I mentioned in an earlier chapter, and the Republican Party's firmest, truest foundational base.

Disillusionment with President Reagan did not materialize in the way it did with President Carter. Why? Probably because the reality of what is possible in the politics of any presidency became apparent by the end of Reagan's two terms. The Reagan presidency proved that, even when the most prominent conservative president of the contemporary era came to power, and despite his best efforts in so many important and historic ways (such as the elevation of William Rehnquist to be chief justice of the United States, the nomination of Antonin Scalia to be a justice on the Supreme Court, the famous tax cuts, etc.), politics came to be seen as having definitive, measurable limits when it comes to impacting the culture.

That recognition was and is good and healthy. The boundary line between culture and politics should remain ever before us. As the late Irving Kristol, godfather of neoconservatism, wrote, "Political problems, even many social problems, are at heart ethical and cultural problems. And improving the attitudes and virtues of a nation is, at best, a slow and halting process."[4] Kristol's analysis, like Moynihan's, was prescient.

Recognizing the limits of politics, while giving the greater emphasis to culture, is now the preeminent conservative task in this new century. Yet many conservatives believe America's most pressing social problems are rooted in the central battle over the size and scope of government. It is widely held that if we can just relimit government, cut taxes, decrease regulations, give free enterprise a wider hand, and find the proper balance between local and central governments, we will recalibrate America onto a better path.

This analysis is powerful and pressing; it is the right one, as far as it goes. But it is not a complete vision. That is because the most pressing problems in our country are cultural and moral matters, rooted in the institutions of family, marriage, and parenting. Problems in this realm are by and large not problems that government can fix, but they are problems government can and will likely exacerbate by overreaching, which is a recurring and dangerous problem during progressive eras like the current one.

We have had two revolutions: the American Revolution and the sexual revolution. Both profoundly impacted our country. But the latter one has resulted in a social and moral decay that, if not arrested, could ultimately negate the original one and destroy our liberty. Our founders rightly warned that we could not have freedom without virtue. Today's deficit of moral excellence strikes at the core of our national DNA. It is a spiritual dearth of the first magnitude.

Russell Kirk posited that social and cultural crises were ultimately spiritual or moral crises. He said that if you want to have order in the commonwealth, you first have to have order in the individual soul. The breakdown of the American nuclear family, the breakdown of marriage, and the breakdown of parenting are the urgent spiritual crises which underlie our cultural crisis and ultimately impact our political and civic lives.

When Moynihan wrote his famous analysis "The Negro Family: The Case for American Action" for President Johnson in 1965, out-of-wedlock births among those families was 25 percent. Today that number is 73 percent. Only 37 percent of black children now live with a mother and a father in two-parent families. That should cause us all to weep.

Among Americans of Hispanic ethnicity, the out-of-wedlock birth rate is 56 percent. Among white Americans, that number is 29 percent, leaving America with an out-of-wedlock birth rate of nearly 40 percent overall. The numbers tell a sobering story. They quantify the brokenness and fragmentation that William J. Bennett was writing about when he said the hearth is broken.

Forty percent of American marriages end in divorce, and 75 percent of second marriages. Fatherlessness is of epidemic proportions in many American communities and is probably the most pressing social problem in urban America today.

Patrick Welsh, who has taught English in a public high school in Alexandria, Virginia, for nearly forty years, regularly writes on education for the *Washington Post*. "Focusing on a 'racial achievement gap' is too simple," he wrote in a column in 2009. "It's a gap in familial support and involvement, too."[5] Welsh is right. If we want a healthy economic climate overall, it can be traced back to the health or illness of the American family. The family is the central institution of American culture, both the bedrock and the foundation.

One of his students urged Welsh to ask the class "just how many of us have our fathers living with us." Not a single hand went up. He commented later, "It hit me that these kids understood what I know too well. The lack of a father in their lives had undermined their education." And presumably much else, too.

Similar examples abound: an NBC *Dateline* program said that in the city limits of Detroit there are four hundred liquor stores and zero supermarkets. The Manhattan Institute's Heather MacDonald has found that "around 80 percent of Chicago's black youth are born to single mothers, creating a dysfunctional culture that is failing to civilize young males." Most of America's major cities now have gangs comprised of tens of thousands of young boys and men who never spent a single night in the same home as their natural-born father.

Roger Scruton, the Anglo-American conservative writer, observes that in addition to external enemies, we in the West confront "a belligerent atheism at home,"[6] which is among the greatest threats to our way of life. Herbert London, chairman of the Hudson Institute, makes a related point in contending that there exists a "spiritual dimension" to nationhood, and if this transcendent dimension is stripped away, you strip away the foundations of a great country. We are testing that proposition.

So, what is the way forward toward a healthier culture? It is to actively reenergize what Burke called "the little platoons," those voluntary associations the American philosopher Robert Nisbet termed the "intermediary institutions" of family, church, synagogue, fraternal groups, neighborhoods, healthy communities, and civil society in general. These are the institutions that can most effectively address our most pressing social problems, and of these primarily the healthy, intact family and not more government.

Government cannot cause a family to fall in love again; government cannot repair a broken marriage; government cannot parent a single child, much less millions; government cannot tuck a child into bed at night.

More Washington-directed solutions will not work, and attempts to force them will make already difficult matters worse. In fact, more government is a trap and does not offer the solutions to the human need that is so great and so profound in our land.

The Dream and the Nightmare, Myron Magnet's magisterial history of the Great Society, powerfully shows how all the promises and best intentions in the world—the dreams—of the politicians and the social engineers of the 1960s ultimately ended up in a spectacular nightmare, inflicting on countless millions of Americans only more misery and worsened conditions.

With more government comes more potential for tyranny. Intentions may be good, but they result in "strangling community spirit and works of charity,"[7] in the words of Chuck Colson, who was Moynihan's colleague in the Nixon administration all those years ago. Burke was right: Morals and manners are actually more important than laws because the former are rooted in personal responsibility and are the fabric of the cultural tapestry of any great and confident nation.

David Brooks of the *New York Times* titled a column "The Limits of Policy." He warned that "when we're arguing about politics, we should be aware of how policy fits into the larger scheme of cultural and social influences. Bad policy can decimate the social fabric, but good policy can only modestly improve it."[8] This is a near-perfect summation of where America is as we step off into a new century.

Hope is just ahead, but it will depend on what the American historian Gertrude Himmelfarb calls a "remoralizing" of our basic institutions and our basic assumptions. We need to focus like a laser beam on healthy families, marriages, and parenting. Their breakdown is a crisis government cannot fix. It is up to us.

If those fundamental institutions are healthy, a healthy cultural and social life will surely follow. Government overreach will be less of a temptation. We'll be better defended against misplaced utopian faith in politics. The challenges are great, but if we are successful, a new American renaissance may await us.

Reprinted with permission of the Centennial Institute, Colorado Christian University, 2010.

Chapter 20

George W. Bush Was Right

*I believe the ultimate responsibility of a leader is to not do
what is easy or popular but to do what is necessary and right.*
—George W. Bush[1]

In great deeds, something abides.
—Joshua Lawrence Chamberlain[2]

George W. Bush was right on the most consequential decisions of his
presidency. In fact, he had signal achievements in a host of areas
where he governed as a conservative. American conservatives have forth-
rightly and consistently set out their disagreements with the president on
the No Child Left Behind legislation, the Medicare health supplement, the
original TARP bail-out legislation, immigration policies, increased federal
spending, and the president's decisions not to veto major federal funding
bills. These have been written and spoken about endlessly and will continue to be debated long into the future. These are all major parts of the
Bush record to be sure. But other important parts of that record and legacy
are conservative successes—often overlooked, forgotten, or obscured by
time. It is important to remember them too, beginning not only with the
war but also with how it was conducted and led.

First and foremost, the Bush presidency will be remembered as a war
presidency. The president understood from the first attacks of 9-11 that
we were and are engaged in a lethal threat to our national security from

Islamic extremism. He believed rightly that this was, without peer, the gravest threat to our country in this new century. He was correct in that judgment at a time when others took a different view. His early conclusion about that threat dated from the minute he learned of the attack while visiting a Florida classroom. And dating from those early decisions about taking the country to war, he has taken all the slings and arrows possible yet remained above cynicism and skepticism that sought to bring down his presidency. That is also a foundational consideration of his achievement. I believe he found his ballast and his confidence, in large measure, because he is a man serious in his faith, who began each day in the White House in prayer, who reads and believes the Bible, and who found daily solace there. Concurrent to his faith, he believed America was an exceptional country without peer, providential in our history and in our future. He believed America had been called out of human history to be a great beacon of liberty, freedom, and democracy to the world. For this view, most notably after his second inaugural address, he was called a unilateralist, which was demonstrably false.

Because he identified the greatest external threat to our liberty early in his presidency, he was able to successfully navigate and prosecute the war in such a way that allowed him to pivot at critical times when the conflict was taking bad turns and twists, and ones that could have resulted in failure. Because he was unstinting about preventing another attack on our homeland, he kept us safe on our domestic soil. We have the benefit of looking backward and making judgments, but neither he nor his best advisors knew how it would turn out. The flurry of decisions that needed to be made, which came across his desk and which were made rightly, prevented a second attack. I believe Providence used him as an instrument in His hand during those years, just as I believe Providence used other war presidents—Lincoln, Franklin Roosevelt, and Reagan in other wars.

Every problem imaginable comes across your desk when you're the president of the United States, but history will be kind to George W. Bush, I believe, because historians will conclude that—through a series of important war decisions, both tactical and strategic—his leadership, his personal character, and his integrity with both the American people and other world leaders added up to the prevention of another attack. His foresight laid a new foundation for foreign and security policy in a new, dangerous era that are now viewed as the correct trajectory by our closest allies. That is an equally important vindication of President Bush's leadership in both the prosecution of the war and in the promulgation of the Bush Doctrine in the Near and Middle East.

The United States Constitution says the first and most important duty of the chief executive is America's national security. President Bush took that oath seriously until the last hour of his last day in office. Like George Washington, George W. Bush had the ability to see things as they were and not as he or others wanted them to be. This is a unique gift of statesmanship. Not only did he know we were at war after that initial attack on 9-11, but also he saw immediately the nature of the evil powering that existential threat to America and our allies. That all seems so clear now, but it was not clear at the time; and in fact two others who ran against him for the presidency disagreed strongly about the nature of the threat. Their opinions have now been categorically dismissed. The existence of countless jihadist cells, in a worldwide matrix, comprise a comprehensive threat to our security and freedom. President Bush faced it head-on and led the largest reorganization of the federal government ever to oppose this new menace. The result has been a security infrastructure to guarantee, as much as is humanly possible, our national security without compromising our constitutional liberties.

Specifically, the president successfully led the effort to create this new firewall with confidence and boldness. For instance, his establishment of the National Counterterrorism Center allows CIA and FBI agents to work closely with one another to detect plots and compare key information. Creating the U.S. Department of Homeland Security galvanized America's ability to prevent acts of terrorism on our soil and react quickly to any successful attempts. The president's championing of the Patriot Act officially removed a dangerous and unnecessary wall preventing the FBI from sharing information with the CIA and vice versa. That legislation allowed the FBI to listen in on potential terrorists in the same way it listened in on domestic organized crime. All of the president's successors will benefit from these reforms and many others, and these reforms were rooted first in the president's own vision about the next necessary steps for our national security. This new infrastructure accrues year by year in the Bush account.

In no small manner his alliance with Tony Blair will be seen, in the light of history, as another and related achievement. Just as Churchill and Roosevelt teamed up in World World II and Reagan and Thatcher did the same to win the Cold War, so the Bush-Blair friendship and strategic alliance sewed up the historical American-British relationship in defense of the great Anglo-American tradition of the preservation of freedom. Their alliance, in a time of such grave danger, saw us through with boldness and confidence. There was no doubt about who was in charge, and they always had the West's best interest at heart. The president knew our enemy; he knew the serious nature of Osama bin Laden's commitments and murderous vision; he took our enemies at their word; and he led a worldwide coalition, which fought back with all the muscle and force it could muster. The net result was a secure America without any consequences for our constitutional liberties. He knew America's enemies were well funded, well educated, and patient, often knowing more about our country, culture, and civilization than many of our fellow citizens. It is because of the Bush-era policies that bin Laden was killed.

In his book *The Leaders We Deserved*, Alvin Felzenberg said: "George W. Bush's willingness to wage preventive war, his undertaking to spread democracy in the Middle East, and his readiness to act unilaterally on the international stage were certainly 'bold and creative,' even if they were at times 'foiled and frustrated.'"[3] This is not a wholly inaccurate description and in fact evokes the larger principles of the Bush foreign policy even if we were not acting unilaterally, as he charges.

The president's heavy emphasis on international religious liberty, basic human rights, free elections, and an open society consistent with economic and global security was a major achievement. The Iraqi adoption of a constitution, voting rights, and purple-inked fingers were symbols of a successful foreign policy, rooted in the president's unwavering view that every person on every continent yearns to be free. Some twenty-five million Iraqis live freer, better lives because of what America and her allies accomplished there. President Bush visited with more dissidents in the White House and on visits abroad than any other president, yet another major achievement consistent with his larger vision. Those dissidents, men and women of the profoundest courage on the face of the planet, knew they had a steady and loyal friend in the Oval Office, and they knew they were never forgotten. The "freedom and democracy agenda," outlined in the president's second inaugural address, for which he was roundly criticized, grew in part from his interaction with these dissidents, some of whom I was honored to meet during their White House meetings with the president.

Our ambassador for international religious liberty at the State Department, John Hanford, knew how important this narrative of freedom and human rights was to the president personally. I worked a lot with him and his team to help get the religious liberty and human rights message out to wider audiences. The president was influenced in this regard by the former Soviet dissident Natan Sharansky, with whom he held an Oval Office meeting specifically to discuss his book *The Case for Democracy*, and by Eliot Cohen, whose book *Supreme Command* was also influential regarding the models of war leadership found in Lincoln and Churchill. I heard the president talk about Lincoln often during Oval Office and Roosevelt Room meetings, almost always in the context of keeping the country unified in war without losing the necessity of explaining why we were fighting; he was keen to keep human liberty, dignity, and enfranchisement at the center of the discussion.

In addition to his achievements in the war and in defense of basic religious liberties and human rights, the president also understood that nuclear proliferation was another major threat to America's future, and he made sure the greatest contributions to missile defense since Ronald Reagan's presidency were kept on the front burner. The Bush record on missile defense has never gotten the credit it deserves, and in this regard President Bush's accomplishment was a natural successor to that of Reagan's vision. It is amazing the progress missile defense made under President Bush's leadership, at the direction of General Henry A. "Trey" Obering, but nary a word about it is known to the general public. During my work in the White House, we held several briefings on missile defense, and I kept in touch with the Pentagon and with my National Security Council colleagues on this policy area.

The reason the president made missile defense such an important cornerstone of his military policy is because he understood that a psychopath headed North Korea; that there was the potential for a nuclear-tipped confrontation between Pakistan and Afghanistan; that the Iranians were serious about developing a nuclear weapon; and that the Pakistan-India relationship was equally fraught, nuclear tipped, and where the volatility of Kashmir always loomed. The president designed a major nuclear pact with India that fundamentally changed our relationship with that country, the fastest emerging superpower, planting the seeds of a new, unique, and important friendship as a counterweight to China.

President Bush paid special attention to the Iranian question and was deeply troubled by the evil man who headed that regime, a thug who doubted the veracity of the Holocaust, who said he would love nothing more than to incinerate Israel, and who believed the United States orchestrated 9-11. It is likely that, had Saddam Hussein not been removed from power, Iran and Iraq would be involved in a major Middle Eastern arms race. President Bush developed a special relationship with Israel during his time in office and was the most reliable friend Israel has had in an American president.

Despite their often vague public rhetoric, the leaders of the nuclear hot spots knew they had a formidable defender of liberty in President Bush, who would not be easily persuaded by antics or false and hollow promises. This has not always been the case with presidents of the United States, who too often telegraphed pliability and weakness. It is easy to forget that, in his strong support of missile defense, President Bush took America out of the ABM Treaty, which hamstrung our nuclear policy. This was yet another major success of the administration. The ABM was a Cold War relic and handcuffed us from achieving the Reagan vision for missile defense. President Bush was able to negotiate missile defense agreements with both Poland and the Czech Republic, which was a tectonic shift in American security policy and which was undone in part by his successor. The president proposed the placement of a radar station in the Czech Republic, and ten ground-based interceptors in Poland. The goal was to offer our allies solid protection from a potential attack from Iran. But in late 2009, the Obama administration did away with the Bush proposals, and our allies, the Czechs, eventually pulled out of a missile defense partnership as a result.

The president's commitment to a robust defense budget following the Clinton-Gore years was rooted in his belief that America's national security was his unparalleled constitutional priority as commander in chief. He worked to prevent a hollowed-out military budget, which was the trajectory America was on when President Bush came to office. This was motivated by a reality in budgeting few wanted to discuss, namely that our spending on defense, while increasing, was doing so at a significantly lower pace than our spending on domestic issues and this has real ramifications for America's ability to defend herself.

His commitments to hard power were as important as his commitments to soft power, none more so than the way he chose to telegraph his compassionate conservatism on the world stage in the creation of PEPFAR, the most significant anti-AIDS program in American or world history, saving or sparing millions of lives in Africa and now accounting for a quarter of all international financing to combat HIV/AIDS, with which thirty-three million people worldwide are infected and growing by one million people a year. With good reason President Bush is much loved in Africa because he was the first president to order the delivery of antiretroviral drugs, food, and to authorize a major antimalarial program that halved the disease in fifteen African countries. His compassionate conservatism was both a domestic and an international narrative, rooted in his faith, and expressed in a host of policies.

Additionally, President Bush unbound and untangled the United States from other treaties not in our best interest: The Kyoto Treaty, the International Criminal Court, the Convention on the Elimination of All Forms of Discrimination (CEDAW)—which is a pro-abortion, antifamily international treaty—and the United Nations Convention on the Rights of the Child, another antifamily measure. In all the international institutions and beginning with the United Nations and the United Nations Educational, Scientific, and Cultural Organization (UNESCO), which the president brought us back into, President Bush installed as his and the country's chief representatives men and women who advocated and defended his own pro-family, pro-life, pro-human rights, pro-religious liberty values. Ambassador Louise Oliver, a prominent conservative, served as UNESCO ambassador in Paris and did a sterling job.

Those last two treaties especially point to a whole other area of major achievement for President Bush. His devotion in public policy to the sanctity of human life, sacredness of marriage, and attendant protection of religious liberties is without equal in the history of the contemporary presidency. His record in this regard is worth reviewing because of its depth, length, and width and beginning from his first week as president, when he reinstituted the Mexico City Agreement, barring taxpayer dollars from funding or promoting abortion overseas. Also that first week in office, he addressed the annual pro-life march in Washington to commemorate the ignominious *Roe v. Wade* ruling which is responsible for more than forty-five million abortions since 1973. After eight years of silence from the White House, thousands of marchers cheered when the newly inaugurated president spoke to them by telephone connection. President Bush was the only American president to have spoken to the annual Right to Life March each year of his presidency. That march, held annually on the anniversary of *Roe v. Wade* has drawn millions of Americans to Washington since its inception in 1974. Thousands of Americans gather yearly to remember the grisly decision where only two brave justices—Byron White, a John Kennedy nominee, and William Rehnquist, a Nixon nominee—voted for human life while their other seven colleagues, in an infamous opinion written by Justice Harry Blackmun, condemned millions of preborn children to death.

Also, the president signed the Unborn Victims of Violence Act, the Born Alive Infants Protection Act, and held a massive public bill signing banning the gruesome procedure known as partial-birth abortion, which former President Bill Clinton vetoed twice and which former U.S. Senator Daniel Patrick Moynihan rightly called "legal infanticide." Hundreds gathered at the Ronald Reagan International Building for that signing, including all the leaders of the pro-life movement. The well-financed, pro-choice groups in America fought the ban through the federal court system for the rest of the Bush administration; and at each turn the Bush Justice Department battled back, consistent with the president's pro-life commitment. The defenders of abortion on Capitol Hill rarely missed an opportunity to criticize the Bush record on life, chief among them the radical exemplar of the pro-choice forces, U.S. Senator Barbara Boxer (D–CA). Columnist George F. Will wrote: "It is theoretically impossible to fashion an abortion position significantly more extreme than Boxer's, which is slightly modified infanticide."[4]

The president's pro-life stance favoring ethical stem-cell research but opposing unethical embryonic stem-cell research was one of the defining domestic policy chapters of his presidency, which I discussed earlier in this book, but it was also a policy decision opposing human cloning research, which had equal importance and value and which was gaining steam during the Bush years. When President Obama came to office, he overturned not only the Bush policy on stem-cell research but also opened the floodgates on human cloning research. Twice during the Bush administration, the president welcomed to the East Room the snowflake babies. They were embryos seemingly frozen in perpetuity and forgotten but then adopted by loving couples who then allowed the embryos to be implanted in the mother's womb. The snowflakes and their parents were inspiring, and I don't think there were ever two more moving or powerful gatherings in defense of life in the White House than those two gatherings hosted by the president.

Also, President Bush created conscience-clause protections for doctors, nurses, and other health-care workers in the medical professions, protecting them from being coerced into taking part in abortions, while formally protecting them in the law, another protection revoked by the Obama administration.

At the Department of Health and Human Services (HHS), the president fully funded pro-marriage programs in the states, as well as abstinence-before-marriage education programs. The success of both programs was an important policy benchmark and almost always trashed by the opponents of those policies on ideological grounds, despite the fact both programs worked. The Bush administration promoted the effectiveness of abstinence education as the only 100 percent effective form of birth control and funded 169 abstinence programs, serving one million students—programs extinguished in the Obama years. The Bush policy was clear: Promoting sexual abstinence until marriage, and fidelity within marriage, should be the central focus of government policy. This was consistent with his endorsement of a federal marriage amendment and is what he meant when he talked about "the sacredness of marriage."

Also at HHS and for the first time in federal government policy, the president allowed an unborn child to receive federal medical coverage under a program called the State Children's Health Insurance Program SCHIP if the child met certain federal guidelines. Dr. Wade Horn, who served as deputy secretary of the Department of Health and Human Services during a key part of the Bush years, was highly instrumental in all these areas and was routinely vilified by opponents who disagreed with the president's pro-life, pro-family policies. No one in the administration took more personal criticism on domestic policy than Horn did.

One the greatest moments of the Bush pro-life record came in the East Room on November 5, 2007, when President Bush posthumously conferred the Presidential Medal of Freedom, the highest civilian award in our country, upon the late Representative Henry Hyde (R–IL) who was the most pro-life leader in the history of the United States Congress. Hyde's family joined the president to remember the unparalleled contribution Hyde made to the pro-life cause. It was one of the most moving ceremonies I have ever attended. The president's pro-life record was summed up in the beautiful sentence I heard him use countless times to underscore the sanctity of all human life, that "everyone who was ever born mattered."

It is immoral and illogical, ethically and technologically, to continue to promulgate anything other than the pro-life position. There are no more excuses left in the pro-choice camp just as there were no more excuses by 1861 in the proslavery camp. We know it is a baby from the moment of conception. Even the pro-choice Supreme Court Justice Ruth Bader Ginsburg has said the *Roe* decision should not have been imposed on the American people. There was no consensus on abortion in 1973; the pro-life statutes in all fifty states should not have been struck down in one fell blow by the Supreme Court. The judicial arrogance in that ruling still astounds and was a terrible decision jurisprudentially.

On this issue there cannot be compromise, but our differences must always be stated and expressed civilly and diplomatically if unapologetically. The law is instructive, and we are a nation of laws not men. President Bush was motivated during his time in office to give a voice to the voiceless. He was part of the majority of Americans who support the pro-life position, especially among the rising generation of young people. This is, it seems to me, the most important civil rights issue of our time, and the pro-life movement never had a better friend in the Oval Office than George W. Bush.

The novelist Walker Percy wrote:

> The current con . . . is that since there is no agreement about the beginning of human life, it is therefore a private religious or philosophical decision and therefore the state and the courts can do nothing about it. . . . It is commonplace of modern biology, known to every high school student . . . that the life of every individual organism, human or not, begins when the chromosomes of the sperm fuse with the chromosomes of the ovum to form a new DNA complex that thenceforth directs the onto-genesis of the organism . . . Nowadays it is not some misguided ecclesiastics who are trying to suppress an embarrassing scientific fact. It is the secular juridical-journalistic establishment.[5]

All of human life, from conception to natural death, is a testimony to the goodness of God. The president's pro-life convictions were deeply impacted when he first saw the sonograms of his twin daughters, Barbara and Jenna. Those images underscored the entirety of his pro-life record. He wrote, "The fact that they could not speak for themselves only enhanced society's duty to defend them. Many decent and thoughtful people disagreed, including members of my family. I understood their reasons and respected their views. As president, I had no desire to condemn millions as sinners or dump new fuel on raging cultural fires. I did feel a responsibility to voice my pro-life convictions and lead the country toward what Pope John Paul II called a culture of life. I was convinced that most Americans agreed we would be better off with few abortions. Bob Casey, the late Democratic governor of Pennsylvania, said it best: 'When we look at the unborn child, the real issue is not when life begins, but when love begins.'"[6]

Also, President Bush commemorated the National Day of Prayer in the East Room all eight years of his presidency. He and Shirley Dobson, Dr. James Dobson's wife, developed an easy rapport, and it was a disappointing break when the Obama presidency refused to commemorate the NDP at the White House. The Dobsons had become personal friends, dating from the first Bush campaign, and we remained in regular touch from the first Bush inauguration until the close of the second administration. Focus on the Family had become one of the most important evangelical ministries in American history.

In other domestic areas, George W. Bush was the first president to sign a major school choice provision, which became the Opportunity Scholarships Program for the District of Columbia. I was with him at Archbishop Carroll High School in Washington when he signed that bill. He sat on the stage with mothers, grandmothers, and other family members who told him, without the school-choice legislation, their sons and daughters, grandsons and granddaughters would not have access to the best possible education. In fact, they pleaded with the president and country to understand that not only were some of the existing public schools subpar in a variety of ways but they also represented a physical danger to the boys and girls who attended them. During the campaigns President Bush promised to promote and defend school choice and vouchers, and he made good on those promises once in office. By contrast President Obama ended the D.C. school-choice program with the help of his Secretary of Education and Washington's mayor. Meanwhile, all their children attended safe, excellent public or private schools.

There were plenty of other achievements to be sure, few more important than the two major tax cuts that were fully in keeping with the greatest tax-cutting presidents in American history: Coolidge, Kennedy, and Reagan. Under the Bush tax cuts, every American who paid income taxes had their taxes reduced. The president not only succeeded in persuading Congress to lower taxes on income, inheritance, capital gains and dividends, but also was vindicated when he said his tax-cutting commitments would result in a significant uptick in the economy. That is precisely what happened. Concurrent with his free-trade, free-market, free-enterprise commitments, the president also presided over the signing of no less than thirteen free-trade agreements. The Bush fiscal record will rightly be debated and criticized for decades to come, but the president himself says during his eight years in office, the national deficit as a percentage of the Gross Domestic Product GDP was about 2 percent. That is below the average of the previous fifty years and below the averages of his contemporary predecessors.

Also, George W. Bush was the first president to try to reform Social Security; he grabbed the proverbial third rail in order to inject fiscal responsibility into that massive entitlement. The influential lobby AARP led the charge against the Bush administration's historic Social Security reforms with a fury. The president's plan was simple: It allowed young Americans to put some of their own tax money into private accounts for their retirement. That funding would be invested in the stock market, but AARP and its allies did not like the sense of risk and refused to allow the status quo to be changed. The terrible irony is that everyone in Washington, Democrats and Republicans alike, knew that by 2036 Social Security's reserves would be drained, leaving the program able to pay only 80 percent of the benefits it promised. The rest would have to be borrowed by Uncle Sam, a tragedy. The irony is that six years later, AARP acknowledged it would support reform, vindicating President Bush's own analysis of the problem.

President Bush saw the necessity and the utility of reaching out to America's largest minority community, Hispanics. He made strides with these voters, garnering 34 percent of their support in 2000 and rising to 40 percent in 2004. The conventional wisdom is those numbers were powered by the president's immigration policies, but I do not believe it explains all or most of that support. The president's willingness to be outspoken about his faith had a lot to do with his strong appeal to these voters, the fastest growing of all American voter blocs, and so did his pro-family, pro-life and pro-marriage stances. The Pew Hispanic Center found that 56 percent of Hispanics sixteen and up are pro-life, and 44 percent oppose same-sex marriage; only 34 percent support it. They knew they had an ally for their values in the president.

One of the major areas of accomplishment for the Bush presidency, which is given far too little attention, is the area of culture, where the president governed from a conservative and traditionalist viewpoint with the aide of creative and talented leadership. The two chairmen of the arts and humanities agencies during the whole of the Bush presidency were nothing short of stellar, and I worked closely with them during my time in the White House. Dana Gioia, the chairman of the National Endowment for the Arts (NEA), and Bruce Cole, the chairman of the National Endowment for the Humanities (NEH), were probably the most imaginative leaders of those agencies in their history and had many great successes rooted in their love for American history and Western civilization. We had a close working relationship from the beginning of their respective tenures. Both their programming and the humanities and arts medalists they and their councils chose to honor and spotlight were of the highest caliber and refreshingly free of political correctness. The standard was excellence, and the Gioia and Cole tenures will bear out legacies of achievement in the Bush administration.

At the NEA, Gioia created the first major victory for serious reading on a nationwide scale in nearly thirty years with his *Reading at Risk* report and the *Big Read* national literary project rooted in the classics. He also created a successful model of how arts education ought to proceed by encouraging a broadly promoted study of the masterpieces of literature, which reached tens of millions of Americans through the performance of the Shakespeare in American Communities project, the Jazz in the Schools program, and the Poetry Out Loud project. There was an attendant commitment to the promotion and playing of classical, jazz, and American songbook music, and perhaps the most definitive promotion and celebration of opera ever at the federal level.

At the NEH, Cole established the highest standards for grant making, which had been a huge problem before he arrived. He and his team never wavered from making sure only excellence was awarded with funding and not the faddish or ideological novelty of the moment. He established the wonderful *We the People* program to improve the teaching and understanding of American history, which eventually reached millions of Americans. Cole's signal and illustrious *Picturing America* program reintroduced to young Americans the most important American paintings and photographs of our heritage, reaching eighty thousand schools and public libraries. At both agencies during the Bush administrations, there was an incomparable commitment to programs promoting the important story of America's visual, literary, historic, and diplomatic heritage.

In this realm of culture, among the most important things any president does is confer the Medal of Freedom, the highest honor a civilian can receive. The list of recipients singled out for this distinction by President Bush is impressive: Walter Wriston, Gary Becker, Robert Conquest, Edward Teller, James Q. Wilson, Charlton Heston, Jacques Barzun, Robert Bartley, Paul Johnson, William Safire, Paul Harvey, Laurence Silberman, Peter Pace, Henry Hyde, Irving Kristol, and Norman Podhoretz.

The same was true in the conferring of the Medal of Humanities by President Bush: Richard Brookhiser, Myron Magnet, Thomas and Jordan Saunders, Stephen Balch, Victor Davis Hanson, Roger Hertog, Richard Pipes, Ruth Wisse, Fouad Ajami, James Buchanan, Bernard Lewis, The Hoover Institution, Walter Berns, Richard Gilder, Lewis Lehrman, Mary Ann Glendon, Alan Charles Kors, Gertrude Himmelfarb, Hilton Kramer, Harvey Mansfield, Shelby Steele, Midge Decter, Joseph Epstein, Elizabeth Fox-Genovese, Donald Kagan, Thomas Sowell, and Tom Wolfe.

These two lists read as a conservative intellectual brain trust, and President Bush was serious about singling out the lifelong excellence of these men and women. The president believed that, in the words of the conservative philosopher Richard Weaver, "Ideas have consequences."[7]

The president was an avid reader of history and biography, and many of these individuals had an impact on his own thinking and governing.

Also, he made a point of selecting important, high-profile, high-exposure conservatives with a national reputation to key posts, none more important than the selection and retention of Vice President Dick Cheney. It is easy to forget the major debate in 1999 and 2000 whether George W. Bush would select a committed conservative as his running mate. The selection of Cheney put that debate to rest immediately. Other important conservatives to serve during the Bush years were United Nations Ambassador John Bolton, Deputy Director of the National Security Council Elliott Abrams, Labor Secretary Elaine Chao (the only cabinet officer to serve all eight years), Office of Management and Budget Director Mitch Daniels, the White House's chief economist Eddie Lazear of the Hoover Institution, the White House speechwriters Bill McGurn and Marc Thiessen, and John Walters as the director of the National Drug Enforcement Agency, to name just a few. They all proved the conservative leader Morton Blackwell's view as the correct one: "Personnel is policy."

One of the best conservative staff choices President Bush made was the selection of Tony Snow to be his White House press secretary. I don't believe there was ever a better presidential spokesman than Tony. We were great friends before he came to the White House, during his tenure at 1600, and after he departed to spend time with his family in light of the disease that would eventually take his young life. Tony was smart, funny, loyal, and able to craft a sentence, an argument, or a quip that seemed to fit just perfectly. When he died, I thought of the line from Ralph Waldo Emerson so fitting for Tony's life: "It is not the length of life, but the depth of life."[8] He was singular.

Power is ephemeral and so are the people who staff any administration, and both are fleeting. Yet achievements last. The successes of the Bush administration were significant. Many of the president's most important decisions were rooted in his innate wisdom. The clarity of wisdom comes into view more sharply across the years. President Bush said repeatedly, while still in office, there was a difference between opinions and wisdom and that he was much more interested in the results of a decision. Those results prove the validity of his view. The president's harshest critics were always asking him to justify himself in order to vindicate large decisions, often involving our national security, and to offer his apology when they felt his decisions had gone astray. But George W. Bush is a man of long views and innate confidence. The wisdom of his actions, I believe, will be validated over time. His constant inner strength was undergirded by a sincere Christian faith and moral rectitude, powered by his view that all men and women deserved to be free and that every life has value, an idealistic but also hopeful worldview.

Chapter 21

Toward an American Renaissance: Faith, Liberty, and the Future of Conservatism

What is conservatism? Is it not the adherance to the old and tried against the new and untried?
—ABRAHAM LINCOLN[1]

The conservative movement has become the dominant intellectual force in American politics, on the strength of writers and thinkers like Whittaker Chambers and Bill Buckley and Russell Kirk. The movement has inspired many hundreds of fine Americans to run for office and to serve in government. It's easy to understand why. On the fundamental issues of our times, conservatives have been right. . . . Conservatives were right that a free society is sustained by the character of its people, which means we must honor the moral and religious heritage of our great nation.
—GEORGE W. BUSH[2]

Some conservatives believe America's best days are behind us, that nations have life cycles and that history teaches us rise and decline are

inevitable. The reasons for decline are various: materialism and extrava-
gant wealth; moral and social decay; a loss of strong marriages and families;
a culture that is decadent; the surrender of elites; a collapse of confident
exceptionalism; but above all, a collapse of faith. I am decidedly not in the
declinist camp. I believe an American renaissance is possible, even likely,
yet it is important to take stock of the health or illness of our country,
culture, and civilization, and to see it whole as it really is. George Orwell
said the first duty of intelligent people is "the restatement of the obvious."[3]

In all the best conservative writing and thinking, Benjamin Franklin
rarely if ever appears as an icon, but he wrote: "There is no freedom
without order and no order without virtue."[4] That single sentence
is the best summary of conservatism I have read. Ordered liberty is
conservatism's most important credo because it understands that our
country cannot have freedom in the truest sense without the morals and
manners that provide the underpinning of our constitutional republic.
Those morals and manners have given our country a civil society and way
of life defined by its continuity and stability, derived from the great Anglo-
American tradition of individual freedom and personal responsibility. The
law does compel us, but virtue is rooted in duty and obligation. High levels
of personal and moral responsibility have given our country high levels of
liberty. No group of Americans ever believed this with greater passion,
insight, or conviction than our founding fathers, and it was as true for
them in the eighteenth century as it is for us in the twenty-first century.

Conservatives believe law flows from revelation. The Founders
believed this too, and it was captured powerfully by the influential British
legal scholar William Blackstone: "When the Supreme Being formed
the universe and created matter out of nothing, He impressed certain
principles upon the matter from which it can never depart without which
it would cease to be . . . Man considered as a creature must necessarily be
subject to the laws of his Creator . . . It is necessary that he should in all
points conform to his Maker's will . . . This will of his Maker is called the
law of Nature . . . Hence it follows that the first and primary end of human
laws is to maintain these absolute [God-given] rights to individuals."[5]

Conservatives believe Western civilization and American history
find their firmest, truest, and most bounteous foundations in the Greco-
Roman, Judeo-Christian traditions; that human freedom and flourishing
find their taproot in moral excellence, which is virtue. This assumes the
centrality of high character at every level of American life as the genesis of
the confidence necessary to produce a great, free, and prosperous country.
In America such virtue, even from before our country's formal founding

in the mid eighteenth century, always found its genesis in that Judeo-Christian tradition's greatest contribution to Western civilization, the Holy Bible. The Scriptures were and are the ancient and lasting moral code for the overwhelming majority of Americans then and now. This makes us fundamentally distinct from our European allies.

The dissenting Protestants who founded and built America believed the King James Version of the Bible and the attendant Book of Common Prayer were the greatest expressions of Christian truth and organized our young, constitutional republic in accord with these two books. The British also gave us the English language in all its versatility; our literary tradition; our legal code and style of government; our tradition of vast religious liberty; and countless other large and small building blocks that comprise our culture, none more important, than law, language, and the moral code of the Bible.

America was always a predominantly Christian country animated and defined by Christian ideals and principles yet welcoming and tolerant from its earliest days of a soon to be flourishing Jewish community. This has made America all the richer and more complete. Christianity and Judaism were in sync, both expressing a set of norms and a moral code that came to define our young country. These two great faith traditions together provided the dynamic necessary for a vibrant, constitutional republic defined by its work ethic, free-enterprise system, fair play, and open religious expression in the public square. These have been the defining aspects of the best of American life. From these religious traditions a foundation was laid, and from it grew our culture—our culture from religion—and from this culture grew our government, our legal structure and code, our schools and universities, our military, and all the institutions that comprise the uniquely American way of life. From the beginning no institutions were more important or more necessary or more foundational than the unquestioned sanctity of marriage, family, and parish/church/temple life. These provided the faithful sustenance for our flourishing.

These were the three indispensable supports that nourished the "little platoons," in the words of Edmund Burke, upon which America grew rapidly and fanned out from the East Coast across a large and geographically diverse continent. Each American family was a little civilization unto itself and collectively comprised the personification of the stability, continuity, and ordered liberty that propelled our country forward. The parish/church/cathedral/synagogue life was the reliable authority for how the country's moral and ethical life was to be organized, linking the living, the dead, and the not yet born (again, a "Burkean" view) into a religiously holistic and contiguous way of life, giving human existence purpose and meaning far beyond the needs of self, and providing ample room for individuality. The basic tenets of American life were a sense of localism, neighborhood, community, and a knowable and identifiable place called home. These are "the permanent things" of which Burke wrote, spoke, and defended. America inherited these traditions from England, though we were always more egalitarian and less class conscious.

This was the founding of America and the institutions from which conservatism sprang. These are the institutions worth conserving and preserving, then and now. Because of this sense of localism and community, informed by faith, Americans naturally helped their neighbors most in need through the institutions closest to them. Americans believed it was not the role of government to be the primary institution serving the orphans, widows, prisoners, homeless, and the down and out. It was the church, the synagogue, the neighborhood, the civic groups, the fraternal groups, the ethnic groups. Robert Nisbet's magisterial *Quest for Community* shows how the rise of the superstate attempted to break this widely held consensus.

Even before our official founding in 1776, the early Americans had absorbed and created a country of ordered liberty in the best British traditions of the seventeenth and eighteenth centuries. They viewed tyranny as a threat, having lived through it; and as the idea of British common law was absorbed, a republic began to emerge, shaped and molded by English tradition. Our founders believed the Magna Carta expressed an apogee of human liberty, and it loomed large as the leitmotif of our young country's founding documents.

The historian Michael Novak says from the beginning of America, we were a country "on two wings," each wing independent and yet each helping the other flourish. On one wing was religious faith, indispensable to the creation of America. On the second wing was common sense rooted in reason. Faith and reason—and not one without the other but both together—ushered in the narrative of young America. Novak says America was and is a "religious republic," and therein rests the firm basis of our founding and our maturation.

George Washington was particularly supportive of the role of religion in American life, as he made so clear in his great farewell address. His military and government career was defined by key decisions supporting religion: his use of military chaplains, his advocacy of tax subsidies for the churches in his native Virginia, his engagement with a host of religious groups, his speeches undergirded by faith, and his insight and advocacy of the relationship between good citizenship and conscience rooted in religion.

This broadly and deeply felt and agreed-upon consensus of the transcendent in American life is among the things that made us exceptional as a country from the start. It was widely believed that Providence had His hand on our proverbial shoulders from the founding and that America was to be a leader for freedom and moral conviction. These inform the central American narrative of what it means to be an exemplary country. Faith, family, freedom, and the institutions that support them naturally go together and are of a piece. A faith of humility and common sense always found a shared mission on American soil, dating from the genesis of the country. The legion immigrants who poured into the country in those first, early waves shared those principles and over time acculturated themselves and their progeny to an identifiable American way of life first established by the largely white, Anglo-Saxon Protestants who came to American soil, but also by the growing minority of Catholics and Catholic missionaries.

The Judeo-Christian tradition in America provided a sense of civic order consonant with liberty, and as Russell Kirk has shown, this widely shared tradition of faith contributed both "an inner order of the soul, the outer order of society" in America. Faith and reason abiding side by side were the glue. These were the "visions of order" the seminal American philosopher Richard Weaver saw as the unparalleled essential of a healthy culture. The natural expression of faith and reason working in tandem gave to America the social and moral principles of a free society and upheld our nation through some of its most difficult and trying chapters of war, depression, and other crises. This consensus was the basis for America's birth and growth into a great country.

Just how central faith has been in America and in public life has been written everywhere in our nation's capital city—embedded in the friezes of major buildings, engraved on important monuments and memorials, written into the founding documents, and reminding Americans that the framers, for all their diversity and geographical differences, agreed that the author of American liberty was God, not man. They agreed the most basic rights of mankind came not from any government but from God, that Americans "are endowed by their Creator with certain unalienable rights." Providence authored our liberty, and we were to be a nation under God.

Arlington Cemetery, the White House, the Library of Congress, the Supreme Court, the U.S. Capitol building, the National Archives, and the Washington, Jefferson, and Lincoln memorials attest to this history of our religious republic—that our public square, from its earliest days, was one that welcomed religion, which in turn informed our most important debates about the abolition of slavery, giving women the right to vote, coeducation, the civil rights movement, and the pro-life movement, which is consonant with the others. The tallest structure in the most powerful city in the world, the Washington Memorial, has the words *Laus Deo* ("Praise Be to God") inscribed on its highest peak. In bold letters, on all U.S. currency, are the words "In God We Trust." Our national greatness finds it roots in this transcendent story. This is what George Washington, the father of our country, meant when he said, "It is impossible to rightly govern the world without God and the Bible."[6]

This prompts a perennial debate of the relationship between what is owed to Caesar and what is owed to God, the proper balance between the political process and religious belief. It also prompts key questions about what are the moral and ethical foundations upon which discourse in our civic life should proceed in this new era. In other words, what is the ethical basis for our political choices, and on what foundation do those choices rest?

Freedom and Christianity go together, not only in the lives of believers but also in the lives of nations. This is what the Gospel writer John meant when he wrote, "Where the Spirit of the Lord is, there is liberty." The faithful soul is free and unshackled. It can be true in the souls of nations too. The poet Samuel Taylor Coleridge wrote, "In fine, religion, true or false, is and ever has been the center of gravity in a realm, to which all other things must and will accommodate themselves."[7]

In America, there exists from our founding an inseparable relationship between revelation and government. Politics cannot be drained of faith because they are of a piece. There is a natural, deep unity between America's political life, and the life of a transcendent moral order that precedes our nation's founding. In order for the United States to thrive in this new century, we need both a thriving realm of faith and a thriving realm of limited government which makes ample room the practicing of that faith. Does revealed religion consecrate a country like ours? Yes, I believe it does, and I believe it is the source of our vitality.

There is a divine dimension to our legal structure which grows from our Judeo-Christian taproots. American society and American faith go hand in hand, and have an entwined fate. The spiritual reality is that there exists a kind of divine contract between mankind and God. From this relationship our national body of ethics, morality, and duties are derived. Therein lies the seedbed of the American concept of justice. A restoration of this worldview has implications for our economy, for education and how our kids are raised and schooled, for our culture and what it values, and for the direction of America in foreign and security policy. Alienation of religion from our country's national life makes us a lesser country. Restoration adds energy and the imagination necessary for the way forward.

Such restoration adds the kinds of social cohesion and shared purpose central to the life of a great nation like ours. This is the heart of the conserving and restoring function that will act as natural antidotes to the nihilism and futility that too often animate contemporary culture. This is conservatism that puts the preservation of America's social order and cultural norms at the center.

This balance of religion and public life is how all Americans understood the country they had been born into, or chose to come to. The laws and institutions of American civilization were arrived at after centuries of debate and consensus resulting in America's greatest achievement, our Constitution. This document is the guardian of our liberty.

A separate but parallel and related outgrowth of this achievement was the emergence of an American culture of painting, poetry, public monuments, music, bridges, and public and private architecture that is beautiful, sublime, and excellent. Our greatest public buildings, our most beautiful monuments and sculptures, our most sacred houses of worship, our most meaningful paintings, our most powerful poetry, our most deeply felt music and hymnody, our most memorable films all grew up along side the same standards of that cultural commitment to greatness, adding transcendence to the natural beauty of America. This was both popular and fine culture at a high level and standard.

For a host of reasons—beginning in the late nineteenth century but gaining massive speed into the twentieth century, most prominently with the advent of the sexual revolution of the late 1960s—this American consensus of achievement began to tear apart at the seams, first slowly and then commencing with an almost breathtakingly speed. The decoupling, divorcing, ungluing of the old norms and mores, undergirded by faith, has been sad and disappointing to study and watch. This moral revolution has impacted every American institution without exception and has had a special impact on the sacredness of life, marriage, family, and faith—the institutions that formed the basis of that which is worth conserving in the American experience. This has been an unprecedented social and cultural tsunami.

The toll upon our nation's political, economic, and religious life is incalculable, hastened by a secularism and political correctness unequalled in its ferocity for most of American history. The unity and confidence that defined American culture have been attacked and the challenges we face from those who oppose ordered liberty are among the most serious challenges we have ever faced. America's spiritual and intellectual traditions are under assault as never before, powered by a combination of atheism, nihilism, ugliness, and lack of standards.

It would have been inconceivable that justices of the Supreme Court, in any period before the twentieth century, could have written a plurality opinion that "At the heart of liberty is the right to define one's own concept of existence, of meaning, of the universe, and of the mystery of human life. Beliefs about these matters could not define the attributes of personhood were they formed under the compulsion of the State."[8] This view, written by Supreme Court justices Sandra Day O'Connor, David Souter, and Anthony Kennedy, from the *Planned Parenthood v. Casey* case twenty years ago, was as much a cultural statement as a judicial one. Their understanding of liberty as libertinism is rooted in personal choice.

What does it mean when a culture excludes God, faith, and virtue from our public life and from public considerations in the law contra to our own founding? Pope Benedict XVI spoke eloquently about this during his visit to England in 2010. He said a society that promotes such exclusions ultimately ends up with a "reductive vision of the person and his destiny."[9] His point was that such moral relativism is a kind of de facto atheism, often evoked in the name of democracy but ending up undermining and imperiling it.

Both American liberty and Western civilization have become targets of this decoupling of faith and reason. The erosion has been alternately slow and fast, mostly subtle, yet real and measurable. The damage can be observed in almost every American institution of note: colleges and universities, public schools, museums and foundations, the theater, and old and new media. The debasement and undermining of good taste and excellence have been deep. Scholar Roger Scruton writes that ours is a time when both "faith and feeling [exist] in a world besieged."[10] In the name of "progress," Herb London says the new orthodoxy is comprised of "opposition to traditional religion; multiculturalism and cultural relativism; materialism; [and a] belief in scientific rationality as the ultimate arbiter of human value."[11] This is the new matrix, all at war with the "traditional roots of America . . . an anemic remodeling of our culture,"[12] he writes.

Thus we have arrived at a sober moment. The Judeo-Christian tradition that provided the roots of ordered liberty in America, is undergoing a historic revision that seeks to undermine American resolve and forever change the nature of America and with it our culture, our freedom, our way of life. Secular humanism seeks to replace the Judeo-Christian faith traditions and replace it with hollowness, isolation, and an atomization and factionalism of a new order. In Herb London's words, this new humanism represents "the rise of a new national religion"[13] that is something different from anything we have seen before in American history.

This is abetted by the federal superstate, which grows exponentially, year by year, seeking to insert big government into the historic and necessary role of the intermediary institutions that have always operated outside government; by higher and more taxes at the local, state, and federal levels; by a tangle and snarl of ever-increasing regulations pouring out of Washington and the state capitals making free enterprise and entrepreneurship more difficult and needlessly complex; and above all, undermining the traditional values and principles that have given us strong families who provide the foundation for strong economies and national confidence.

This is the startling crossroads at which twenty-first-century American conservatives find ourselves. It is tempting to conclude if we can just elect the right politicians, if we can just get the right legislation into place, if we can just arrive at the correct political consensus, then we can find our way forward. But politics, while central and instrumental, will not provide the way forward alone even as we continue to have an ongoing and necessary debate about the size and scope of government, about the size and scope of taxes, about the nature of regulations and government involvement in the average American's daily life. We need a cultural basis for addressing the most important problems we face, apart from the political fray.

The greatest poet and literary critic of the last century, T. S. Eliot, said art is not religion; poetry is not religion; humanism is not religion; only religion is religion, and all cultures spring from religion. He said a refreshed and renewed dedication to the ancient faith may offer a way forward for a culture in peril. He believed the healthy spiritual life of a nation produced the confidence and hope necessary to sustain ordered liberty, while spiritual crisis produced chaos and confusion. Eliot said genuine faith provided a useful and important way to think about, discuss, assess, and evaluate the way forward for a culture in crisis. This was his paradigm for thinking about the future of Europe after 1945.

I would modify his paradigm slightly and suggest conservatives need to think about how the promulgation of a refreshed and renewed Judeo-Christian consensus in America might aid our way forward as a country in this young century. Eliot believed a wrecked spiritual life in a country equaled a wrecked cultural life and thus a weakened country. This consensus was certainly widely held long before Eliot's time. It was the consensus widely believed in America's founding era. If we are to redeem the time—a phrase Eliot borrowed from Saint Paul—and thus redeem America, we must conceive of a way to discuss and evaluate the cultural challenges that are impinging on our freedoms and way of life, but we must do so in a way fully in sync with our founding principles, norms, and mores. Perhaps we need to return to go forward, to find the past in the present, and to imagine a Judeo-Christian culture in sync with this new era. We need a creative community that will challenge the idols of our present age. This worldview is consonant with ordered liberty, with a vibrant, healthy culture for the arts, and with a rededication to the first principles of family, marriage, parenting, and faith.

Conservatives give an incomplete answer when we communicate conservatism as a political and economic program of lower taxes, small and limited government, fewer regulations, and a strong national defense. All of these things are utterly fundamental and foundational and at the heart of what we believe. Yet the scope needs to be widened to include spiritual and cultural matters that reflect our historical consensus in America, one consonant with our founding. It encompasses the institutions most worth defending, has a larger appeal, and provides a hopeful way forward to the kind of American renaissance we should be articulating. If we are seeking a restoration of America, then we must articulate a rebirth of a culture that springs from religion. This could be the heart of an American renaissance.

This allows conservatives to discuss learning and education; America's legal community and the discourse and rhetoric flowing from it; the nature of our civic and social lives; and the precarious nature of our political institutions. Burke said conservatives wanted to reform in order to preserve and not to pull down. The latter was the revolutionary way, and conservatism was not revolutionary but rather reforming in its essence. Allowing the great Judeo-Christian tradition to help us reposition and reanchor ourselves to that which is worth conserving must be part of this renaissance. Faith puts purpose, vision, and meaning back at the center of American life.

In cultural matters, the fields are ripe for an imaginative conservatism, beginning with an emphasis on man's chief end, which is not material but rather spiritual. Art is not some spiritual escape, a kind of neo-religion of its own. Art can never be religion. We must help steer the culture away from reductive trivialities and its current state of ugliness and novelty and toward a renewed emphasis on beauty, sacredness, the things of the spirit, and the ineffable. We must match this vision with the tools available to us—colors, forms, canvasses, paints, meter, rhyme, and sketchbooks—but we must not cloud or fog them. Rather we must give them a general accessibility to draw people upward. This pursuit of beauty, of excellence, of truth is the thing. Pope Benedict XVI said artists must be "capable of restoring enthusiasm and confidence [about] what can encourage the human spirit to rediscover its path, to raise its eyes to the horizon, to dream of a life worthy of its vocation."[14] Too often conservatism has been silent on culture, ceding it to the Left and to others. We must reengage at the highest and most popular levels.

The poet and former chairman of the National Endowment of the Arts, Dana Gioia, has shown the danger of walling off great poetry and indeed all great art from the mainstream of American life. Artists have a public and important role to play, rooted in excellence, and to avoid what the president of the Trinity Forum Cherie Harder has called "our culture's rush toward efficiency, speed, quantification, and distraction" but rather to seek "the time and attention required to find the best words and images and then to hold them together in ways that illuminate . . . is now wildly countercultural. It is inefficient. Its value is not readily quantifiable. Its utility is intangible."[15]

Conservatives believe the artist's subject is history, existence, and experience. We need beautiful and true ways to convey that narrative rooted in the principles of order, composition, and harmony instead of chaos, dissonance, and fracture. We might begin by renewing our interest in classical and realist figurative styles in painting, architecture, and sculpture, which are evergreen and ever new, all rooted in aesthetic values derived from a return to order and craft. But we must not exclude abstraction or contemporary art; there is greatness there too. The vital place of revealed religion and tradition in civilized society, as expressed in its highest artistic forms and aspirations, will act to counter nihilistic and atheistic extremism.

The purpose of great art, at one remove, is a beautiful continuity and rooted in excellence, not trying to fit itself into the prevailing values of any one age. This dedication to a renewed excellence in the arts will take persistence, commitment, and a singleness of purpose to counter self-doubt.

This renaissance in the arts and in culture in general will allow us again to ask the big questions: For what purpose did God create us? Why are we supposed to be good and to do good to others? What does it mean to be alive and how are we to remain true to ourselves and to others? The goal must be, to paraphrase Ezra Pound, "To make it new"—"it" being the best of Western civilization. To transmit culture from one generation to the next, we must restore the teaching of history, not ideological attitude, in our schools.

The sociologist Robert Nesbit said fads start from the top down but movements begin from the bottom up. Movements are what change a country and a culture. Politics is a reflection of the values of a culture. If we want to change politics, we have to impact the culture. Any cultural renewal and reform will take a long while, perhaps decades or more.

The cultural narrative of which I speak longs for faith and hope, but also engagement and imaginative freedom. As a nation we long for a common destiny and a common culture, and we must return to what the writer James Ppieson calls "the objective of a liberal education" which is "to identify the permanent and perennial issues in the midst of flux and change."[16] Literature, art, music, architecture, and philosophy are the foundations of Western civilization, and we are duty bound to convey them to this generation free from ideology.

There has been a massive revisionism to Western civilization and American history that in the twenty-first century seems normal enough, but as late as the early 1960s seemed utterly outré. This revisionism has now deconstructed our constitutional republic and the rule of law, traditional faith, the values of hard work, thrift, and entrepreneurship; it has obstructed our heritage of the fine arts and excellence in culture in the most condescending and dehumanizing tone possible; it has politicized and erased the Judeo-Christian imprint on science; and it has employed technology to change human nature. This is what we are up against.

We have a country, a culture, and a civilization to preserve and to reform. This is the task before us, and the primary challenge of our era. To do so we must refocus on the spiritual values and beliefs common to our national life and its founding. American conservatives must offer a renewed vision that embodies the ideal community where everyone is welcomed and which remains true to the fundamental and vibrant religious truths of the Jewish and Christian traditions upon which America was founded and which in turn impacted and influenced the scope of our greatest national institutions, none more so than our families. We must place renewed emphasis on order in each soul. To paraphrase Flannery O'Connor, we must push back against the culture as hard as it pushes against us, and instead of relegating religion to the corner of the debate about American renewal, we must instead recenter it where our founders always placed it, in a place of prominence, reflecting the inherent spiritual nature of man and recognizing that healthy culture grows from it. We must do so civilly, diplomatically, and prudently, just as the framers did. Contemporary conservatism needs not only strong leaders who show unbridled fortitude, passion, and imagination; but also it needs those moral principles, rooted in religion, that will in fact help renew the civil and social order that has eroded and decayed precipitously.

Whittaker Chambers, one of the most astute, eloquent, lucid observers of the twentieth century, said Western civilization was experiencing a "total crisis." What he meant by that, in the words of writer Brian Anderson, is the West was abandoning "the traditional Western vision of man under God. That understanding provided meaning and depth to human existence, as well as a sense of limits and . . . a justification for sacrifice and suffering"[17] and as a counterweight to relativism, materialism, and self-centeredness. Chambers believed "meaningful freedom directed man to transcendent ends," and he "elevated a counter-canon to modernity's reigning masters Marx, Nietzsche, and Freud,"[18] in Anderson's view. Chambers was calling for moral renewal as a bridge to the free society—underpinned by virtue and derived from religion.

Decoupling God from our public square creates a vacuum for an overweening, too-powerful federal government to fill. Our most foundational institutions are systematically usurped and decreased when government and attendant secularization grow and spread. As Ryan Messmore, the William E. Simon Fellow at The Heritage Foundation, has said so well:

> Government power is inherently limited by the role of other
> social institutions, such as families, religious congregations,
> schools, and businesses. The rightful authority of these institu-
> tions helps to check the authority of the state. . . . As government

claims responsibility for more tasks, it absorbs the allegiance that citizens once placed in other relationships and forms of association. When the federal government assumes more responsibility for fulfilling the moral obligations among citizens, it tends to undermine the perceived significance and authority of local institutions and communities. This encourages citizens, instead of looking to their families, churches, or local communities for guidance and assistance, to depend on the government. . . . As individuals begin to look more consistently to the government for support, the institutions that are able to generate virtues like trust and responsibility begin to lose their sway in the community. Excessive bureaucratic centralization thus sets in motion a dangerous cycle of dependence and social decay.[19]

As social and moral decay have beset America, government has filled the vacuum historically filled by families, faith organizations, and other private entities. It is a breathtaking exchange.

James Madison, the principal author of the United States Constitution, wrote, "The powers delegated by the proposed Constitution to the federal government are few and defined."[20]

A little-known U.S. president, Franklin Pierce, sagaciously observed, "The constitutionality and propriety of the Federal Government assuming to enter into a novel and vast field of legislation, namely, that of providing for the care and support of all those . . . who by any form of calamity become fit objects of public philanthropy. . . . I cannot find any authority in the Constitution for making the Federal Government the great almoner of public charity throughout the United States. To do so would, in my judgment, be contrary to the letter and spirit of the Constitution and subversive of the whole theory upon which the Union of these States is founded."[21] In this new century the federal government has become more centralized, its ends more intrusive.

The essential nature of twenty-first-century American conservatism is a view that the federal government is too large and should be relimited; that governments like families should live within their budgets; that the market economy is the road to prosperity and is consistent with human nature; that our defense budget must be robust in defense of our liberty; that above all we need to preoccupy ourselves with the moral framework of our freedom; and that we need to preserve the values of Western civilization in the Greco-Roman but especially the Judeo-Christian traditions as the bulwark of virtue that nurtures freedom. We must reject moral relativism and the transgressive renorming of American values, which continues apace. We must work to restore a normative culture that is the antidote to moral bankruptcy.

To redeem, restore, recover, renew, and reconcile our country for another century of liberty and self-government, we must replenish virtue among all our citizens. This is the antidote to overweening government. Social regeneration must be the heart of an American renaissance. It is a return to ordered liberty. The founders saw this as the essential capstone of the country.

Government should never compel people to follow a religious viewpoint, but neither should it exclude religion from our public life. But for Christians and Jews, it is a central tenet of faith that we get involved in the public life of our nation and not view government as evil or unworthy. For Christians, Romans 13 instructs us that government should be God's servant for good ends. Some Christians believe that we should do evangelism but stay out of government, that we should be involved in spiritual matters but not secular ones. But we know that God calls us to do good works in the public square and that we were created for such works. How Christians influence and impact culture and government are consistent with that view.

We are to seek to persuade others to our views through discussion, dialogue, and debate but always with civility and mutual regard. This has always been America's great and best tradition of faith in the public square, a biblical responsibility to influence culture and government for good from a providential guidance that is just and fair. Christians and Jews must never remain silent when the great moral and social arguments and questions of our era are being waged, whether that be the legalization of abortion, the explosion of pornography, the expansion of gambling, or other issues that directly impinge on the family and marriage.

Religion must have a public role against a rising tide of secularism; it must have a role in politics and education that contributes to authentic pluralism, and it gives to our nation a nourishing of its heritage. Its role is consistent with liberty and our founding. Freedom of conscience and freedom of association are paramount pillars in American life.

Any restrictions on these freedoms put restrictions on ordered liberty. The founding fathers welcomed and encouraged public expressions of Catholicism, Protestantism, and Judaism; they knew that faithful men and women would proclaim their faith in private and in public and they felt those contributions were vital for the strength of the new republic.

This view is consonant with science, too. Science should not have a moral preeminence, but faith and science are not at war; they are of a piece, and a religious sensibility in science is a good and necessary thing as exemplified by Frances Collins, the head of the National Institutes of Health, who is only the latest in a long and distinguished line of major scientists who are Christians bringing to bear their ethical and moral framework on the issues of our time. Scientific discovery does not undercut our faith; but rather advances the limitlessness of God's creation; spiritual and scientific knowledge are compatible.

John Cardinal Henry Newman set out the need for an intelligent, well-rounded laity as necessary for the promulgation of faith in public life, "not arrogant, not rash in speech, not disputatious, but men who know their religion, who enter into it, who know just where they stand, who know what they hold and what they do not, who know their creed so well that they can give an account for it, who know so much history that they can defend it."[22] Defending faith's wisdom and vision in the public forum is one of the bedrocks because this will help foster a faith-friendly dialogue on contentious issues of our time. We must not demur from recognizing and discussing the relationship between reality and morality; the latter defines who we are as humans and allows us to see more completely. The Judeo-Christian tradition should be seen as a timely, vital, healthy contributor to our most pressing social, economic, political, and cultural challenges. Any marginalization in the name of tolerance is detrimental to the vitality of our country and an affront to the guarantees of religious liberty in the U.S. Constitution. Religion is neither a subjective nor a private matter, a kind of private opinion that ought be restricted.

The largest historical questions are these: Can a society like America's survive without a religious base? If a nation loses faith in a Godhead, can it endure? Europe is an important paradigm for America, a continent being ravaged by a rising tide of secularism intolerant of the Judeo-Christian tradition and an aggressive Islamic extremism. When he was still Cardinal Ratzinger, before becoming Pope Benedict XVI, he delivered a remarkable speech to the Italian Senate in 2004 in which he said, "Europe seems hollow as if it were internally paralyzed by a failure of its circulatory system."[23] A necessary rekindling of a dialogue among church, synagogue, and civil society in America is overdue. Extremism of secularity is erasing from our culture the ancient values of true tolerance and traditional religion.

Conservatism is about community, with civic responsibility at its core, about love of country and patriotism rightly rooted in the best we have to offer. Our exceptionalism is rooted in our founding documents, the Declaration of Independence and the Constitution, and in the transcendent view of America deriving from our Judeo-Christian heritage. We must reintroduce to the rising generation of young Americans this great heritage and patrimony—the heroes; the great battles and generals; the great music and composers; the great paintings and artists; the great poems and poets; the great novels and writers; the great turning points of history; the great buildings and architects; the great monuments, sculptures, and sculptors; the great discoveries, explorations, scientific achievements, and inventors; the great books and great authors; and the fundamental narrative of why, in Russell Kirk's historic pentagon Greece, Rome, Athens, Jerusalem, London, and Philadelphia comprise the five anchor cities in the Greco-Roman, Judeo-Christian story of Anglo-American freedom and liberty.

Noah Webster, writing in his *On the Education of Youth in America*, said: "Every child in America should be acquainted with his own country. He should read books that furnish him with ideas that will be useful to him in life and practice. As soon as he opens his lips, he should rehearse the history of his own country."[24]

Ken Myers wrote: "Education rightly ordered must properly train the sentiments, sensibilities, and affections of students. . . . A person so trained will understand that the chief end of a truly human life is to conform the soul to reality, not . . . to attempt to remake reality to fit our dreams."[25] This is what gives students moral certainty and a consensus about our public life.

The writer Theodore Dalrymple has placed America's cultural challenge in the right context, saying we need to learn from Europe's slide into aggressive secularism. He says we need "a defense of all that is best . . . in American history. . . . That is why the outcome of the culture wars in America is so important to its future. A healthy modern society must know how to remain the same as well as change, to conserve as well as reform. Europe has changed without knowing how to conserve; that is its tragedy."[26]

The way forward for American conservatism is not to detach economic prosperity from the great moral issues of our time; economic deficits are rooted in moral and ethical deficits first. Character, personal integrity, and its consequences are inevitably tied up with economic dynamism, technological creativity, and the vitality of the marketplace. This strong sense of duty and economic flexibility go together because virtue is the other side of freedom; they are inextricably entwined and linked.

Pope Benedict XVI eloquently said: "Let us never forget how exclusion of God, religion, and virtue from public life leads ultimately to a truncated vision of man. . . . In our time, the price to be paid for fidelity to the gospel is no longer being hanged, drawn, and quartered, but it often involves being dismissed out of hand, ridiculed, and parodied."[27]

We need people of faith in politics, in the professions, in science, and in the arts because they help suffuse life with moral ballast. This will be one of the central tenets of our national restoration. Politics and religion operate in the same sphere because both deal with how we organize our lives together. It is why we can and do formally separate church and state but not religion and politics. This formally recognizes reality: a civic order on the one hand and a moral and religious order on the other.

William F. Buckley Jr.'s assertion in *God and Man at Yale* is as apt today as it was when it was first published in 1951, that in writer Roger Kimball's words, "The dual between Christianity and atheism is the most important in the world." Buckley wrote, "The struggle between individualism [by this he meant conservatism] and collectivism is the same struggle reproduced on another level."[28]

Once-great countries that forget their patrimony, and especially their faith, in a kind of general amnesia have a few things in common. They become more brutal and vulgar, but they also forget the things that made them great: their literature, their national songs and hymns, the heroes who died in wars or made incredible sacrifices to make them free and to give them a future of hope and prosperity. Secularization and decline go hand in hand.

Of all the paintings by Norman Rockwell, my favorite is titled *Lift Up Thine Eyes*. The painting is centered on a majestic cathedral and in front of it a host of people. All are too busy and preoccupied to notice the cathedral's splendor, giving it not even a glance. Heads are down, eyes are averted to the sidewalk. Ill cultures are like that. We need a cultural renaissance to battle a cultural forgetfulness that sometimes seems pervasive, meretricious, empty, and void. There is much spiritual vitality in our land still, but it is too often attenuated. Burke warned about just how fragile civilization can be, and our culture is worthy of our robust defense and nurture.

The writer Evelyn Waugh, speaking of Rudyard Kipling, wrote: "He believed civilization to be something laboriously achieved which was only precariously defended. He wanted to see the defenses fully manned. . . ."[29] Waugh, who penned these comments in 1938, observed: "At a time like the present it is notably precarious. If it falls we shall see not merely the dissolution of a few joint-stock corporations, but of the spiritual and material achievements of our history."[30] In commenting on Waugh's observations, Kimball wrote, "The contest between barbarism and civilization is perpetual. There are no permanent victories, only permanent values."[31]

This is consonant with T. S. Eliot's view of the kind of tradition worth preserving. He believed that in both politics and religion, tradition was dynamic, not static, and I agree. Eliot said it was dangerous "to associate tradition with the immovable; to think of it as something hostile to all change; to aim to return to some previous condition which we imagine as having been capable of preservation in perpetuity" and that "tradition without intelligence is not worth having."[32] There are things in the past worth preserving; there are things in the past worth discarding. Innovation is a part of tradition but always with fixed principles. With Burke, Johnson, Coleridge, Newman, and especially Eliot I believe conservatism at its finest nurtures and conserves the beautiful, the true, and the just in our culture. That is what Eliot meant when he said there was a kind of pastness in the present that keeps contemporary life vital. It is what makes the ugly and deliquescent in our culture so heartbreaking.

Our founders were comfortable and encouraging of religion's role in American public life and in politics itself. They did not seek to separate the two because they rightly believed faith promulgated a moral citizenry, which was essential for the survival of our young republic. It is no less true today. It is impossible to understand America, in our founding and in the present era, without understanding the centrality of the

Judeo-Christian tradition, a tradition of faith so powerful that it is not only not static; it is the primary vehicle for much of the major social changes in our history. And it is the model for the very forward for America now.

Epilogue

Final Thoughts on Redemption, Grace, and George W. Bush

Thou hast given so much to me,
Give one thing more—a grateful heart.
Not thankful when it pleaseth me,
As if Thy blessings had spare days;
But such a heart whose pulse may be
Thy praise.
—GEORGE HERBERT[1]

Even among these rocks,
Our peace in His will.
—T. S. ELIOT[2]

The founder of the Salvation Army, William Booth, wrote, "The greatness of a man's power is the measure of his surrender."[3] This is the lesson I have learned, that contentment does not reside in worldly victories or material things, in the level of one's intelligence, or in any other earthbound barometer. My contentment resides in my relationship with God, my relationship with my wife and kids, my relationships with my family and friends, and my relationships with my colleagues and professional associates. I have come to see that putting God first, others second, and myself last not only gives life a joy and unparalleled contentment but also

224

imitates Christ's humility. My own trajectory has been a story of professional success, followed by a crushing fall, followed by redemption. My faith in God and His boundless tenderness carried me through. He has provided the way forward.

The remarkable thing about America is that one really can begin anew; grace is fathomless and ineffable, and people want you to do well. This is the land of second chances. It is the genesis of my own love affair with America, and it is the point George Washington meant to convey when he admonished his fellow citizens to "labor to keep alive in your breast that little spark of celestial fire called conscience."

I have viewed my time in and out of public service as of a piece, defined by and rooted in duty to God and country, informed by the culture of my upbringing—the centrality of my Lutheran Christianity and its confessional, liturgical, and effervescent hymnody; my conservatism; my love of tradition and of Western civilization with its music, painting, history, and literature. In this changing world I have found great satisfaction and continuity in home, family, friends, parish life, and my colleagues. All of this is animated in a sacramental vision of my life in Christ—the humility of communion, the power of the law and gospel, and the purpose of the baptismal font and my prayer life.

My wife, my sons, and my parents have been central in my redemptive life and none more so than my own dad, my best friend, with whom I traveled to Northern France in 2009 after a year of crisis. We stood there together on the bluffs of Normandy, in the sands of Omaha Beach, and walked together among the rows upon rows of crosses and stars of David in the American cemetery, eventually ending in a contemplative, elegant, silent little chapel in the midst of that cemetery. My father affirmed me during that trip, reminding me of his love for me and the kind of man God wanted me to be. I was deeply impacted by it all. It was my dad's way of saying that beginning again was not only possible but a good thing and a gift from God.

Also, in 2009, I began to reread some of Russell Kirk's most important work to remind myself why I entered politics in the first place. He taught me as a young man to think less about politics and more about principles and to think seriously about both means and ends and their ramifications. In this, he said, tendencies toward ideologies would best be warded off. He wrote that the conservative "thinks of political policies as intended to preserve order, justice, and freedom. The ideologue, on the contrary, thinks of politics as a revolutionary instrument for transforming society and even transforming human nature. In his march toward Utopia, the ideologue is merciless."[4] So much of my life became entwined with day-to-day politics, but Russell took me back to first principles. This gave me great hope because it helped drain the toxicity from professional life that kicked into overdrive and gave me a new perspective of what political life should really be about. I believe in a moral order that is eternal, that the fount of that moral order flows from a God who loves and cherishes us, that all human life is precious because it is finite this side of heaven, and that if grace were not real I would be broken by the weight of my sins and failures. Yet I know that forgiveness is real, rooted in the supernatural love of my Redeemer who lives.

This was a vision deeply at odds with the regnant political culture. The cultural and political imperative for the conservative in our time is to restore the federalist's vision that was the genesis of our country, its founding vision. This will be a task of monumental proportions. But hope is real, and I believe the majority of Americans seek that restoration. Who will lead us is foundational to the task at hand, and it is the preeminent project of conservation in our time. The United States of America is an exceptional country without peer; the genesis of our greatness, this side of eternity, is the United States Constitution and the Declaration of Independence, which grew out of the Judeo-Christian tradition at the heart of Western civilization.

I have seen in the lives of the men I have worked for and admired most in public life—Dan Coats, Gary Bauer, and George Bush—a truly common bond—a faith that gives them the gift of humility in public life despite what their critics might say. I love and respect them deeply for this. I owe a debt to President Bush that I can never repay not only for his personal grace and mercy toward me when I needed it most but also for modeling for me and the country a professional and unwavering personal integrity that will be the portal to his becoming a statesman in the years ahead.

President Bush was asked about his legacy all the time, even while still in office. He always said if the historians were still arguing about George Washington's presidency, surely they would be arguing about his own presidency for years to come. This is the statement of a confident man, and I learned about this inner confidence for the first time in the 2000 presidential campaign and again in the 2004 campaign. Had he lost either race, I think he would have returned to his ranch with the same dignity and humility he did after he left the White House, with a clear conscience. This is who the man is.

George W. Bush, before making the most consequential decisions of his presidency, prayed about the decisions he faced; gathered the best evidence and consulted the best minds; pondered the available options; and then, having made his decision, took heart and found inner peace. His confidence could not be shaken, and that is why I am confident and hopeful that in the years ahead, with the benefit of time and space, historians will look back at those incredibly eventful eight years and conclude he made the right decisions about the biggest things during his time in office.

The last thing to say about George W. Bush is probably the most important: He was a man of prayer and faith. I was honored and humbled to pray with him on several occasions in the Oval Office and elsewhere. He always preferred that those praying together continue a Bush family tradition and hold hands while speaking to God; he was one of the most reverential men I have known. From his prayer life flowed the way he treated his wife and daughters, his senior and junior staff, his friends, and all the people who worked for him. It is all bound up in his prayer life. He is earnest not only about reading the Scriptures but also living the life of faith. He is a serious Christian.

I remember a famous American walking into the Oval Office and with barely a pause asking if the president believed in the literal six-day creation of the world. The president smiled and said that debate has been going on since the dawn of man. He demurred, but then said, "Let me tell you what I am confident of; I am confident that I am a sinner, that Jesus died for my sins on the cross, that He rose on Easter Sunday. That is what I believe."

I close with a powerful observation from the British World War I veteran and writer F. L. Lucas. His salient observations about the fleeting sense of power and influence, and the importance of meeting and exceeding one's duty despite fame or fortune, is a fitting capstone to this memoir. It is a tribute to the caliber of men and women I have been honored and privileged to serve with during my time in public service in the U.S. Senate and at the White House: "It is unlikely that many of us will be famous, or even remembered. But not less important than the brilliant few that lead a nation or a literature to fresh achievements, are the unknown many whose patient efforts keep the world from running backward; who guard and maintain the ancient values, even if they do not conquer new; whose inconspicuous triumph it is to pass on what they inherited from their fathers, unimpaired and undiminished, to their sons. Enough, for almost all of us, if we can hand on the torch, and not let it down; content to win the affection, if it may be, of a few who know us and to be forgotten when they in their turn have vanished. The destiny of mankind is not governed wholly by its 'stars.'"[5]

Supplementary Reading

A number of excellent essays, articles, and books that touch on timely topics, issues, and trends, which have impacted my own thinking. In this supplementary section I offer a few of them worth reading.

Essays

Bush, George W. President Bush's Speech from the National Cathedral Service of Remembrance. September 14, 2001.

Graham, Billy. Sermon from the National Cathedral Service of Remembrance. September 14, 2001.

Articles

Buckley, James L. "Needed: Foot Soldiers for a New Conservative Surge." *Human Events*. October 4, 2010.

Cherlin, Andrew, and W. Bradford Wilcox. "The Generation that Can't Move On Up." *The Wall Street Journal*. September 2, 2010.

Coburn, Senator Tom. "Less Could Be More." *American Spectator*. September 2010.

Coulter, Ann. "How Many Times Did Goldwater Run for President Again?" *Human Events*. 27 September 27, 2010.

Cromartie, Michael. "The Dead Are Not Raised by Politics." *Patheos*. August 11, 2010.

Eberstadt, Mary. "The Weight of Smut." *First Things*. June/July 2010.

Evans, M. Stanton. "What Wall? The Framers Would Be Surprised to Hear that the Constitution Says Religion and Government Should Not Mix." *National Review*. January 23, 1995.

"George W's War." *Investors Business Daily*. September 2, 2010.

Hanson, Victor Davis. "Why We Miss Bush." *The New York Post*. September 7, 2010.

Mukasey, Michael B. "America and the Meaning of Courage." *The Wall Street Journal*. June 5, 2010.

Rasmussen, Anders Fogh. "Remembering 9/11 on the Battlefield." *The Washington Post*. September 11, 2010.

Rector, Robert. "Poverty Explodes: Root Cause Is the Collapse of Marriage." Web Memo, The Heritage Foundation. September 2010.

Schambra, William. "Conservatism and the Quest for Community." *National Affairs*. September 14, 2010.

Schlafly, Phyllis. "Push Marriage to Make Dent in Deficit." Investors.com. October 11, 2010.

Stein, Ben. "Ben Stein's Diary." *The American Spectator*. July/August 2010.

Tubbs, David L. "The Politics of Humanity." *The American Spectator*. November 2010.

Some key books have guided my own thinking.

God and Christianity

Chesterton, G. K. *The Everlasting Man*.

Chesterton, G. K. *Orthodoxy*.

Chesterton, G. K. *What's Wrong with the World*.

Lewis, C. S. *The Abolition of Man*.

Lewis, C. S. *How Christianity Changed the World*.

Lewis, C. S. *Mere Christianity*.

Lewis, C. S. *The Weight of Glory*.

Stark, Rodney. *Victory of Reason: How Christianity Led to Freedom, Capitalism and Western Success*.

Conservatism and Political Science

The Anti-Federalist Papers

Constitution of the United States

The Declaration of Independence

The Federalist Papers

De Tocqueville, Alexis, *Democracy in America*.

Goldwater, Barry. *The Conscience of a Conservative*.

Kirt, Russell. *The Conservative Mind*.

Magnet, Myron. *The Dream and the Nightmare*.

Weaver, Richard. *Ideas Have Consequences*.

Biography and History

Boswell, *The Life of Johnson.*
Buckley, William F., Jr. *God and Man at Yale.*
Chambers, Whittaker. *Witness.*
Kirk, Russell. *Edmund Burke: A Genius Reimagined.*
Kirk, Russell. *Eliot and His Age.*
Burke, Edmund. *Reflections on the Revolution in France.*
Solzhenitsyn, Alexander. *The Gulag Archipelago*

Economics

Hazzlitt, Henry. *Economics in One Lesson.*
Smith, Adam. *The Wealth of Nations.*
Von Hayek, Frederick. *The Road to Serfdom.*

Culture

Burke, Edmund. *A Theory on the Sublime and the Beautiful.*
Eliot, T. S. *Ash Wednesday.*
Eliot, T. S. *Choruses from the Rock.*
Eliot, T. S. *Four Quartets.*
Eliot, T. S. *The Waste Land.*
Hirsch, E. D. *The Schools We Need and Why We Don't Have Them.*
Nesbit, Rober. *The Quest for Community.*
Newman, Cardinal John Henry. *The Idea of a University.*
Newman, Cardinal John Henry. *Loss and Gain.*
Smith, Adam. *A Theory on the Moral Sentiments.*

Special Note of Gratitude

During my White House years, some of the great and important friendships of my life were formed with Nick Stathis, James Cooper, Greg Wyatt, Bill Bright, Adrian Rogers, Frank Wright, Bob Becker, Sue Keeler, Lew Lehrman, Bob Tyrrell, Fred Barnes, Owen Frisby, Clark Judge, Michelle Easton, Bill Fay, Henry Cashen, Marion Harrison, Marjorie Dannenfelser, Barbara Ledeen, John O'Keefe, Dan Robinson, Harold Holzer, Nile Gardiner, Melinda Ronn, Cleta Mitchell, Ann Corkery, former U.S. Senator Rick Santorum, Bill Wichterman, Representative Robert Aderholt, Representative Trent Franks, Representative Mike Pence, Don Hodel, Mark Earley, Richard Land, Dan Carter, Al Regnery, Hilton Kramer, Seth Lipsky, George Will, Michael Barone, Mike Grebe, Michael Joyce, Steve Moore, Midge Decter, Dan Oliver, Rob Schenck, Brent Bozell, Steve Mays, Donna Rice, Joel Vaughn, Peggy Nienabor, and all my White House interns.

These men and women, and others, enriched my life beyond measure. They transformed the tackling of a tough task into a vocation bathed in joy and gratitude.

Notes

Frontmatter

1. *The Dartmouth Review* (January 13, 1999), http://s14929.gridserver.com/issues/1.13.99/index.html, accessed December 4, 2010.

2. *William Warburton Quotes*, http://thinkexist.com/quotes/william_warburton.html, accessed June 15, 2011.

Prologue

1. *Marcus Tullius Cicero Quotes*, http://thinkexist.com/quotations/a_thankful_heart_is_not_only_the_greatest_virtue/173426.html, accessed June 24, 2011.

2. Margaret Thatcher quoted Walt Whitman in her Foreign Policy of Great Britain speech on December 18, 1979. See http://famousquotes.me.uk/speeches/Margaret_Thatcher.html, accessed June 24, 2011.

3. *Works on Paper: The Craft of Biography and Autobiograph* by Michael Holroyd, 2002, http://bit.ly/1954JO, accessed June 10, 2011.

4. Proclamation 4882: Information from Answers.com, http://www.answers.com/topic/proclamation-4882, accessed December 4, 2010.

5. John Adams Quotes, http://www.revolutionary-war-and-beyond.com/john-adams-quotes-3.html, accessed December 4, 2010.

6. Lewis Carroll, *Through the Looking Glass*, www.cleavebooks.com, accessed June 10, 2011.

7. MetaBlog: 7/23/06–7/30/06, http://metabole.blogspot.com/2006_07_23_archive.html, accessed December 4, 2010.

8. "Can You Define the Term Neo-Con?" http://answers.yahoo.com/question/index?qid=20081121083438AAAOZEz, accessed December 4, 2010.

Chapter 1

1. G. K. Chesterton, *The Innocence of Father Brown*, www.fiction.eserver,org/short/innocence/hammerof.html.

2. John Milton, *Paradise Lost*, B., x., 1087.

3. "Those Who Mourn: Blackaby Devotional," www.bit.ly/mTwDvV, accessed June 10, 2011.

Chapter 2

1. Edmund Burke, *Reflections on the Revolution in France* (1790). Found online in The Russell Kirk Center for Cultural Renewal, "The Moral Imagination" by Russell Kirk, www.kirkcenter.org, accessed June 10, 2011.

2. George Plimpton, "Tom Wolfe, The Art of Fiction No. 123," *The Paris Review*, www.theparisreview.org, accessed June 10, 2011.

3. Joseph Sobran, "The Reluctant Anarchist," December 2002, www.sobran. com, accessed June 10, 2011.

4. G. K. Chesterton, *Orthodoxy: The Ethics of Elfland* (1908).

5. Alexis de Tocqueville, *Democracy in America* (1935).

6. De Tocqueville on religion and freedom, OrthodoxNet.com Blog, http://www. orthodoxytoday.org/blog/2005/06/27/de-tocqueville-on-religion-and-freedom/, accessed December 4, 2010.

7. William Wordsworth, "Surprised by Joy—Impatient as the Wind," www. poemhunter.com, accessed June 24, 2011.

8. Evelyn Waugh, *Come Inside* (Excerpted from *The Road to Damascus* 1955), Catholic Education Resource Center, www.catholiceducation.org, accessed June 10, 2011.

Chapter 3

1. Book review by Chris Banescu on *Mere Christianity* by C. S. Lewis, posted December 9, 2005, www.orthodoxytoday.com, accessed June 10, 2010.

Chapter 4

1. GoggleBooks, *The Use of Poetry and the Use of Criticism* by T. S. Eliot (1933), www.bit.ly/kvA7Am, accessed June 10, 2010.

2. Dante Alighieri, *Divine Comedy* (1300–1321).

3. Text of Al Gore's concession speech, http://www.usatoday.com/news/vote2000/bush11.htm, accessed December 4, 2010.

Chapter 5

1. *Theodore Roosevelt Quotes*, www.goodreads.com/author/quotes/44567. Theodore_Roosevelt, accessed June 10, 2011.

2. T. K. Titus, *Critical Study of T. S. Eliot Work*, Goggle Books, accessed June 9, 2011.

3. Online Library of Liberty, "Jay to William Wilberforce," http://oll.libertyfund. org/?option=com_staticxt&staticfi"le=show.php%3Ftitle=2330&chapter=220775&l ayout=html&Itemid=27, accessed December 4, 2010.

Chapter 6

1. "More for Montana!," http://www.moreformontana.com, accessed December 4, 2010.

2. Corpus Christi Caller Times Caller.com, "Bush OKs Limited . . . ," http://www.caller2.com/2001/august/10/today/national/7963.html, accessed December 4, 2010.

3. Pope John Paul II, *Evangelism Vitae*, www.bit.ly/mNlwxe, posted March 25, 1995, accessed June 10, 2011.

4. "The President's Decision: The Overview," http://www.nytimes.com/2001/08/10/us/president-s-decision-overview-bush-gives-his-backing-for-limited-research.html?pagewanted=2,accessed December 4, 2010.

5. BBC News | AMERICAS | "Bush Facing Stem Cell Storm," http://news.bbc.co.uk/2/hi/americas/1484139.stm, accessed December 4, 2010.

6. "US Judge Refuses to Stay Stem-Cell Ruling" | Real Time Market, http://www.automatedtrader.net/real-time-dow-jones/15485/us-judge-refuses-to-stay-stem_cell-ruling, accessed December 4, 2010.

7. "Illinois Federation for Right to Life: Appeals Court Rules," http://ifrl-blog.blogspot.com/2010/09/appeals-court-rules-tax-dollars-for.html, accessed December 4, 2010.

8. "Decision Time," http://www.wnd.com/index.php?pageId=10427, accessed December 4, 2010.

Chapter 7

1. PineandLakes.com: "Taxpayers Have Been Lulled to Sleep," December 24, 2004, http://www.pineandlakes.com/stories/122204/opinion_042.shtml, accessed December 10, 2010.

2. Frontline: "The Jesus Factor: The President and His Faith," http://www.pbs.org/wgbh/pages/frontline/shows/jesus/president/public.html, accessed December 4, 2010.

3. "Americans for Community and Faith-Centered Enterprise—," http://rightweb.irc-online.org/profile/Americans_for_Community_and_Faith-Centered_Enterprise, accessed December 4, 2010.

4. "U.S. Catholics Want to Believe in Bush's Presidency," http://newsinfo.nd.edu/news/6250-us-catholics-want-to-believe-in-bushs-presidency/, accessed December 4, 2010.

5. Denver Catholic Register—World/Nation, http://www.archden.org/dcr/archive/20010530/2001053004wn.htm, accessed December 4, 2010.

6. "Nudging Church-State Line," http://omega77.tripod.com/bushfederalaid.htm, accessed December 4, 2010.

7. "On the Right by William F. Buckley Jr.," uExpress.com, http://www.uexpress.com/ontheright/?uc_full_date=20010130, accessed December 4, 2010.

8. "On the Right by William F. Buckley Jr., uExpress.com, http://www.uexpress.com/ontheright/?uc_full_date=20010130, accessed December 4, 2010.

9. "The President at Notre Dame," http://www.breakpoint.org/commentaries/3357-the-president-at-notre-dame, accessed December 4, 2010.

10. "Definition of Liked," http://www.brainyquote.com/words/li/liked184957.html, accessed December 4, 2010.

Chapter 8

1. Ronald Reagan's Speech on January 15, 1983, "Remarks on the Anniversary of the Birth of Martin Luther King Jr.," posted July 19, 2010, Famous-reagan-speeches. blogspot.com, accessed June 10, 2011.

2. T. S. Eliot, *Quartet No. 4: Little Gidding*, www.tristan.icom43.net/quarters, accessed June 10, 2010.

3. "Islam Never Changes—It Has Always Been a Religion of War," http://www. thefreepressonline.co.uk/news/1/2051.htm, accessed December 10, 2010.

4. "American Rhetoric: Billy Graham," http://www.americanrhetoric.com/ speeches/billygraham911memorial.htm, accessed December 10, 2010.

Chapter 9

1. Grace Bible Church, www.gracevice.com/blog-thoughts/contentment by Paul Toms, posted May 10, 2011, accessed June 10, 2011.

Chapter 10

1. Quotation by C. S. Lewis, *The Quotation Page*, www.quotationspage.com/ quote/25736.html, accessed June 10, 2011.

2. Greetings from Mecosta—Crunchy Con, http://blog.beliefnet.com/ crunchycon/2006/10/greetings-from-mecosta.html, accessed December 10, 2010.

3. Roger Kimball, "The Greatest Victorian," www.ly/mL4WEs, accessed June 10, 2011.

Chapter 11

1. Quotation by Thomas Jeffereson, *The Quotation Page*, www.quotationspage. com/quote/27616.html, accessed June 9, 2011.

2. Speech by President Bush in the Oval Office on March 19, 2003.

3. Edmund Burke, *Reflections on the Revolution in France* (1790).

4. See http://www.weeklystandard.com/articles/semper-fly_574087.html, accessed June 21, 2011.

5. "Reid: Iraq War is Lost, U.S. Can't Win," www.msn.com, April 20, 2007, accessed June 9, 2011.

Chapter 12

1. Patrick Henry's "Liberty or Death" speech on March 23, 1775, www.u-s-history.com, accessed June 10, 2011.

2. "Hillary Clinton: Petraeu's Reports Require Willing Suspension of Disbelief by CSPAN," September 11, 2007, accessed June 10, 2011.

3. "The Rhetoric of 9/11: Bullhorn Address at Ground Zero," September 14, 2001, http://www.americanrhetoric.com/speeches/gwbush911groundzerobullhorn. htm, accessed December 11, 2010.

4. Thomas Sowell, "Good Riddance," *The Crescent News*, www.crescent-news. com, April 22, 2010, accessed June 9, 2011.

5. Paul R. Shockley Home Page, http://www.prshockley.org/, accessed December 11, 2010.

6. "Non-War off the Battlefield," www.anchorrising.com/barnacles/2010_11.html, November 20, 2010, accessed June 9, 2011.

7. "Michael B. Mukasey: America and the Meaning of Courage," http://online.wsj.com/article/SB10001424052748704875604575280771383483024.html, accessed December 11, 2010.

Chapter 13

1. Quote by Martin Luther, *The Quotation Book*, http://quotationsbook.com, accessed June 9, 2011.

2. "Transcript of Bush Statement," http://www.yuricareport.com/Dominionism/BushTranscriptConstAmendMarriage.html, accessed December 12, 2010.

3. "Bush Urges Amendment to Ban Same-Sex Marriage," excerpt from speech on February 24, 2004, www.Zenit.org, accessed June 9, 2011.

4. "Bush Tolerates Civil Unions, Thinks States Should Decide," http://www.crosswalk.com/1293061/, accessed December 12, 2010.

Chapter 14

1. "A Shepherd's Voice: Lee Harris on 'Restoring Honor,'" http://johnmalloysdb.blogspot.com/2010/09/lee-haris-on-restoring-honor.html, accessed December 12, 2010.

2. "The Collapse of Marriage and the Rise of Welfare Dependence," lecture by Jennifer Marshall, Robert Lerman, Barbara Whitehead, Honorable Wade Horn, and Robert Rector, The Heritage Foundation, www.heritage.org.

3. Catherine Snow, "Friday Five: Phyllis Schlafly on the New Generation of Conservative Women," www.citizenlink.com, accessed June 9, 2011.

4. Patrick Haynes, *In Defense of the Religious Right* (Nashville, Thomas Nelson, 2006).

5. Ibid.

6. Ibid.

7. Alexander Hamilton Institute,– "Wisdom of the Founders Conference," http://www.theahi.org/news-events/2010/9/30/wisdom-of-the-founders-conference-nyc-9-november.html, accessed December 12, 2010.

Chapter 15

1. B. A. Robinson, "Judicial Philosophies: How Judges Interpret Constitutions and Laws," www.ReligiousTolerance.org, accessed June 9, 2011.

2. Stated by John Jay in a letter to William Wilberforce. See johnjayinstitute.org/leadership-programs/executive-leadership-seminars, accessed June 9, 2011.

3. "Kennedy Closing Statement on Nomination of Judge John Roberts," http://www.freerepublic.com/focus/f-news/1494020/posts, accessed December 12, 2010.

4. Andreas Cala, "In Spain, Pope Benedict XVI Lambasts 'Aggressive Secularism,'" *The Christian Science Monitor*, November 7, 2010, www.csmonitor.com.

5. Dallas Morning News | News for Dallas, Texas | Reporting from . . . , http://www.dallasnews.com/sharedcontent/dws/news/washington/djackson/stories/093005dnnatroberts.a5bd3f9b.html, accessed December 12, 2010.

6. "Roberts Sworn In as Chief Justice," http://www.crosswalk.com/1354087/, accessed December 12, 2010.

7. "Roberts Confirmed as 17th Chief Justice," The Washington Post, September 30, 2005, http://washingtonpost.com, accessed June 9, 2011.

Chapter 16

1. Quote by G. K. Chesterton, http://quotationsbook.com, accessed June 9, 2011.

2. Timothy Williams, "Bush Names Counsel as Choice for Supreme Court," The New York Times, www.nytimes.com, accessed June 9, 2011.

3. Ibid.

4. Ibid.

5. "Bush Nominates Alito," http://www.kktv.com/news/headlines/1932962.html, accessed December 12, 2010.

6. "Alito '72 Tapped for High Court," The Daily Princetonian, http://www.dailyprincetonian.com/2005/11/07/13675/, accessed December 12, 2010.

7. "Confirmation of Alito Would Shift Court Firmly to the Right, Experts Say,", Associated Baptist Press, http://www.abpnews.com/content/view/755/, accessed December 12, 2010.

8. "President Picks Judge on Appeals Court for O'Connor's Seat," The New York Times, November 1, 2005, www.nytimes.com, accessed June 9, 2011.

9. Ibid.

Chapter 17

1. Alexham, "President Bush At His Best," http://bit.ly/iscQdh, accessed June 9, 2011.

2. Ronald Reagan quote, www.quotationspage.com, accessed June 9, 2011.

3. "Embryonic Stem Cell Research and Religion," http://lawreview.law.pitt.edu/issues/68/68.1/Pittman.pdf, accessed December 12, 2010.

4. "Pope Meets Bush, Condemns Stem-Cell Research," ABC News, http://abcnews.go.com/International/story?id=80666&page=2, accessed December 12, 2010.

5. "Pope John Paul II to President Bush on Stem-Cell Research," http://www.americancatholic.org/News/StemCell/pope_to_bush.asp, accessed December 12, 2010.

6. "Pope Chastises Bush over Death Penalty, Stem Cell Research," http://www.mindfully.org/Reform/Pope-Chastises-Bush.htm, accessed December 12, 2010.

7 "Pope Meets Bush, Condemns Stem-Cell Research," ABC News, http://abcnews.go.com/International/story?id=80666&page=2, accessed December 12, 2010.

8. "Bush Hails Pope as 'Strong Symbol of Freedom,'", ZENIT, https://www.zenit.org/article-10277?l=english, accessed December 12, 2010.

9. "President Bush Attends Pope's Funeral," http://uruguay.usembassy.gov/usaweb/paginas/346-00EN.shtml, accessed December 12, 2010.

10. Mark Silva, "Bush Said He Was Awed by Ceremony," Chicago Tribune, April, 9, 2005, www.chicagotribune.com, accessed June 9, 2011.

11. "President Bush Attends Pope's Funeral," US Embassay's Montevidro Archives, April 8, 2005, http://bit.ly/iQRNFi.

12. "George W. Bush: Interview with Reporters Aboard Air Force One," http://www.presidency.ucsb.edu/ws/index.php?pid=64016, accessed December 12, 2010.

13. "Pope and Bush likely to Discuss Iraq," ZENIT, http://www.zenit.org/article-19785?l=english, accessed December 12, 2010.

14. George W. Bush Christian Quotes from Boycottliberalism.com, http://www.boycottliberalism.com/George-W-Bush-Quotes.htm, accessed December 12, 2010.

Chapter 18

1. "Playing the High Card," The American Spectator, http://spectator.org/archives/2010/11/13/playing-the-high-card-arguing, accessed December 10, 2010.

Chapter 19

1. John Adams Quotes, http://www.revolutionary-war-and-beyond.com/john-adams-quotes-5.html, accessed December 4, 2010.

2. Quote by G. K. Chesterton, The Quotations Page, www.quotationspage.com, accessed June 8, 2011.

3. Quote by Daniel Patrick Moynihan, Good Reads, http://goodreads.com/quotes/show/116754, accessed June 9, 2011.

4. "The Great Seduction of Modern Politics," http://www.estatevaults.com/bol/archives/2009/09/22/the_great_seduc.html, accessed December 12, 2010.

5. Patrick Welsh, "Making the Grade Isn't About Race. It's About Parents," The Washington Post, October 28, 2009, www.washingtonpost.com, accessed June 9, 2011.

6. "Liberty and Civilization: The Western Heritage," htt://goodreads.com.book/show/8527363-liberty-and-civilization, accessed June 9, 2011.

7. Chuck Colson, "Devotions by BreakPoint: Tea and Charity," www.oneplace.com, March 30, 2010, accessed June 9, 2011.

8. David Brooks, "The Limits of Policy," The New York Times, May 3, 2010.

Chapter 20

1. "Bush Breaks Ground on Library, www.Spokesman.com, November 17, 2010, http://www.spokesman.com/stories/2010/nov/17/bush-breaks-ground-on-library/, accessed December 12, 2010.

2. "Colonel Joshua Lawrence Chamberlain," The American Civil War, www.brotherswar.com/civil_war_quotes_4e.htm, accessed June 10, 2011.

3. "The Schlesinger Syndrome, Updated," The American Spectator, http://spectator.org/archives/2010/10/20/the-schlesinger-syndrome-updat, accessed December 12, 2010).

4. Family Research Council, http://www.frc.org/get.cfm?i=WU10H01&f=RF07B06, accessed December 12, 2010.

5. "Pro Ecclesia * Pro Familia * Pro Civitate," http://proecclesia.blogspot.com/2009/04/creative-minority-report-quotes-late.html, accessed December 12, 2010.

6. Deborah Gyapong, "Dubya's Book Is Out," http://deborahgyapong.blogspot.com/2010/11/dubyas-book-is-out.html, accessed December 12, 2010.

7. Dr. Enrico Peppe, "IC's Top 25 Philosophical and Ideological Conservative Books: No. 21-Richard Weaver: Ideas Have Consequences," www.intellectualconservative.com, accessed June 9, 2011.

8. Amityville Union Free School District, http://www.amityvilleschools.org/schools/high_cutillo.asp, accessed December 12, 2010.

Chapter 21

1. "Abraham Lincoln Quotes," www.searchquotes.com, accessed June 10, 2011.

2. "President Bush Takes His Campaign Message to Conservatives," http://www.crosswalk.com/1262869/, accessed December 12, 2010.

3. Herbert I. London, "Terrorism's Victory," http://www.herblondon.org/6844/terrorism-victory, accessed December 12, 2010.

4. "Serenity in Storms: A Sermon Preached to President Bush," http://catholicexchange.com/2004/09/11/93871/, accessed December 12, 2010.

5. Sir William Blackstone, Commentaries on the Laws of England in Four Books, vol. 1 [1753], edited by George Sharswood, http://oll.libertyfund.org, accessed July 1, 2011.

6. "It Is Impossible to Rightly Govern the World without God," http://www.ccfla.org/accesscart/owBasket/owAddItem.asp?idProduct=25196, accessed December 12, 2010.

7. Samuel Taylor Coleridge, The Constitution of Church and State, According to the Idea of Each, edited by H. N. Coleridge (London, 1852), 79.

8. "Is Christmas Unconstitutional?" Legal Lad, http://legallad.quickanddirtytips.com/Christmas-constitutional.aspx, accessed December 12, 2010.

9. "Encyclical Letter Caritas In Veritae of the Supreme Pontiff Benedict XVI to the Bishops Priests and Deacons Men and Women Religious the Lay Faithful and All People of Good Will on Integral Human Development in Charity and Truth," www.vatican.va, accessed June 9, 2011.

10. Brandon Ragle, "Culture Counts: Faith and Feeling In a World Besieged," www.brandonragle.com, posted August 23, 2008, accessed June 9, 2011.

11. "Book Review: America's Secular Challenge," http://sheepcrib.blogspot.com/2008/12/book-review-americas-secular-challenge.html, accessed December 12, 2010.

12. Ibid.

13. Ibid.

14. "Pope in Landmark Meeting with Artists in Sistine Chapel," AFP http://www.google.com/hostednews/afp/article/ALeqM5hnjsRbsVJJizG7b6tjaG68mBz2QA, accessed December 12, 2010.

15. Trinity Forum Update, http://www.ttf.org/index/update/september-2010-2/, accessed December 12, 2010.

16. A Boat against the Current: Quote of the Day, James Piereson, http://boatagainstthecurrent.blogspot.com/2010/09/quote-of-day-james-piereson-on-columbia.html, accessed December 12, 2010.

17. Brian C. Anderson, "More Relevant Than Ever," http://bit.ly/mRPCQt, posted November 4, 2010, accessed June 9, 2011.

18. Ibid.

19. "Loving the State or Loving the State Out of Existence," http://blog.heritage.org/2008/08/25/loving-the-state-or-loving-the-state-out-of-existence, accessed December 12, 2010.

20. Kevin Craig, "Enumerated Powers: Liberty under God," http://kevincraig.us/enumerated.htm, accessed December 12, 2010.

21. "Franklin Pierce's 1854 Veto," May 3, 1854, Disability History Museum, www.disabilitymuseum.org, accessed June 9, 2011.

22. "Rome of the West: Blessed John Henry Cardinal Newman," http://www.romeofthewest.com/2010/09/blessed-john-henry-cardinal-newman.html, accessed December 12, 2010.

23. Joseph Ratzinger and Marcello Pera, "Without Roots: The West, Relativism, Christianity, Islam," Catholic Education Resource Center, www.catholiceducation.org, accessed June 10, 2011.

24. "912 Patriots Of South Jersey," http://www.912patriotssj.com, accessed December 12, 2010.

25. "Irrigating Deserts," Touchstone Archives, http://www.touchstonemag.com/archives/article.php?id=23-05-008-c, accessed December 12, 2010.

26. "The American Conservative: Suicide of the West," http://www.amconmag.com/article/2010/mar/01/00014/, accessed December 12, 2010.

27. "Row after Pope's Remarks on Atheism and Nazis," http://www.abovetopsecret.com/forum/thread612033/pg1, accessed December 12, 2010.

28. "Eric Mayforth's Review of God and Man at Yale," http://www.amazon.com/review/RP7Z7EQ0E6H69, accessed December 12, 2010.

29. "The New Criterion Is Probably More Consistently Worth Reading than Any Other Magazine in English," http://cliftonchadwick.wordpress.com/2010/06/30/%E2%80%9Cthe-new-criterion-is-probably-more-consistently-worth-reading-than-any-other-magazine-in-english-%E2%80%9D/, accessed December 12, 2010.

30. "A Criterion for Compromises," http://www.firstthings.com/on_the_square_entry.php?year=2007&month=08&title_link=a-criterion-for-compromises, accessed December 12, 2010.

31. *The New Criterion* Is Probably More Consistently Worth Reading than Any Other Magazine in English," http://cliftonchadwick.wordpress.

com/2010/06/30/%E2%80%9Cthe-new-criterion-is-probably-more-consistently-worth-reading-than-any-other-magazine-in-english-%E2%80%9D/, accessed December 12, 2010.

32. "The Critic as Radical," The American Conservative, http://www.amconmag.com/blog/the-critic-as-radical/, accessed December 12, 2010.

Epilogue

1. George Herbert quote, "Janice Campbell: Taking Time for Things That Matter," http://janice-campbell.com/2007/11/20/gratefulnesse-by-George-herbert, posted November 20, 2007, accessed June 10, 2011.

2. T. S. Eliot, *Ash Wednesday*, www.msgr.ca/msgr-7/ash_wednesday_t_s_eliot.html, accessed June 10, 2011.

3. William Booth, founder of the Salvation Army, "William Booth Quotes," www.Great-Quotes.com, accessed June 10, 2011.

4. "Russell Kirk: 1918–1994," www.conservativeforum.org, accessed June 10, 2011.

5. F. L. Lucas, Style, www.richochet.com/member-feed/on-writing-and-serving, accessed June 21, 2011.